Just Julie

Julie
Goodyear

Just Julie

MACMILLAN

First published 2006 by Macmillan
an imprint of Pan Macmillan Ltd
Pan Macmillan, 20 New Wharf Road, London N1 9RR
Basingstoke and Oxford
Associated companies throughout the world
www.panmacmillan.com

ISBN-13: 978-0-230-01433-6
ISBN-10: 0-230-01433-X

Typeset by SetSystems Ltd, Saffron Walden, Essex
Printed and bound in Great Britain by
Mackays of Chatham plc, Chatham, Kent

In loving memory of my grandma
Elizabeth Ann Duckworth
and my mam and dad
Alice and William Goodyear

For my only son Gary Goodyear
and my three grandchildren
Emily, Elliot and Jack Goodyear

Acknowledgements

Richard Milner at Pan Macmillan

Jan Kennedy at Billy Marsh Associates

Paul O'Grady, Dale Winton, Scott, Vicki, Carol,
Val, Edna, Janet & Gwen, Danny, Norma, Irene, Graham,
Kim & the Twins, Jan & Paul, Sister Margaret, Tony Warren,
Margaret Forwood, Jill Shaylor, Jackie Sweeney, Lois & Roy,
Norman Frisby, Leita Donn, Peter & Alan, Martin & Digby,
Joan Rivers, Harold Singer, Roger Harper, Dr Eva Jacobs,
Janice Troupe, Tim Toulmin, Guy Black.

Contents

Preface

This book cannot be anything other than searingly honest because that is how I am – and I am not changing *that* for anybody.

I can only tell my story how it was and as a result there will be times when names will have to be changed to protect the guilty. Yes, I know names are usually changed to protect the innocent. But then my life has not followed usual patterns and often has been as much of a surprise to me as it has been for others.

'So what have you done wrong now, Julie?' is a refrain that will recur frequently throughout the pages of this book! What can I say? We are not responsible for every aspect of the people who enter our lives or all the events and happenings that come our way, but we can choose how to interact with them, how to avoid becoming bitter, angry and twisted, and how to appreciate the black comedy.

My life, so far, has run the entire gamut of human emotions and there have been as many heartbreaks and sorrows as there have been joys and happiness along the way. To write this autobiography I have had to delve deep within myself and my emotional reserves, and revisit places I would much rather have remained filed away forever and never had to visit again. But I've done it!

When I agreed to tackle this book – which charts twenty-five years of playing Bet Lynch, the loveable, sexy, brassy barmaid I played such a huge part in creating for *Coronation Street*, three marriages, four same-sex relationships, my nervous breakdown, being diagnosed with cervical cancer and being told I'd only a year to live, and then being charged with fraud in 1982 when I set up a charity to help other patients – I said, 'My background dictates that if you can't think of owt nice to say about someone, you should say nowt – a rule I observed for sixty-four years. But *enough*! I am ready now to stand up and be counted and set the record straight.'

This book, then, is a no-holds-barred account of my life, a book written in blood, sweat and tears. And, as I placed the final fullstop on its pages, I felt what? Happier? Freer? At peace with myself and others?

Purged is the word that comes to mind. And knackered!

To those people in my life who aren't mentioned – and you know who you are – all I can say is, 'Think yourselves bloody lucky. You got off lightly.' And, anyway, it would have been beneath me to put you in. I can only hope that my other readers will laugh with me, cry with me and, above all, find some inspiration in this book; and that it will allow them, like me, to appreciate once and for all that we *can* survive the slings and arrows – *can* live and tell the tale!

And, if anybody should be interested in an epitaph for my life, I would like them to consider: 'At least she tried. . .'

JULIE GOODYEAR
Manchester and Spain,
spring and summer 2006

PROLOGUE

Losing My Mind

It could have been night, could have been morning. I could have been a baby, child or adult, fully dressed or stark naked. I wouldn't have known. I thought I was running, but moments later realized I was motionless, lying face down on the grimy dog-stained pavement, and there was grit in my mouth, blood on my hands and blood dripping from my bare feet.

It was the sight of blood that saved me. I knew then that I needed help — needed a hospital — knew that was where I had to go. As I levered myself up from the kerbside, I heard screaming and shrank back, terrified, clapping both my hands over my ears. What was happening? Why was somebody screaming? Then I realized that my mouth was open, that it was me making those terrible piercing sounds.

But who was *me*? I didn't know my name, didn't know who I belonged to or where I lived. Why was I wearing a mud-spattered, bloodstained nightdress? Where was I going when I stumbled and fell?

No answers. Just darkness, ripped apart by more screams, deafening me, enfolding me. Then all went quiet again, and there were no more questions, no more thoughts on the rampage.

How did I get from where I was that night to the lodge gate of the hospital, where the night porter lifted me up? Was it the kindness of a stranger that helped me to that place, which was not so very far from the little bungalow where I lived? If so, I will never know for sure. But sometimes, in my mind's eye, I fancy I feel the roughened skin of a woman's firm hand tugging on mine, and I see a gentle face mirroring my anguish, and murmuring, 'It's all right, luv. It's *all right*.'

The next thing I remember with any kind of certainty is somebody screaming again and the porter's voice saying, 'There, there, luv. You're in good hands now.'

'Please stop the screaming,' I said, choking the words into his chest. '*Please stop it.*'

'That's just what we're going to do now,' a different disembodied voice replied, 'and then you'll have a good night's sleep.'

And I did! He, she, they must have given me a mega-dose in that injection. I don't know how long I slept following it, but it felt like a lifetime. Oblivion. Blessed nothingness. Healing heaven.

Later, I learned that during those first two weeks they attached electrodes to my temples and gave me several rounds of ECT – electroconvulsive therapy.

Later still, I was informed that I had had 'a complete nervous breakdown'. Complete! What did incomplete feel like?

'There's no shame in that,' they told me. They would 'get me well again'.

Please, oh please. My heart was still pounding, the sound of its beats deafening, obliterating all but the nearest sounds.

'There . . . there.' Another gentle voice, another reassuring hand, another syringe. 'We'll soon 'ave you right as rain, luv. Right as rain. You'll soon be going home.'

Home! *Oh no!*

The terror returned, the screaming started up again. But whether the screams were audible or silent that time, I'll never know. I only remember, as my hands frantically tore the air and my legs tried to run away again, that there was another hand floating towards me, another long silvery needle dribbling peace into one of my veins.

It was the only time in my often traumatic life that I remember drawing my knees up to my chest in a tight fetal ball and sobbing out loud, but still tearlessly, because I was somebody who never ever, whatever the circumstances, cried, 'Don't let me die. P-l-e-a-s-e don't let me die.'

Even at that moment in the midst of all that mental anguish, shock and horror, I had not given up on myself. I wanted to live, wanted to get back to the set of my beloved *Coronation Street*, wanted to feel Bet Lynch's wind beneath my wings, and fly-fly off to that glorious golden oasis where I always left Julie Goodyear – and all her troubles – behind.

'So what 'ave you *done* now? You must 'ave done summat wrong?' were two of Alice, my mam's, most familiar expressions where I was concerned.

They were never said, though, in exasperation; more in resignation that summat dreadful had happened – or was about to happen – again in my life. And such events, which somehow

3

I never seemed to see coming, were frequent – as regular as clockwork you might say!

The straw that broke this camel's back, however, came comparatively late in the saga that is my life – in 1973 when I was thirty-one years old. And, for now, all you need to know is that my nervous breakdown and arrival at an NHS hospital, and subsequent admission to a private clinic, followed a second marriage that didn't even survive the wedding day. Why? Having bundled me into the wedding car after the ceremony, the bridegroom left with the best man and returned to his mother's apron strings. What timing! Our guests, including most of the cast of *Coronation Street*, were all waiting and the wedding reception hadn't even got under way.

Consummated? He couldn't even look at me, let alone kiss and make up when I asked him in the car what on earth was the matter; what had I done to upset him?

But enough of that for now.

Nervous breakdowns, both complete and incomplete, I suspect, are frequently born of more than one event. They're more commonly a sum total, the result of a step-by-step process that chips off little bits of your heart and slowly undermines your sanity until there's a brainstorm, a frightening bewildering jumble that needs immediate help. I was lucky. Both within the NHS and the private clinic I found myself in the hands of good, caring doctors and nurses and a brilliant psychiatrist; and this good fortune, which saved my sanity and doubtless my life, came just in the nick of time.

I wasn't always so lucky with medical teams when I really needed them. When, for example, at just eighteen years old I was in a labour ward, giving birth, I found myself at the mercy of a ferocious sister and nursing staff who were terrified of her. The labour lasted for forty-eight hours and, even though I was married, I was subjected to total disapproval from that sister throughout.

No one had prepared me for the birth and for two days I lay in that ward like a frightened, bewildered animal, screaming with the pain every time I had a contraction. It was horrendous! The only thing I knew to ask for, because my mam had told me, was gas and air to help ease the agony of the contractions. But when these became unbearable and I cried out for it, the sister just laughed and wheeled it away. Unbelievable. I've had more nightmares about that woman than any other person in creation – and that's saying summat!

But that kind of behaviour, I've learned, was common in those days. There was no pity for girls who were 'caught out', not a bit, and I know she got pleasure from inflicting pain on vulnerable people. All the other nurses were under her, and although they might have disagreed with what she did and said, they never questioned her authority, never spoke up. As far as they were concerned, she was in charge; and they were too frightened of her, too afraid of losing their jobs.

I had no idea what birth entailed; never even knew that babies entered the world from between your legs. I thought a nurse would come in with a knife and, on the other side of the screen that covered the end of my body while I lay there, my legs in those horrendous stirrups, would cut me open, tracing a line from my belly button to my lower stomach, and yank the baby out.

Natural childbirth be buggered. There I was lying in an old hospital bed, wide-eyed with terror, waiting for someone to come and put me on the birthing trolley cum table, when I felt a surge of summat damp and a head coming out between my legs.

'Get on with it,' was the sister's attitude throughout the rest of the birth. When I was writhing in pain from a particularly vicious contraction, I remember the sister leaning over me and saying in a harsh tone, laughing in my face, 'Now, was it worth it, *was* it?' I was shaking too much, was too frightened to say anything.

When, at last, my baby was born on 28 April 1960, one month after my eighteenth birthday, it wasn't handed to me. There was no precious moment allowed when I could gaze down at its features and count its fingers and toes, stroke its tiny eyebrows, and bond. Hastily bundled into some flannelette thingy, it was placed in a far corner of the delivery room. Then the sister left and I lay there watching the hands of a clock on a wall. Was the baby alive? Was the baby dead? Had I really heard a slap, followed by an indignant cry? I didn't know, couldn't tell. My legs were still in stirrups, which I thought was normal practice then, but now I know wasn't, and I could feel blood trickling from me.

The pain, too, was horrendous. This wasn't surprising. The sister had been very rough with me when she was pulling the baby through and dealing with the afterbirth, but no rougher than she had been throughout the entire labour and birth. She seemed to have particularly enjoyed giving me the pre-labour enema, had really hurt me badly with that. But now it was all over. I'd no choice but to continue lying there, legs splayed in that humiliating position, and watch the hands of the clock go round agonizingly slowly.

Not until I'd been lying in that delivery room for many hours, staring blankly at the walls, did I receive my first words of kindness. A youngish, lean-faced doctor came in, took one look at me and immediately sized the situation up. 'How long has this girl been lying here like this?' he called over his shoulder, shocked – and I could tell he was really angry.

Having gone out of the room, closing the door behind him, he then came back with a nurse in tow who I hadn't seen before. Then, remaining in the room, he instructed her to wash me and get my legs down. Throughout this, he talked to me kindly, but I was suffering so badly from cramp in my legs and lower back that I could hardly take in anything he said. Then he began to explain that because I was so 'badly torn' I would unfortunately have to be 'hurt again' while he 'stitched me up'. So my legs had to go back up into the stirrups.

Once all that had been done, he asked the nurse to bring the baby to me and, at last, I was able to hold my sound-asleep nine-pound ten-ounce baby in my arms. It was the first time I'd seen the fruits of my labour, the first time I realized I'd given birth to a son. From that moment on, though, all my misery faded into oblivion. As I held Gary in my arms it was love at first sight, and I knew then that he would always be the most important man in my life. I just couldn't stop looking at him, and the love I felt for him was almost overwhelming. Come hell or high water, I knew I'd want to protect him, shield him from all harm, even if it meant laying down my own life. That's how deep those initial emotions were.

The doctor made it very clear to me throughout the rest of the time he was in the room that he was very angry with that sister, and for years afterwards I longed to get my hands on her.

One day, by which time I was playing Bet Lynch in *Coronation Street*, I did! And she was still inflicting pain on the helpless and vulnerable. It really is a small world, but more of that later.

My troubles on that ward weren't over yet. Having been stitched up and allowed to hold my baby at last, I was put back in the ward, still in shock, and that same sister was suddenly there again at my bedside. Without a word of explanation, she pulled the curtains around my bed and, as I shrank away from her in terror, she yanked up my hospital gown and clamped rubber-suction thingies onto my nipples. Within seconds, milk started to flow out of my breasts.

Throughout this procedure, which she repeated several times, causing painful contractions, she expressed the milk into a container, and then took it away. It was only later I found out that this milk – *my* breast milk – was being used to feed tiny babies in the premature baby unit. I wouldn't have minded if somebody had explained; I would never have begrudged anybody's baby the chance of life. But I hadn't even been given the opportunity to feed my own.

The next time I was able to bond with Gary was two long days after I'd given birth to him. That would be unheard of today. And even then I had to do it like a thief in the night, without permission.

The nursery was at the far end of what was a very long ward where every bed was taken, and I could hear a baby crying. It was the most compelling sound I'd ever heard and I knew it was *my* baby who was crying, *my* baby who was hungry and desperate for attention. The instinct to get to him was overpowering and I sat up in the creaky bed. Nobody moved a muscle without Sister's permission in that ward – *her* ward – and I was terrified I'd get caught.

Somehow I managed to slither out of bed in the dark and began, despite the searing pain in my body, to crawl underneath all the other mothers' beds. Flattening myself to the floor and absolutely terrified that somebody would catch me and be cruel to me again, I persevered for the whole length of the ward.

'So far, so good,' I kept whispering to myself for reassurance, then, prising open the door to the nursery, I was able to see that I was right. It was my baby crying; I didn't need the label on his wrist to tell me that.

God, he looked so like Ray, his father. He had the same dark hair, same features – same everything. He was a perfect miniature clone of his twenty-two-year-old dad. I put my hand inside the cot and lifted him out. At that moment I would have risked fire, hell and brimstone to bring him comfort and stop him crying.

Laying him gently down on the linoleum floor beneath me, I got into a half-crouch, half-kneeling position over him and, resting on all fours like an animal, I managed to get a nipple into his contorted crying mouth. The crying, thank God, stopped immediately. It was magic. I couldn't believe that something so simple could be so effective. He was so tiny, so frail, yet he was suckling with such eager ferocity, such contentment, and I'd given him that comfort, that consolation, absolutely instinctively. For the first time, some of the horror of that day and the awful months leading up to it fell away. Despite it all, I'd done something right. I'd comforted and fed this tiny scrap of humanity. He was my baby; I was his mother. Nothing and nobody could take that moment away from me, not now, not ever.

When Gary eventually stopped suckling and drifted into a contented sleep, I eased my tired body into a better position, placed him back in the little cot and gently released my little finger from his grasp. That done, I knew I had to face the long crawl back. But, sliding under all the beds like before, I did it. I got back to my bed. Oh God, the relief.

I lay there trembling from all that effort, my heart pounding, praying that he wouldn't wake up and start crying again. If he did, I'd have to go through all that again, and I'd no strength left. He didn't wake up. I'd got away with it, or so I thought. Wrong.

As the first shaft of daylight entered the ward, there *she* was, mouth open and face contorted with fury. I couldn't hear what she was saying through my terror, but I knew she was accusing me of what I'd done. How had she found out? Had one of the other mothers seen and grassed me up? No. The truth was simpler than that. When I'd crawled from my bed to the nursery then back again, I'd left a trail of blood which ran all the way from my bed to his cot.

Within seconds, she had her own back. She clamped the pump to my now cracked and sore nipples, the terrible contractions started again, and I felt as if I'd died and gone to hell.

A bit later she wrenched off Gary's umbilical cord with such ferocity it made him scream with shock and pain. And when we at last managed to escape her clutches ten days later and got home it took a long time for the place where the cord had been to heal and lie flat. I had to place a penny on it and wrap a binder around him. This was summat I'd seen my grandma do many times with little babies. And it came back to me.

As she wrenched the cord off him, I remember her saying, 'We get your sort back in here every year.' 'Your sort!' What did she mean? I didn't understand. What sort of girl was I? As far as I was concerned, I was just Julie.

I'd had a baby, yes. But that's what women did, wasn't it? And I was married to Ray Sutcliffe, the baby's father. We had done the right thing. Our baby was not illegitimate, was not a bastard. His father's name would be on his birth certificate. The fact that I was married, though, counted for nowt. 'I've got to find out what "your sort" means,' I remember thinking over and over again. 'I *must* find out what it means so that I will never ever have to go through this again.'

I was left with such a fear of pregnancy, labour and birth after that experience, that I knew there would never be any more children – and there weren't. I loved, and love, Gary unconditionally. From the day he was born I really would have laid down my life for him. Nothing of what happened during his birth was his fault – kids don't ask to be born. But once was enough. Pregnancy and birth, for me, would be a one-off.

My time on the maternity ward, however, was not the only time I was to suffer at the hands of medical staff or, for that matter, suffer full stop. But all that will become clearer as my life story unfolds. I am now sixty-four years old. It's been a long and winding road, and I've trodden it, step by step, to where I am now. And I've still got a sense of humour!

I remember people saying over the years, 'It's only the nice girls that get caught out. The clever ones, the ones who do *it* more often – the promiscuous ones – don't get caught.'

At first, I was so naive; I wasn't sure what all that meant. But I know now! Ray and I only did it once – and we were caught out. Honest to God, I was a virgin the night I got pregnant with Gary and, although I remember the circumstances well, the details are still a bit of a blur!

What I do remember is that I left school on 29 July 1958, when I was sixteen, and that the late 1950s was an era that became known for a new breed of post-war youngster: the *teenager*. Teenagers, according to the newspapers and magazines at the time, were 'rebellious' and questioned their parents' values. Elvis Presley and Buddy Holly, who rocked into our lives around then, were 'setting us on fire'. Teenage girls had also, apparently, discovered their sexual allure. Hey! What were those journalists on? We Heywood girls were never slow at moving with the times but we weren't quite that forward, and the lads weren't exactly drooling over us either. There were wolf whistles, yes, but those were given and received more from bravado and to preserve your street cred than anything else.

The dance craze, though, was certainly jiving – and rock 'n' roll – in Heywood. We were forever flipping each other over our shoulders, floating each other through our legs and twirling each other around our backs. My mate Sue and I spent every spare minute practising these incredibly fast moves, and as I was taller than Sue, I did the flipping, while she did the leaping, swinging and spinning. It was all good, glorious, manic fun!

Our nearest rock 'n' roll venue was a Mecca dance hall called the Carlton, which had one of those sparkly spinning mirrored balls hanging from the ceiling. On Saturday afternoons we would all flock to Rochdale and launch ourselves into hectic jives – and slow waltzes sometimes – to huge dance bands. Our practice sessions paid off. Sue and I won quite a few competitions at the Carlton. At some point in the evening the band would launch into what was known as the Carlton Capers, the dance hall's version of the hokey-cokey, which was always hilarious.

To go to the dances, we had to pretend we were at each other's houses being good little girls, heads down, pens in hand, doing our homework. Carrying this off needed careful planning. We used to sneak out in ordinary clothes, in case we were spotted, and then change in the ladies' loos at the dance hall into sleeveless polo-neck tops or sleeveless blouses with stand-up collars and felt skirts, which we bought from C&A with our pocket money. We'd soak the net underskirts in sugar to make them stiff, and with an elasticated waspy waistbelt you were away. I've always loved white and often wore it in those days. We also wore fluorescent knickers – either lime green or pink – matching socks and black velvet ballet flats so we could really get into the jiving.

Bill, my dad since he'd married Alice when I was seven years old, would have gone mad if he knew, because he never liked me wearing clothes that he thought were 'too revealing' or made me look older than I was, which is, of course, what most teenagers want to be!

Ray was a trainee draughtsman at Avro, an aviation company where I got my first job after leaving school. He lived in nearby Moston, which back then was a bit posher than the area we lived in. He was quiet, and then, as now, I always went for quiet people. I've learnt, though, that the quiet ones are often the worst!

With his dark curly hair that he teased into a quiff and large tortoiseshell glasses, Ray looked like Buddy Holly, and his workaday clothes – white shirt, bootlace tie, drainpipe trousers and winkle-picker shoes – reflected his passion for rock 'n' roll.

In the evenings he used to change into a powder-blue suit, which at the time was really 'with it'. About five feet ten inches tall, he was always very body-conscious and, as I soon found out, did a lot of weight training. Lots of the girls at work fancied him but, for whatever reason, he picked me and we went out a couple of times to the pictures. He was intelligent, hard-working and certainly not a Jack the Lad. Far from it. He just really enjoyed his keep-fit trips to the gym, where he went as often as possible with his friend Derek.

Once I got to know him, he opened up and I started to appreciate his dry sense of humour. He told me I was his first 'serious' girlfriend. I must have found him attractive and I remember thinking that we made a nice couple. I was aspiring to be a bit of a Diana Dors lookalike then and he was a muscleman – Mr Atlas! I was quite chuffed when we started going out together regularly. I thought I was in love but, if I'm being honest, I wasn't. I was in love with the idea of being in love.

I can't remember how many dates we went on before *it* happened. I only remember that it did on a night when I was wearing a green A-line trench coat with a mandarin collar, and that Ray took me out for a meal to a rather expensive restaurant where we drank a wine called La Flora Blanche. It was white and sickly sweet and, to this day, I can't think of it, let alone drink it, without feeling ill. I drank a lot of it that night, though!

Although I loved being spoiled – did then, do now – and my eyes must have been as big as saucers from being in a restaurant with real napkins. I was only seventeen and it was all a bit overwhelming. Ray's parents must have been away on holiday because, after the wining and dining, we went back to his house, which I thought was very nicely furnished. At some point that night I lost my virginity and, bingo, got pregnant. Since then, I've heard it said that your first time is special, very special, and you never forget it. Sorry, but mine wasn't! Although I'd not had one over the eight, I was certainly a bit drunk and, for that reason, I don't remember much about losing my virginity except that it was all a bit of an awkward clumsy fumble which was quite painful at one stage. And the green mac never came off!

I didn't know it then, of course, but there was worse to come.

It might have been the new era of teenagers casting off old traditions and practices, but I was totally ignorant of the facts of life. Nobody ever told us. We were left to find out the hard way. I didn't even know I was pregnant, didn't connect the feelings of constant early-morning sickness with anything other than a bug; not, that is, until Alice, my mother, sat me down and, with eyes blazing, exclaimed, 'Now look what you've gone and done. Your father will go mad.' It was awful!

Once I was made to accept what had happened to me, and everybody was yelling and shouting about the terrible shame I'd brought on them and on myself, I wanted the ground to open up and swallow me. Alice and Bill said they wanted to see Ray to find out what he had to say for himself, and then his parents, too. When my father told Ray, he looked like a rabbit caught in the headlights, and made it clear he couldn't believe what he was hearing. Then he promptly denied he was the father. When he did tell the truth and admit his 'wrongdoing', he added, 'If it's any consolation, Mr Goodyear, it was my first time, too.' That just made my dad even madder.

'Well, *why* pick my bloody daughter to practise on?' he yelled, his fists clenched. Then the dog joined in and, snarling, went for Ray. Jesus, it was awful. Everybody's faces were as black as thunder and my mam was rocking and sobbing, 'Not our Julie.' Poor me, poor parents, poor Ray. I really do think he was telling the truth and that it had been his first time, too.

The sickness that came over me then continued right through the pregnancy. I even had to take a paper bag to be sick in on the bus when I went to work as a shorthand typist at Avro's.

From the minute my mam had sat me down and told me I was 'pregnant', I was in shock. To be unmarried and having a baby then was such a social stigma, and I was left in no doubt that my dad was beside himself with fury and very disappointed in me. It really was a devastating time. There were three choices: a shotgun wedding, a dangerous illegal backstreet abortion, or having the child and putting it up for adoption. That was it and, in truth, I had no say in the matter.

Neither Ray nor I was keen to get married, but there were no legal abortions then and a lot of girls died as a result of backstreet botch-ups. In an attempt to avoid the shotgun wedding, though, I remember being put into a scalding hot bath and made to drink a bottle of gin. This wasn't done to be cruel, but in the hope that your period would restart and the problem would go away. But, even though the water scalded my skin, and the gin (which I can't drink to this day) made me violently sick, it didn't work. I was still pregnant.

It's tough being a girl was one of the lessons I learned back then. Boys can get away with it but girls can't. They have to pay the price. Since then, I've said on more than one occasion that if I have to come back again, I'll come back as a fella.

Word, of course, soon got round. Hardly surprising. I was

throwing up all the time and the fellas who used to catcall and wolf-whistle at me at work and in the streets stopped. Instead, the jeering started and taunts such as 'Eh up. A bun in the oven?' and 'You'll never miss a slice off a cut loaf!' were thrown at me. Bastards. I don't know for sure, but I think Ray's experience was very different. He probably got pats on the back for being such a good stud and having 'lead in his pencil'.

Once all the decisions had been made, I just went along with it. I asked a mate, Sue Skelton, to be my bridesmaid and the wedding preparations began. Sue's parents weren't best pleased because I was pregnant. It couldn't be a white wedding for obvious reasons – and my mam certainly wouldn't have allowed that anyway! It just wasn't done then. Edna Barlow, who lived across the road, was asked to make my wedding dress and Sue's bridesmaid dress. They were 1950s style with sticking-out knee-length skirts. Mine was blue, as a mark of shame, flocked with white roses, and hers was pink. My headdress was a coronet made of little white plastic pearls whilst Sue's was a coronet made of tulle and pink carnations. I remember Edna had to stitch me into the back of the dress, because it had been made up in such a hurry and didn't fit that well.

When the so-called big day arrived, I didn't want to have any part in it, but Sue and I spent the morning getting ready. As I was only two months pregnant the bump didn't show. Before we left for the church, I decided to have one last jive as a single girl. I put on some rock 'n' roll and, all dolled up in our frocks and headgear, Sue and I had a fifteen-minute jive before we set off. I was still only a kid. The wedding itself took place at St Luke's Church, Heywood, on 26 September 1959. Overall, I remember it as a rather downbeat affair. Looking back, no bloody wonder.

After a honeymoon in Rhyl, Wales, where I was constantly throwing up (much to Ray's disgust) we rented a terraced house at 37 Torrington Street, two doors away from the Bay Horse Hotel which my parents ran, and I continued to work at Avro up to two weeks before Gary was born.

That's how it was for me. I then returned to work two weeks after I was discharged from the hospital. I just went straight back into my pre-motherhood life, still bleeding and very self-conscious that I might seep breast milk.

'But at least,' I thought, 'the worst has to be over.'

Wrong.

From day one Ray and I weren't happy living together, and there were no precious shared moments when we looked forward to the arrival of our baby. We were two immature innocents, locked together in a two-up two-down terraced house, both wanting to return home to the safety of our parents; how could it have ever worked?

Ray was never that interested in his baby. Later I made excuses for him, constantly telling Gary that, although Ray was four years older than me, he was too young to be a dad. I made these excuses because I didn't want to bring my son up with any feelings of resentment or bitterness towards his father; didn't want him to know just how awful, heartbreaking and lonely that period was for me. The truth was certainly not a burden I was going to place on the shoulders of an innocent child.

Ray, though, was not a considerate husband, and made no effort to be one. We were never close, never really had any moments of happiness together. I suppose some shotgun marriages work, but ours didn't. Apart from everything else, I was terrified of becoming pregnant again and very reluctant, therefore, to resume full marital relations. I'm sure Ray found that hard but he never said anything – just went to the gym with his friend Derek more often.

The only good news was the moment Alice and Bill set eyes on Gary, their grandchild, that was it – love at first sight. And, because I was so young, he was more like their child, really – the child they had never had together. To say that Alice and Bill adored Gary would be an all-time understatement, and I was so glad, so thrilled about that. As a bonus, it also meant that when I went back to work they were only too happy to look after him, and I had peace of mind knowing that he was in safe, loving hands.

I'd no choice, of course, but to go back to work to support him. Babies, I quickly discovered, don't come cheap, and motherhood can be hard graft. There were no disposable nappies back then. It was all terry towelling and safety pins, but I never minded changing him. I was just so proud to see the white nappies hanging on my washing line in the backyard. That, I thought, said something about me as a mother! I couldn't be all bad if I was keeping my son so clean and well fed.

I have to say that, throughout my pregnancy and Gary's birth, I was so convinced my baby was going to be a girl I didn't even consider I might have a little lad. The few bits and pieces that I had got together – and, believe me, I didn't have much – were all in pink. That sort of thing mattered far more in those days than it does now in these unisex times. Fortunately, however, the girl in the opposite bed had a little daughter, so I was able to give her all my pink bits and pieces. She was so grateful, because she was also very young and, even worse, an unmarried mother! God help her. I truly hope she managed to cope. Gary's first outfit, though, was pink, and very cute he looked, too!

Often, when you come from the backstreets and a poor background, one pregnancy after another is all that you have to look forward to in life. That was a woman's lot back then, and still is today for far too many girls and women. It was – *is* – a case of Friday night, half a bitter and a packet of crisps (if you were lucky) followed by a good hiding, sex and another kid on the way.

That, I vowed, was not going to be my lot in life. It was not going to happen to me. The experiences I'd had before the age of seventeen had forged my resolve in steel! I would turn them to good use – would make good. I had aspirations. I had dreams. Yes, I was a mother now, but I was also Julie and, much as I loved my son, and because I wanted better for Gary and my mam and dad, I would continue to be *just Julie* for some of the time. Just watch me. Just watch me fly!

ONE

The Way We Were

My own birth on 29 March 1942 was no less traumatic, it seems, than my son's eighteen short years later – and, over the years, my entry into the world became a bit of a family joke. Because I was born in 1942, when the Second World War was well into its deadly jackboot stride, my mam said that bombs were dropping and exploding throughout her labour, the blackout curtains were tightly drawn, and, as I obviously didn't want to come out to such chilling events, I had to be dragged by forceps into the world. It was, I gather, a very prolonged and difficult birth, and Alice, bless her, was badly damaged and couldn't have any more children after me.

Apparently, there was another hazard in those days that today's new mums do not, hopefully, have to face. 'It was quite common,' Mam told me, 'for newborn babies to be swapped in hospitals.' Yes, she did say swapped!

If there was an unattractive couple who had a particularly ugly baby, or a good-looking couple who had had a particularly beautiful baby, a deal might be struck, and if the money was right the babies would be swapped. And this, Mam told me, was exactly what was suggested to her by a well-to-do lady in the next bed, who thought I was a particularly desirable 'golden baby'. I know. Unbelievable!

I'm delighted to say that, although there was a good offer hovering over my so-called golden head, perfect body and tiny limbs, my mother said no.

One of the reasons I wanted *Just Julie* as the title for this book is that when I was born my grandma wanted me to be called Julianna, and all the nursing staff wanted me to be called Pamela, because I was born on Palm Sunday. But my mam stood her ground and said, 'No, it's just Julie.' And just Julie it still is.

My mam was eighteen when she got married to George Kemp, my biological father, at the Baptist Chapel, Heywood, on 13 April 1940. She was twenty when I was born, and at the time George was away fighting in the war. So she was still young to be a mother but she did want me. She's always insisted I was the very best thing that ever happened to her. It was, though, as I gathered over the years, one of those wartime marriages – the 'marry in haste, repent at leisure' variety. I was never told whether my father was granted leave to come home and visit me.

Alice and I were like sisters to look at and, as the years went by, she was often taken to be my sister. She enjoyed the compliment, but on another level the confusion also used to annoy her. The fact that I called her Alice probably didn't help people to understand the true nature of our relationship, but I never called her Alice from a lack of respect. She was just young and liked me calling her that, so, according to the mood of the moment, I either called her Mam, Mother or Alice.

She wasn't a very demonstrative mother in the sense of showering me with cuddles, hugs and kisses, but she was no less

demonstrative than any other Northern working-class
her family. Hers was more an unspoken love, a love th
deep that it didn't need putting into words. I just knew;
always knew that because she was still young she needed to have
some fun in her life. I was always happy for her to go out with
her girlfriends and do that. Anyway, I enjoyed being with my
grandma most of all. Elizabeth Ann Duckworth, my mam's
mam, was a lovely lady and I adored her.

Alice always worked. Her first job was at Woolworth's. She
started as a shop assistant on light bulbs and worked her way up
to the make-up counter, which was much more her cup of tea.
She was slim and very attractive. The first perfume I remember
her using came in a midnight-blue bottle in a white plastic
seashell. It was called Evening in Paris. For make-up, she used
Panstick and always put a bit of lipstick on each cheek as rouge.
As she worked throughout my babyhood and childhood, I
spent nearly all the time with my grandma, who didn't work.
I virtually lived with her. Alice, who was the youngest of
Grandma's four children, was petite and small-boned, and my
grandma was bigger (or so it seemed at the time) and a much
stronger personality. She had tremendous strength and was a real
matriarch. My grandma lived at number 8 Pickup Street, Heywood, and my mother at number 4, just a few doors down.
Who in their right mind calls a street Pickup Street anyway?

My earliest memory is of the inside hood of my pram. White
rambling roses from a tree behind my pram hung over the hood
and I loved the smell of them. As I was born in March and most
roses bloom from June to July I must have only been three
or four months old – not bad eh? I still have a great love of
perfumed roses, especially white ones, and I top these up in my
garden whenever I get half a chance.

My other earliest memory is being placed inside a box just in case there were air raids or a gas attack. I was then picked up and, hopefully, taken to safety. I hated being put in that box and always made my feelings felt. Our air-raid shelter, which was very deep, dark and earthy, became a play den for me when the war ended. I loved that shelter, thought it was absolutely fab, and whenever I could scrounge some candle ends I made a brick altar in it. Money was always in short supply and we were pretty poor. But as I didn't know any different way of living as a child and anyway thought everybody lived like us, I never felt deprived.

Heywood, a Lancashire mill town situated ten to fifteen miles north of Manchester, snakes between the larger towns of Rochdale and Bury. The belching chimneys of the cotton mills and the smoky coal fires used to engulf all the cobbled streets, red-brick houses and washing pegged out to dry on lines with a sooty pollution that often turned everything grey. The scene then, and now, is totally reminiscent of an L. S. Lowry painting. The houses were typical two-up two-down, with an outside toilet and coal bunker in the backyard. The front doorstep was always kept immaculately scrubbed and you could have, if you wished, eaten your dinner from it. At the front a little row of flagstones led from the living room into a tiny garden, which was where my pram used to be parked during that first summer, and where I first saw and smelled real scented roses.

When you entered the house through the front door, there was a heavy curtain, suspended from a pole fixed to the ceiling, which was placed there to keep draughts out and the warmth of the coal fire in. In the one living room there was a horsehair sofa, a rocking chair, a sideboard with a brass clock and two Shy Girl ornaments standing on it, and a black-leaded fireplace. In the winter there was always a fire to cheer you up and a pot of something that smelled lovely cooking on the coals. A tin bath was kept in the backyard and brought in for bath times, and there was a wooden airing rack for drying clothes that you could pull up and down from the ceiling. Men got the first bath, then women, then kids – by which time the water was filthy, but I didn't care cos I didn't know any different.

My grandma's bed, which was in the left-hand corner of that downstairs living room, was always made the minute she got out of it. She really was a spotlessly clean, tidy woman. There was an upstairs in the house, but this, probably for money reasons – heating and furnishing and all that – was not used very often.

In the kitchen there was an old wooden mangle, the dolly tub, which you filled with water for thrashing clothes up and down using the posser, and dolly blue bags for whitening. There was an old slop-stone sink and a cool cubbyhole, which was the pantry where milk would be kept with other things that might go off. It was the poor version of a modern fridge, but like a walk-in one.

On the floor in the main living room there was coconut matting and my grandma used to make peg rugs out of bits of clothing fabric and old blankets, and one of these would be stood in front of the fire. I thought they were beautiful. There was gaslight but, more often than not, we used candles.

One of my jobs when I was about three was to go to the corner shop to buy a new gas mantle, and as they were gossamer-thin and very fragile I had to be careful not to break it on the way back. They cost good money. Two of my other childhood jobs were weeding the flagstones in the kitchen and setting and lighting the fire. The firelighters we used were little bundles of wood soaked in paraffin, again bought from the corner shop. Later I was allowed to put a match to the fire, which was a very special treat!

I was absolutely terrified of the tippler, our name for the outside loo, because whenever our cat had kittens, they'd all be dropped down the inside of the tippler and left to die. A barbaric practice, yes, that certainly sits unhappily with today's animal rights sensitivities, but that was normal practice then. If you had a cat, it was because the cat had a job to do, which was to catch mice and other rodents; and if nobody needed another cat, then the kittens had to go.

My fear came from believing that the kittens remained alive down there in the tippler, and that when I went to wee or pooh, they would all rush up the sides and fly up my bum! The wooden top of the tippler had to be scrubbed and bleached and, as it was a very long time before you heard the splash of wee or the plop of a pooh, I knew it was a very long drop before anything reached the sewer. As it was, I only had a candle to take out there and that blew out pretty quickly in the cold wind. Also, as I was such a thin, scrawny specimen, I once got stuck inside the tippler's hole, and my grandma had to come and pull me out. That *was* frightening – reminiscent of my forceps delivery! For night times in those days, adults had buckets to pee in and children had enamel pots called pos. My grandma, bless her, used to boil some water and use the steam to warm the rim of mine. I was spoiled, I know, and I loved it.

I am left with only very sketchy memories of George Duckworth, my grandfather, who was employed at the local ironworks. I always got the impression, though, that my grandma married beneath her. Whether he had been unfaithful, 'played away from home' at some stage, I don't know for sure, but I always got the feeling that he had. He was a welder, which was a tough job, but he was always the life and soul of any party. He loved going to the pub, which wasn't something my grandma ever did, and was regarded as the pub's comedian. He was a long-suffering man. I remember sitting up on the table once and pouring a jug of warm water over his head and him not minding in the slightest. I was probably pretending to wash his hair.

I must have been very young when he went into hospital, but I was aware that my grandma didn't visit him before he died. His body was brought back home, as was the custom at the time, and his coffin, which had a glass viewing panel in the top, was put underneath the window. The fact that the coffin was sealed was very unusual. Normally it would have been left open for a few days, but they had removed the top of his skull at the post-mortem (apparently he'd had a seizure). I wasn't the least bit frightened, though. I was just interested and pleased that he had been brought home, and I peeked at him several times through the viewing panel and said little prayers.

The reason I wasn't frightened of seeing a dead body is that I used to accompany my grandma when she was asked to lay somebody out. She used to take her own bucket of clean water and a white flannel to wash the bodies and do whatever needed to be done. Then she would place two old pennies to weigh their eyelids down. I felt completely secure with her and just used to watch quietly while she took care of everything. My grandma had a great respect for the dead, which was why people trusted her and why she was always called upon to lay out their loved ones.

My grandma, who had dark hair, was very elegant and often wore a bunch of violets at her neck. When she was younger, she wore a cloche hat. She wasn't a demonstrative woman, but she showed her love for me in so many practical protective ways. She had home cures for everything, and guarded me against all the elements: cold, wind and rain. The preparations just for going to bed took forever, but she never lost patience. As a result, I never seemed to catch anything. We're talking liberty bodices here with tiny rubber buttons, vests, goose grease and hops in the pillows, which pricked your face but supposedly helped you to sleep better. Mustard baths were good, too.

The house was full of herbal preparations, and people would come from miles around for Grandma's remedies. At one stage there was a herbalist's shop in Heywood and I would be sent there with a list of things to buy. When people visited my grandma they would leave a few coppers to help towards another shopping trip. Maybe it would be Epsom salts or Thermogene wool next time. I can remember so vividly all the different mixtures of the herbs and their particular textures and smells. What I would give now for all the books that were chucked out when she died. Herbal medicines and alternative therapies are so popular these days, and she was obviously way ahead of her time. I have known her to cure gallstones with her potions. The old wooden commode next to her bed came in very handy.

Communication with the spirits – spiritualism – was for her (and therefore for me) a way of life. I thought all of that was entirely natural. Holding meetings at home to raise the spirits of the dead in order to communicate with them happened all the time. I remember Mrs Greenhalgh, a neighbour, who had a goitre in her neck, which fascinated me, coming round to the house and she and Grandma would sit talking to spirits on the 'other side'. I thought it was just fab, loved it, I really did. There was nothing creepy or scary about it. I so looked forward to people coming round and the kettle going on. Meetings were always a maximum of four. My grandma was so good at communicating with the spirit world, and while she did this I would usually be sitting in my favourite place under the table, listening and learning.

Growing up in this way, I have always taken seeing and communicating with those who have passed over very seriously. In later years, after my grandma and mam died, they often came back and visited me. Just entered the room and made me aware of their presence. When you've experienced something like that from such an early age, it's just another dimension to your life. A special gift. I don't need any props – perfumes or personal effects or anything else – the spirit of a person is simply either there with me or not.

I'm lucky to have such a gift. It's just like anyone entering a room really, only in spirit form. This can happen at any time and I'm never surprised if someone just pops in for a minute, or if I hear a disembodied voice. That's just normal. They're very welcome, and I always feel happy, comfortable and reassured in their presence. Often, in fact, it proves to be a better relationship with the person than when they were alive!

Thanks to my grandma, I was brought up knowing that we have nothing to fear from the dead; it's only the living we need to be afraid of! That was my grandma's philosophy and now it's mine.

Mentioning fear has reminded me that, during my early childhood, my mother's sister's husband – my uncle – who was a drunk, regularly beat up his wife, and as she always sought refuge with my grandma, he would often turn up at the house, banging on the front door and shouting abuse. Very quietly and with great dignity, my grandma would stand up, walk towards the fireplace, pick up the iron poker, walk past me and open the door. These actions would be followed by a thump, a pathetic whimper from him and then a heavy thud, after which everything would go quiet again. My grandma would then close the door, come back into the room and, without saying a word, wipe the poker with a newspaper and put it back in its usual place. All was peaceful again.

For some reason, it never occurred to me to open the door and see what state the old drunk was in. My auntie always went back to him in the end, and his behaviour, involving endless 'domestics', continued throughout her life. It was truly awful to see a once-beautiful woman, who had been crowned the Cotton Queen of Heywood, regularly beaten up and kicked and regarding it as her lot – she'd made her bed so she had to lie in it. Not for me, I thought, no way.

As I grew up, although I sensed at times that we were poor and that making ends meet was a real struggle, I never felt deprived of anything; and I have never regretted the kind of upbringing that I had. In fact, in many ways that very background has stood me in good stead. I have always had, for example, a great sense of the value of money. Later in my life, Pat Phoenix, my adored mentor on *Coronation Street*, advised me to save as much as I could. She never took her own advice and got seriously into debt at one time, but I listened to what she said. I always paid my taxes and bills and didn't get the swimming pool until I was sure I could afford it and pay for it outright. I have never ever been in debt or owed a single penny to anybody. When a bill drops through my door, I pay it before it lands!

I've never really understood why other people behave differently, and I find it very difficult to understand if I am not paid immediately! I expect others to have the same standards that I have, but I know they don't. Likewise, I wouldn't dream of not answering a letter or returning a phone call. Such behaviour is just plain rude and mystifies me. 'Do as you would be done unto' is my philosophy. All my childhood experiences – good, bad, positive and negative – have made me realize the value of everything and everybody, and taught me not to take anything for granted.

As a child, I was both shy and introverted; later, as an adult, I was just shy! But just how shy and what it costs me to cover that up very few people have ever realized. In fact, I can count on the fingers of one hand those especially sensitive people who saw through the surface bravado to the real me, who was often a quivering wreck underneath.

This didn't mean, however, that there weren't lots of times when, from early childhood, I would sing and dance and put on mock concerts for Bill, Alice and anybody else who was prepared to watch and listen or join in. For me, such activities were pure escapism, a time when I could be someone else, and there was, I am sure, an embryo performer inside me from a very early age. But for much of the time I would just crawl under my grandma's table, which was usually covered in newspaper or a dark red chenille cloth, and get on with living in my own little world.

Christmas was always great fun. I loved making chains out of coloured strips of paper and I was allowed to stick bits of cotton wool on the window panes. Creating this snowflake effect took forever and, however much I scratched at it with my fingernails when Christmas was over, it never seemed to come off altogether throughout the rest of the year. It was wonderful.

For some reason, which was normal back then but I think

very unusual now, my shoes were placed behind the front door for St Nicholas to find. I don't think that is a very British tradition, but my grandma always said, 'If you put 'em behind the door, there'll be a surprise in the mornin'.' And, sure enough, there would be a tangerine or a few nuts, and a silver threepenny bit. Over the years, I kept the silver threepenny bits and had them made into a bracelet. How's that for a saver!

One of my little jobs was to take a bucket out and follow the milkman or coalman's horse and cart so that I could collect the horse manure for the roses planted in the tiny square of garden at the front of Grandma's house. It might have been small but it was beautiful, and there always seemed to be something in bloom there. The ashes from the fire were also collected and thrown outside to stop us from slipping when it was icy.

I remember bitterly cold winters when there was frost and ice inside as well as outside the windows. For extra bedcovers we'd put newspaper in between my one blanket and an overcoat to keep me warm. Newspaper in those days was used for everything. It served as bedcovers, tablecloths, food wrappers, for lighting the fire and toilet paper. One of my favourite jobs was cutting newspapers into squares and threading a piece of string through the corner ready to go outside into the tippler to be hung on a nail behind the door. Much later in life, when the press published yet another offensive and untrue story about me, I used these newspaper squares as defensive weapons: I sent bundles of them to tabloid editors with a little note attached, indicating that was all they had written or published was fit for! I always signed the note, never did this anonymously, which I was told particularly upset them! But not, I bet, half as much as they had upset me in the first place.

Having measles, which was a killer disease when I was a child, was absolutely awful, but having my tonsils and adenoids out was even worse and is a really bad memory for me. Very young, I was taken to somewhere called Doctor Harry's and left there. There were no visitors allowed then and I thought I'd been abandoned forever. There was only one room with cots placed in it and I lay in one of these shaking with terror. A little later, I can remember screaming and trying to fight off the gas mask, followed by excruciating pain when I came round. I was offered ice cream to ease the searing hot pain in my throat. Normally this would have been a tremendous treat, but I couldn't bear to swallow and wouldn't touch it. It was just dreadful. There was no such thing as child psychology in those days and I was convinced nobody was ever going to come and take me home.

That experience, however, was put to really good use in my adult life. Many years later, when it seemed that my son might need the same operation because he was regularly suffering from tonsillitis, I was advised by one doctor that he would grow out of it. I was only too happy to take his advice and save Gary from what had been such an awful experience for me.

Another grim experience in my childhood was school dentistry. For that, as well as coping with my own distress and terror, I had to sit in a queue and cope with the other kids' fears. Since then, even though I now have a fabulous dentist, called Alan Dobkin, who totally understands my fears and has never hurt me, I have had a pathological fear of dentists. The being sick, caused by the gas mask, plus the pain that followed treatment, was just terrible. I can't even have a check-up now without the smell and horror of those times flashing back into my brain, and I know that memory will always remain, tucked in a corner of my mind, to haunt me. I bet a lot of people reading this will remember that, too.

One of the abiding memories of my childhood is taking part in Heywood's famous Whit Walks when I was about six. I was dressed all in white, with little white shoes and socks, and carried a white flower. I thought I looked great. I could hear people saying, 'Ah, doesn't she look a little picture?' Then this voice rang out; it was another kid's mother. 'Julie, hold your lily up, you daft bitch.' My mam said they were just jealous.

But that's how it's always been for me. Just when I think I'm doing everything right, there's always someone who comes along and spoils it. I brace myself waiting for the next attack. Alice had a very no-nonsense attitude about this. She'd just say, 'Take no notice, luv.' That's not always easy, but I do try.

Although I was an only child I don't ever remember feeling lonely or wishing I had a brother or sister. I was very happy in my own make-believe world and, in particular, with my button jar that had been my grandma's before she gave it to me. My favourite daydream when I was about five years old centred on the mass of multicoloured, differently shaped buttons crammed into that jar. Picking them up one by one and holding them up to the light, I pretended they were diamonds, pearls and emeralds – riches beyond belief – and lying on my tummy on the floor, draped in my exotic jewels, I would make up stories about princes and princesses. I was always the heroine, of course! That button jar kept me blissfully occupied for hours. As did painting little paper doilies.

Another real treat was being allowed to take a drawer out of the sideboard and sit there smelling the lovely fragrance of the crackly seeds packed into lavender bags; and then being allowed to take out every single item, one by one, before putting them all back into the drawer again, neatly, properly – *very* properly.

I might not have had any shop-bought toys to throw out of my pram if my nose was put out of joint, but I did have my beloved button jar and a vivid imagination, so I lacked for nothing. Wood crackling and spitting in the grate, coals lighting up the hearth, sparks making a bid for freedom up the chimney – all this was my ever-changing kaleidoscope – wonderful. Even the soot up the back of the chimney told me a story as it glowed in the dark.

Recollections of George, my biological father, are very sketchy, because he remained away from home, still serving as a soldier, throughout the first three years of my life. When he did return in 1945, at the end of the war, he and my mother only got back together again for a short time. I do remember, though, that he used to call me snowball and his eyes were crossed and his skin was very greasy.

One day, when I was about five years old, I recall desperately wanting to get my hands on a shiny penny, which was the in thing then. When I mentioned this longing to my grandma, she said I should go and ask my dad for one, so I skipped out of her house up to number 4 and knocked on the door.

'Can I have a shiny penny, please?' I asked when he appeared at the door, looking somewhat bleary-eyed.

There was a pause, then he replied cautiously, 'Well, have you got the penny, then?'

'No,' I answered, a frown creasing my forehead and hope dying an instant death in my hazel eyes.

'Well, come back then when you've got the penny,' he added. 'And I'll give it a shine for you.'

Feeling incredibly disappointed, let down and angry, I returned to my grandma's house. When I told her what had happened, her nostrils flared a little and she sniffed, but she didn't look the slightest bit surprised. Maybe she thought I needed to learn a lesson and get a sense of what kind of man my father could be. But I'm only guessing.

I did so want the shiny penny, though, that I'd seen other children showing off with, and I kept saying, 'Where can I get a penny, Grandma?' It took me quite a while to achieve my heart's desire, but I'm not one to give up and I got one in the end. Grandma gave me a sterilized milk bottle to take back to the corner shop and I got a penny back for it. I was angry because I knew the moment had passed really and the other kids' interest in shiny pennies had moved on, but I set off back to the house where my dad was living with Alice and knocked on the front door. When he opened it, I gave the penny to him. Looking back now, I can see that it's very telling that I didn't even go into the house, but just stayed outside on the doorstep while he took the penny inside and made it shiny.

'Right! There you go,' he said, as he returned looking very pleased with himself.

In my heart of hearts I was far too hurt, too angry because of the long wait, to rejoice in that penny and, once I'd got it back in the palm of my hand, I gestured that he should come with me.

'What? Where?' he asked, looking puzzled.

'Over there,' I replied, pointing.

And, despite his reluctance, I took him to the nearest iron grid that topped the drain in the nearside kerb and dropped the penny down it. Having waited for the plop I gazed up at him, then said, '*Piss off!*' using the tone of voice I'd heard adults use when they said that. Then, before he could collect himself, I ran off down the street to my grandma's and slammed the front door firmly behind me.

I have no way of knowing now where I first heard that expression, certainly not from my grandma who never swore. I was five years old and bruised by having had to wait so long for that penny, and I obviously wanted to make a point. That incident represented the end of my relationship with my biological father! It was less than a year later when, like so many couples in the aftermath of the Second World War, George and my mam's relationship ended and they got divorced.

Before I tell you about the man who became, to me, my real dad, let me share a few childhood memories about the family pets.

There was always a budgie, called Joey, at my grandma's but, given the length of time we had that bird, it couldn't possibly have been the same one. One of my little jobs was to collect dandelion leaves, wash them and put them in with his cuttlefish and millet sprays. On one occasion when, for some reason, we didn't have a Joey for a short time, a kid up the road gave me some white mice that had incredibly tiny bright pink eyes and the sleekest of furry bodies, and my grandma allowed me to keep them in the budgie's cage.

After a while nature took its course and there were lots of little mice darting about. I found them endlessly fascinating but it was all to end in tragedy. One morning my grandma obviously decided some urgent action was needed. 'Look at the poor little things,' she said, tut-tutting, 'they're sweating. All that running around – they're too hot, luv. I think they'd like a swim to cool them down.'

'Are you sure, Grandma?' I asked, instantly anxious.

'Oh, yes, quite sure.'

And, going over to the slop-stone sink, she started filling the washing-up bowl with cold water. I remember standing on a stool by the sink to look in, feeling very unsure that the mice really did want a swim. But Grandma started to put them in the water and soon the bowl was full of all sizes of white mice thrashing around.

'Look, they're fine, luv,' Grandma kept insisting. 'They're having fun.'

I might have been young but I didn't really believe her. Then, suddenly, it was all over. They stopped moving, sank to the bottom of the bowl and didn't come up again. Later, just like the unwanted kittens, they were taken out into the backyard and put down the tippler – and that was the end of the white mice.

Despite my grief – and it ran very deep at the time – I must have been wise beyond my years because I seemed to understand this event from my grandma's point of view. The mice were just another problem that had to be dealt with. I know today's grandmas and mothers would never do what she did, and certainly not in front of a child, but times were tough then.

For example, I can remember another occasion when a large pigeon came flying into the house and, much to my amazement, I was allowed to keep it in the pantry, give it leftovers to eat, and tame it. Within a few days it became a much-loved friend and I gave it the name of Snoopy. I don't know how long I had Snoopy but one day, after we'd had our tea, Grandma said, 'Did you enjoy that?'

'Yes,' I replied, 'I did, Grandma.'

'Good,' she answered. 'That was Snoopy pie.'

I just made it to the backyard tippler before I threw up all the pie.

Even then, despite my broken heart and great sense of loss, something inside me understood my grandma's reasons. Fur and feather was bred and kept for eating then, not as pets, and I honestly don't think she thought I would be that upset, but if I was then I needed to toughen up.

So, that was the end of Snoopy, and I vowed silently that I would never keep a bird or white mice again, and I would never give anything a name. I did, however, manage to get hold of some tadpoles and brought them home in a jam jar. Watching them was a consolation, and I thought they were the most magical things on this earth. I was devastated – couldn't believe it – when they sprouted legs and pissed off. Oh, no, not them as well!

I didn't know it then, but this was just the first of many betrayals and desertions that were to come. 'Even *they've* gone,' I remember sighing. I didn't even get a chance to kiss a frog, let alone watch it turn into a prince!

Lots of people had allotments then for growing veg and making the housekeeping money go further, so, poor though we might have been, there was nearly always good, fresh, healthy food on the table. Things are going full circle now and allotments are back in fashion, big time. As for today's buzzword 'recycling', that was taken for granted when I was a child. Even washing-up water was recycled: emptied over the rose bushes to kill off greenfly. My grandma, like everybody else, kept chickens in a pen. Having collected the eggs, we would use the chicken poo as fertilizer on the garden. After Grandma had wrung the birds' necks, I was always happy to help pluck and clean them. Nothing was wasted.

Heaven for me in those days was a halfpenny piece of 'Spanish', which had a liquorice flavour and came in little white twisty bags. You dipped this into bright yellow crystals that tasted very tangy and fizzy. One penny for both. Dandelion and burdock, which was a brownish-coloured fizzy pop made by a local firm called Wild's, was my favourite drink. I really enjoyed that. Later on, during my pregnancy, that was my only craving.

As a child, I was always very aware of the difference between Catholics and Protestants. Catholics were called cat-lights and Protestants were called proddy-dogs. We so-called Protestants were not supposed to play with the cat-lights, and I don't expect they were supposed to play with us. I knew we were Church of England, but I didn't see what difference this should make. From an incredibly young age, I thought such divisions and labels were absolutely stupid, and, as I've gone through life I still think they're stupid. I often find myself wanting to shout from the rooftops, 'Listen, you silly buggers! My favourite colour is the rainbow, and there's good and bad in every religion, colour, race, creed, sexual orientation. Why can't we just get on and love each other or, at the very least, be kind to each other?'

Bonfire Night was a great occasion. It was held on a square of dirt at the end of Pickup Street which was called, most appropriately, the end. Wood would be collected, the bonfire would be built, and the scarecrow-guy and treacle-toffee-apples and potatoes in their skins would be put in the fire to cook – and sometimes burn. It was all very exciting. Fireworks then were not the sophisticated ones we have today; they were coloured matches, sparklers, Catherine wheels and bangers. I was never keen on the bangers, though. The local lads would tie these to a cat's tail. Whenever that happened, I was back in the house in a jiffy, biting my lip under the table. I hated cruelty. Still do.

Smells always bring back memories. The smell of mothballs in my grandma's house, for instance, was everywhere. Years later, when I went to India to work on *Road Raja* for Sky TV, the very first smell I noticed when I entered my accommodation was mothballs. Bloody hell – how the stars live!

Brown carbolic soap and green blocks of Fairy soap were also in abundance, and 'Soap and water costs nowt' was a commonly heard expression in my grandma's house. Hers was a 'Cleanliness is next to godliness' philosophy and I have certainly inherited that! Carbolic and Durback soap was also used to help free us from nits. I was quick to notice, though, that these nits were never *your* nits; they were always somebody else's. I wanted my own! Desperately. I also wanted impetigo so I could be painted blue with iodine. No luck there, either.

I enjoyed being de-nitted, though. For this, I was sat on the table with newspaper spread around me. Then my hair was gone through with a fine-tooth comb and the nits were squashed between Grandma's fingernails. I loved her triumphant smile, and the attention. I'd sit as still as a statue while she went through my blonde hair looking for these nits which weren't even mine. If they didn't want to be mine, I thought, let her kill them. See if I care.

Alice and George got divorced when I was six and Mam remarried a year later, this time to a master builder called Bill (William) Goodyear, a confirmed bachelor who was forty at the time. Bill was a local lad who had started work as a teaboy at John Ratledge & Co. and worked his way up to owning the firm.

Soon after they got married Mam took me by bus from my grandma's house in Heywood to Rochdale, where Bill had bought a house for the three of us. He had a car, too, so we'd gone up in the world. 'We're going to knock on the front door,' she told me just before we arrived, 'and when it opens I want you to say "Hello Daddy."'

She obviously wanted me to make a very good first impression, but I'm afraid I let her down very badly. When Bill Goodyear opened the door, I was horrified and just stood there and screamed and screamed. What I saw was a large man, wearing a trilby hat. The hat was bad enough but when he took it off, I could see he was absolutely bald, hadn't a single hair on his head! I'd never seen a bald man before. He had lost every hair on his head overnight when his parents had been killed in a car crash twenty years before.

I really didn't like his bald head – which much later I grew to love – but, to make matters worse, as soon as I was inside the house, he tried to take me down some steps into the cellar. I'd never seen a cellar before and it was a dark, forbidding place. All Bill wanted to do, bless him, was to win me over by showing me he'd got lots of bottles of pop down there (dandelion and burdock), but I didn't know that and I put up one hell of a struggle, trying to wrench my hand from his. I thought I was going to be put down there as a punishment and locked in!

Although, as I said, Bill was forty at the time, he'd never been married and knew nothing about children. In the end, though, none of this mattered because he absolutely adored my mother, worshipped the ground she walked on, and that was all that mattered to me. Everything else, including the fact that my name was changed overnight from Julie Kemp to Julie Goodyear and that he was very Victorian in his attitudes and a very strict stepfather, faded into insignificance. All I ever really wanted as a child was for my mam to be happy – and he made her happy.

Having said all that, I didn't like living in Rochdale because I yearned on a daily basis to be back in my grandma's house in Heywood, which always felt so cosy and safe. When Bill and Alice went out together for an hour or so, I often ran away. I'd get very very frightened about being left on my own, and I'd sneak out wearing my nightie and run barefoot all the way from Rochdale to Heywood. Sometimes they wouldn't discover I was missing until they woke up in the morning. Rochdale is only a ten-minute car ride from Heywood, but it was a very long trek for a little girl dressed only in a flannelette nightie and, if I remembered to put it on, a thin woollen coat.

I never had any bad experiences on the way, though, and it was lovely when I got to my grandma's because the door was always on the latch and she always seemed to be expecting me. The fire was lit, the horsehair sofa I slept on was already made up, and everything felt warm, safe and familiar. I always believed what Grandma told me, that nothing was going to harm or hurt me. Others might let me down, but she would always pick up the pieces, would always be there for me. I used to like the smell of the cologne cloth she put on my forehead. Heaven.

I particularly loved running away in the middle of the night because she had no transport and there was no danger of her taking me back. Of course, Bill smacked me for escaping on such a regular basis and going back to her, but I regarded a few slaps, which weren't that painful anyway, as a price worth paying for being with her.

A couple of years later Alice and Bill moved into a house in Molyneaux Street, Rochdale. The house was what in those days was called a mixed business shop, like a corner shop really. I quite liked the corner shop, as well as Spotland Junior School which I'd started going to, not forgetting my first boyfriend Arnold Lord. He had a hunting horn which he used to blow outside the house as a sign that he was waiting for me. Mam and Bill laughed about this years later, but at the time I thought it was a secret between Arnold and me!

By the age of eight, then, I had a new dad and our new life had got off to a good start. The very upsetting rows between my mother and biological father had stopped at last, but now there was something new for me to get used to. All of a sudden my mam was part of a loving couple and that took me quite a while to adjust to.

I'm sure many children who go through the trauma of their parents' divorce and remarriage withdraw into themselves and are possibly damaged and bear the emotional scars for life. But not me, well, not for very long anyway! I have never been a quitter. I seemed to have an inborn understanding that 'Winners never quit and quitters never win!' Blessed with a naturally sunny disposition that usually found a way to turn negatives into positives, I stumbled on the answer and fought back.

At every opportunity, I began to perform for Alice and Bill and was thrilled to discover that, in this way, I could get their attention. I sang, danced, clowned, turned cartwheels, stood on my head, dressed up, acted – did whatever felt right at the time. Aged just eight, I didn't know it but I'd discovered a way to fight back and escape from any problem that life chose to throw at me. I was up, up and away, rehearsing for what would be my future career. From then on whenever I got the urge, I performed – both at home and at school. Once, when something had upset me, I got up in front of the whole class and sang 'If You Knew Susie', and on another occasion I serenaded the history teacher. I was learning to cover up my shyness by being a clown.

My voice has always been deep and husky and, in those days, I liked to think this made it sound very grown-up – sophisticated even. Much later, at Bury Palais, I got up on stage and started to sing 'Blue Moon' but some clever sod threw a meat pie at me. What did I do? I ate it and got a round of applause.

The summers during my childhood always seemed to be long and hot, and I particularly enjoyed popping the tar bubbles on the road with my fingers. I lived in fear, though, of our family trips to Blackpool, because I knew what *that* would mean.

That meant on the day before these outings a pudding basin would be placed on my head, and all the hair left showing under its edges would be cut off; then what was left after the basin came off would be subjected to a home perm called something like a Tweenie Twink and I would end up as a 'curly top'. Then, to add insult to injury, the knitted swimsuit, which was in green and yellow stripes and always sagged down to my knees when wet, would come out, and *that* was *that*.

Brash, cheerful, legendary Blackpool, with its three piers, its steel finger of a tower and the stretch known as the Golden Mile, was the playground of the North, a favourite destination for day trippers and holidaymakers alike, but I just didn't want to go there! On top of everything else, I was either coach- or car-sick and hated every minute: hated the boarding house, hated going onto the sands in the knitted swimsuit (which became instantly full of grit), and as soon as the sea air hit the perm I looked like an electrocuted wasp!

Punch and Judy shows were no consolation. They absolutely

terrified me – Punch's red face, big nose and stick, Judy's squeals. As if that wasn't bad enough, the baby was murdered and thrown out! The other kids seemed to be enjoying it all and laughing, but I found it horrible, and was constantly told off with, 'Why can't you be like other children? What's the matter with you? Oh, come on, Julie, *try* to enjoy it.' Then, before I'd recovered from that horror, I was put on the back of a donkey, in that wet swimsuit with seaweed dangling from it. And, as if sitting there was not punishment enough, I always got the donkey that bolted and headed for the sea.

No! Trips to Blackpool in those days were certainly not something to look forward to or get excited about and, many moons on, when I was given the great honour of being the celebrity guest who switched on its illuminations, all those child-hood memories came rushing back. But more of that later.

Even going across the main road for a mug of tea was a nerve-racking ordeal. I had to dodge the trams to bring it back and I was forever being told off because there was sand in it. What was I to do, for goodness' sake? There was sand every-where, including places sand should never go!

One other thing, everybody you knew was there because everybody went on day trips and holidays at the same time. I just wanted to go home.

I don't remember much about my first day at school; I think that memory has been blotted out by one humiliating day when the teacher asked, 'Is it anybody's birthday today?' My hand shot up. It was my birthday, which, looking back, I am quite sure she knew.

'How old are you, Julie?' she asked, playing along.

'I'm eight, miss,' I replied, bursting with pride.

'Come to the front of the class, then.'

When I did, and stood there before a sea of expectant faces, she gave me a piece of chalk and said, 'Write the word "eight", then, on the blackboard.'

I was stunned. I knew how to write the number, but I didn't know how to spell 'eight', which you must admit is not the easiest of numbers to spell. I made a good stab at it, but didn't get it right. Subjected to giggles and ridicule from my classmates, my big birthday moment was ruined. My misery and embarrassment was only cut short by the teacher saying, 'All right, Julie, go and sit down,' which I did, very quietly. My humiliation lasted all day. Not a good birthday, that one.

Later, I went to the Queen Elizabeth Grammar School in Middleton, but I was never an academically bright child and I only just got in. I was, apparently, a borderline case. This meant I had to go for an interview with the headmistress. I was just lucky. She obviously took to me and I scraped through, and, joy of joys, got a good education. Alice and Bill were so proud of me.

I regret that I was no genius at school. But, like so many children, I was a late developer where the three Rs were concerned, and only really got off the ground between the ages of thirteen and fourteen. I was always willing to work hard, however, and, once again, was certainly not a quitter. The only drawback of Queen Elizabeth's was its school uniform. The colours were green, red and grey and the kids from the school next door used to sing 'Red and green are seldom seen except on fools and donkeys.' The school, which had the nickname of Quegs, had the motto *Tout bien ou rien*, which, as I soon learned, meant 'All good or nothing'. And, my God, were we encouraged to live up to it! Girls and boys were expected to take up careers in the professions. But even then I knew that I wanted to be an actress. I often think I was born knowing that!

Not surprisingly, I loved drama at school and was a member of the dramatics society. I was over the moon when one of the lady teachers told me that I'd surprised the whole school with a performance which would not have shamed a professional actress! I received this acting compliment – my first ever – at the age of fifteen when I played the lead part of a character called Toni Opera in the school play *We Must Kill Toni*. I can't pretend I didn't love being the centre of attention and I remember glowing with pleasure as the teachers responsible for my hair, make-up and wardrobe fussed over me. I loved it all: the rehearsals, the first-night butterflies in my tummy, the perform-ance and the heady applause as the curtain dropped. I felt part of a team, in which each member was pulling together and working for a common good. That gave me such a warm glow, and a feeling of being loved.

Despite that success, when I confided in one of my teachers, Mrs Maskew, that I wanted to train to be an actress, she just laughed. 'You can forget *that*, young lady,' she muttered. 'It takes far more intelligence and staying power than you have.' She then added that she thought I would make a good secretary or clerk and, when the time came for me to leave school, she would send me to the aviation firm Avro's for an interview. If I was lucky they might just accept me in the typing pool. 'Oh, well, work's work,' I thought. 'Better than nowt.'

I don't think she was being unkind or insensitive when she put me down. She was just being worldly wise. Acting, after all, was then – and is now – renowned for being an incredibly competitive business, and many actors are known to 'rest' far more than they work. Much better was Mrs Maskew's attitude, to be realistic and set my heart on getting a 'proper' job, rather than reaching for the stars and risking a painful crash-landing!

So by the time I was thirteen, life was settled and feeling good. I was happy at school and happy at home with Alice and Bill. We were now living in a little terraced house in Gregge Street, Heywood, an area where Bill owned several houses with his business partner, Jack. As long as I could see my grandma on a very regular basis, which I did without the necessity to run away any more, I was more than content. But things were obviously too good to last. I was about to be hit full on by the worst tragedy of my young life, the very last thing I could have expected to happen.

I was at school when Tom Roberts, a good friend of my mam and dad's, but particularly close to my mam, came to my school in his car to tell me some truly terrible news. I knew that something awful had happened as soon as I saw his car and, although he wanted me to get into it before he spoke, for some reason I just didn't want to. And even when I did finally climb in and he told me, I didn't really believe the words I was hearing until I saw the body for myself back at Pickup Street.

My beloved grandma had been found drowned in a canal opposite our house in Gregge Street. Her body was pulled out a fair distance from her own home but close to ours, so she must, we reasoned, have been on her way to see me. She had, we were soon to learn, apparently been in the water for at least three days. Oh God, how could I not have seen her for three whole days? It didn't seem possible.

When I ran into the house to see her, to prove to myself that this horror was true, she was lying in an open coffin. To my deep distress, doubtless because she had been in the water for so long, there were bluebottles buzzing all around her.

Despite this, though, and given all the other problems involved when people are found drowned, somebody had done a very good job of brushing her hair, and making her look almost as lovely as she had in life; and, having dealt with the bluebottles, I just stood there heartbroken, totally bereft, overcome with shock. The pain went beyond tears.

The one thing that really helped was all those early experiences when, as a small child, I'd accompanied my grandma as she'd laid out the dead. This had obviously stood me in good stead as I wasn't in the least bit scared when I saw her lying in her coffin. I knew that everybody in the house was crying, weeping buckets, but I'd seen that so often I just accepted all the tears as part of the ritual of death. For reasons I didn't understand then, I'd grown out of crying – never cried any more, couldn't cry – and that remained the case for many years to come.

In those days the curtains in a house were closed as soon as somebody died. Death was not the taboo subject it has become today, and funerals were not as removed – sanitized – as they are now. There were no chapels of rest for bodies to lie in until the burial. The bodies were brought home to rest in the midst of their family and loved ones in their own homes.

The verdict brought in at the inquest into my grandma's drowning was accidental death, but that seemed unlikely to me. I couldn't believe that she had just tripped and slipped down the bank into the canal and then just drowned. Although the canal was quite deep, there was a fair amount of open scrubland next to it, so it wasn't easy to just slip down the bank. And what was she doing there? She hadn't been out of her own house for many years then, and it would have been unheard of for her to walk from her home in Pickup Street to the canal near our home. Was she coming to look for me? Had she needed me and I wasn't there?

I know that a note was found at her home because, much later in life, my mother showed it to me. But that note could have been written at any time to meet any possible eventuality. At the bottom of the note, addressed to my mother, my grandma had put, 'Look after Julie for me. She will be a big help to you one day.' Her death remains an unresolved painful mystery. She really wasn't the sort of woman who would commit suicide. The very thought would have disgusted her.

In later years, my mother said that Grandma had been suffering from high blood pressure and that she could have had a dizzy spell. Well, I knew that was true because the doctor used to put leeches on her head and they'd fall off full of blood. I never liked that, really. She was apparently seen on the canal bank by a mother and daughter, who witnessed her helping a little child who had fallen over. My grandma had consoled the child and brushed grit from her knees. Maybe, after that, after they had all moved on, she suddenly felt dizzy from all the bending down, swayed and then fell into the canal.

Like so many things that happened in my life after that tragic event, I was left with so many questions to torment me, and so few answers to put my mind at rest. Whatever had caused my grandma to drown, die, pass over to the other side, that event, terrible though it was, was not the only problem I now had to face. My grandma's death was the beginning of my mother's anorexia. Within hours of the news Alice stopped eating, and that continued, more often on than off, for the rest of her life, until she died aged sixty-four. She never had any real interest in food after that day, always said she'd rather have a bouquet of flowers. Once I got regular work on *Coronation Street*, however,

I was able to pay for vital medical treatment for her. Just to keep her alive took, on average, twice-yearly stays in hospital, being drip-fed. She enjoyed it. A room full of flowers, sherry in one hand, drip in the other. 'Our Julie's in *Coronation Street*, you know. She plays Bet.' What a woman!

Yes, my grandma was my security blanket, but I adored my mother – always felt, even though she had a husband who also adored her, that she was my special responsibility. That was a burden I always carried so lightly, a burden I would gladly have borne for time immemorial. If asked, I would have leapt at the chance to sacrifice my own life for her to go on living. Her happiness meant *everything* to me.

To this day, I never go anywhere without making sure I am carrying her bus pass with me. It's my passport to being reunited with her one day wherever she is now. Her face, a vision of loveliness to me, even on the picture on her bus pass, is gazing up at me as I make ready to put the final full stop to this chapter.

'I know you're here now,' I whisper.

And her answer is always the same: 'Yes, luv. Now and forever.'

TWO

Becoming My Sort of Girl!

As my bedroom overlooked the Gents' toilet, there wasn't much by my first teenage year that I hadn't heard in the way of foul language or the disgraceful way men talked about women. I also witnessed a good few fights as well as some more serious drunken brawls.

This came about when, shortly after my grandma's death, Bill and Alice obtained the tenancy at the Bay Horse Hotel, a small pub in Torrington Street, Heywood, just around the corner from where we'd been living in Greggc Street. This popular backstreet pub was thriving then, always filled with a band of merry regulars who thoroughly enjoyed a pint and a game of darts or dominoes. It was to play a very prolonged and important part in my life – and, I might add, education!

I'm not suggesting that any of this was bad for me, it was just the way it was. I couldn't fail, though, in that environment, to grow up fast and become wiser in some respects beyond my years. It really was an education in itself. Yet, somehow, I remained an innocent, ignorant of what I really needed to know about the facts of life and how babies were conceived and brought into this world.

The nearest I got to all that was a coarse ditty beloved of the local testosterone-driven lads in and around the aforementioned Gents! This went, 'It's only human nature after all, to get a girl up against the wall / To pull down the protection and fit in the connection / It's only human nature after all.' Not, you must admit, very helpful or strong on details for a teenager. And did I overhear the women protesting – giving them a clout round the ear when they heard such chants? No. Their response was nearly always an indulgent 'Well, boys will be boys' and, on rare occasions, 'Well, we all know how much boys love their toys – and, let's face it, luv, that's what we girls are for them: their favourite toys.'

The women could be just as bawdy at times, too. I remember being very puzzled by one expression, which I heard bandied around on a number of occasions. This was, 'You know what? He can get places Vaseline can't!' Spare my blushes! And me only thirteen at the time.

Apart from a brief period after I lost my virginity at the tender age of seventeen and was, as they say, caught out and had to marry and live with Ray Sutcliffe, I remained sleeping in that room above the Gents until I was twenty-six years old.

There had been a few boyfriends before Ray, but those were of the crush variety; the ones where you draw or carve hearts, with an arrow going through and two sets of initials. Nothing more serious than that. Ray was my first real boyfriend after I left grammar school and started work in the typing pool of Avro, which was based in Chadderton, close to Heywood. Despite my aspirations and dreams to become an actress, there was no way Bill and Alice would have allowed me to go to London, the 'wicked city', let alone the Royal Academy of

Dramatic Art, RADA. 'Bad things happened to girls in showbiz.' No one thought that bad things could happen in an aircraft factory, full of lusty fellas. Yeah, right!

It was considered quite a step up when I was employed by Avro, which has since been taken over by British Aerospace. It was a big employer in our area. When I joined in September 1958 nearly 6,000 staff were involved in producing different types of aircraft. The firm accepted me, along with thirty other school-leavers, onto their training scheme for a weekly salary of £2 17s. 6d. a week. For the first three months of the induction course we studied company law, maths and English, then we were split into two groups so that the accountancy recruits could be trained in accounting and the secretaries, which included me, could study shorthand and typing. I was very proud when I graduated six months later as a shorthand typist and became a secretary in the typing pool of the accounts department. My old teacher Mrs Maskew was equally surprised and delighted when Avro distributed a recruitment leaflet to schools. On the cover was a picture of her ex-pupil – me, Julie Goodyear – perched decorously on an office desk. My very first modelling job!

The training school was at the back of the firm's huge aircraft hangar, which stretched two thirds of a mile from end to end. The factory was like a mini-town, bustling with life, different activities and all shapes and sizes of people. The massive building had glass ceilings to let in as much natural light as possible, and there were stepladders leading up to the jigs, and fifteen-foot-high scaffolding towers. Parts of aircraft were suspended on these jigs with men crawling all over them. The noise was deafening, with pneumatic drills making a constant racket. To get to the school meant walking a quarter of a mile past hordes of engineers and other factory workers riveting planes together.

Along with the other girls, I had to learn to hold my head up high and sashay past the lads, who would all go into a frenzy: behave like lunatics, whooping and hollering, whistling and catcalling and banging their hammers on the huge fuselages. It really was a baptism by fire.

The fashion at the time, which I actually hated, was for huge, swirling skirts held out by layers of net petticoats, topped with twinsets and pearls, or shirts buttoned to the neck. On our feet we wore pumps. Always by nature fashion conscious (probably because my mam was so glam), I bucked this trend and started to wear straight skirts, jumpers, high heels and jewellery. I also changed my hairstyle often; one day I would put it up in a chignon, the next day let it hang loose or pile it on top.

On one occasion, out of sheer bravado and because I was being urged on by some of the other girls, I agreed to be photographed for *Avro News*, the company's monthly magazine. For this I was asked to wear a leopard-skin bikini! I remember my bum being very nearly frozen solid while the pics were being taken by the editor, Gordon Allen, who asked me to pose during my lunchtime on the draughty stairs leading from the reception area to the offices.

The moment it was published, I wasn't at all sure I'd done the right thing. I became the plant pin-up and crossing the factory floor became an even greater agony of embarrassment! All the men in the huge hangar started to single me out, calling, '*Julie, Julie,*' and, between wolf whistles, some very dubious 'compliments' winged through the air. At that age – in fact, any age; I am the same now – I found that kind of banter embarrassing. For the sake of my street cred, however, I pretended to take it in my stride. Well, you've got to, haven't you?

Almost as soon as Ray and I got married, he started to behave really badly and was very cruel to me at times. And all this was while I was still reeling from the sadistic nursing sister teaching me the 'error of my ways', not to mention still learning to be a mother to my new son and trying to encourage Ray to take an interest in his child. 'I don't believe he's mine anyway,' Ray would taunt me on an almost daily basis, but especially if I was trying to get him to lend a helping hand. And, for good measure, he would ram it home: 'I never thought he was mine – never *ever* believed it.' There were no DNA tests then, so I couldn't prove that he was, beyond a shadow of a doubt, Gary's father. But, then, he only had to look. The baby was the spitting image of him!

Also, whatever I cooked, because Ray was so body-conscious and always worrying about his weight, he would only drink the juice and throw the rest away. If it was cabbage, for example, he would drink the water it was cooked in, but throw away the vegetable itself. He was absolutely obsessed with his bodybuilding and weight training, and all this at a time when we could ill afford to waste any food. At the very least, he could have left what he didn't want to eat for his son and me.

Things went from bad to worse, and Ray and I decided that, for both our sakes, we should agree on a separation, even if we needed to carry on living in the same house.

Quite unexpectedly, just as my despair was reaching rock bottom, something that promised an end to my woes presented itself. Ray's family – his mother, father, brother, sister and brother's wife – all decided they wanted to take advantage of the £10 passage that the Aussie government was offering Brits, and emigrate. Ray, without consulting me, decided that he was going too. He didn't seem to mind when I then announced that I would ask my mam and dad if Gary and I could move back into my old room in the pub with them. When I did ask this, Alice and Bill thought about it for a few minutes, then said, 'Of course, we'll take you back. But you'll have to carry on working to keep yourself and support Gary.'

'Of course,' I said, so relieved. 'I wouldn't dream of doing anything else.'

So, that's what happened. Gary and I moved in with them, and Ray stayed in the house we'd shared until it was time for him to leave for Australia. I've no idea what his parents – Gary's paternal grandparents – thought about all this. It was never discussed. I suppose they took the line that Ray would be better off without us and could make a fresh start.

I also have no way of knowing whether Ray felt any sense of remorse or guilt about leaving me, unsupported, literally holding the baby. I can only say that I have a vivid memory of him coming to the back door of the pub and my father, who never liked him anyway because of what had happened, saying to me, 'See what he wants, Julie.'

When I went to the back door, Ray, looking rather sheepish, said, 'Well, I'm off now,' as if he was just going to pop down the road to the corner shop for a loaf of bread.

'Right!' I replied, my voice devoid of any emotion. 'I'd better go and get Gary then.'

'No no,' he said at once, adding, 'You're all right.'

It was like, 'Don't bother – look after yourself'!

I was just numb, couldn't feel anything, and that was that. I've never seen or spoken to him since then and, at the time of writing this book, his son is forty-six years old and he'll never know what he's missed. He fathered a son any man would be proud of.

I didn't feel bitter then and I don't feel bitter now. When I read about some of the situations that girls and women find themselves in today – all that acrimony and fighting over access and possessions – I think Gary and I were relatively lucky. Gary, bless him, wasn't caught in a damaging tug of war and neither was I. He had a doting mother and doting maternal grand-parents, and a good male role model in my dad, Bill. I always tried to be a mother, father and friend to my son, and I hope I succeeded. At least I tried.

So, that brief goodbye was it as far as Ray was concerned, and, as far as I know, he is still living in Australia. It would have been helpful in those early years, though, if he had sent the £2 10s. maintenance money, but he never did. Fortunately I was young and healthy and had secretarial skills, so I could get what is called in acting circles a proper job!

Having returned to my old room over the Gents' toilet, Gary had his room, and Mam and Dad had theirs. The experi-ence, to say the least, made me more than a little wary of men. For a year or more, I did a full day's work then came home to look after Gary. But I was still young, still in my early twenties, and I had a lot of living to do. Slowly but surely, I plucked up courage and began to go out again with girlfriends, even having the occasional platonic boyfriend.

My mother was happy about me going out again. She knew that I was absolutely determined – resolute – that I was never going to get into trouble again, so she didn't try to keep me at home. My father, however, was a different matter. He remained uneasy, not at all sure that I would look after myself, and every now and then he would go charging around the flat on the warpath. He used to spy on me and kept a very strict eye on what I was wearing, and he always gave me a hard time if he thought my clothes, which were market versions of the current fashions, were too racy and likely to get me into trouble. I didn't resent this. I understood where he was coming from and knew that, nine times out of ten, his bark was far, far worse than his bite.

Aside from worrying about me, Bill had other problems on his mind. Managing a pub is hard work, a seven-days-a-week slog, and my father didn't like it, didn't enjoy his role of landlord. He had been a master builder, a perfectionist and passionate about the jobs he took on, and had mainly worked in the open air all his life. He just didn't take to being stuck between four stuffy, smoke-stained walls. Likewise, when he met my mam he was comparatively well off – times were good for him – but, over the years, he had lost financial ground.

Things then got worse when he and Alice started, from necessity really, to have separate nights out, and Alice's friend Tom – the one who came to tell me about my grandma – began to take her out on Tuesdays, her agreed night off. They'd go off in a car to have a drink at another local pub. Understandably my dad, who adored my mam, began to fret and feel jealous. It was then that a combination of too much alcohol (an occupational hazard for pub landlords), insecurity and blind jealousy created a highly volatile atmosphere, and after those Tuesday nights Bill would sometimes become quite threatening towards Alice. There was a lot of shouting.

I'd always felt very protective towards my mother, but after the death of her mother I became even more so. It was my job, as I saw it, to bear the brunt of all her troubles and that included, if necessary, fighting her corner. She was now seriously anorexic; she had been off her food since the day we heard that Gran had been found drowned, the same day I'd cooked her a favourite meal of lamb chop, mushy peas and golden chips to tempt her appetite – but all to no avail. The bickering between Bill and Alice soon became routine, and he started to become seriously verbally abusive. I was now scared of him. The atmosphere was claustrophobic and it was difficult to get out of his way. As a result, I started to get hit accidentally when I got between him and Alice.

At this time, my mother was drinking even more than he was, but the marriage never actually broke down. He still adored her, and she constantly denied that there was anyone else in her life. But he was very jealous and, although he wanted to believe her so badly, he couldn't. As far as he was concerned, Alice and Tom, who had been friends for a very long time, were far too close; and as far as Alice was concerned, she hadn't done anything wrong, had not been unfaithful, and had the right to remain friends with Tom.

It was only when Gary, who was just coming up to three, got in on the act that things came to a dramatic head. Thinking the bickering and abuse was a fun, noisy game, Gary started to jump up and down with great excitement during one bust-up between Bill, Alice and me, shouting, 'Hit her again, Grandad. Hit her again!' At that moment something inside me snapped. Before I knew what I was doing, I'd launched myself across the room and gone for my father with my clenched fists. I then continued to punch him around the face and head until I actually knocked him to the floor. This was a real no-holds-barred fight.

Bill slowly pushed himself up from the floor, shook his head a couple of times to clear it, got shakily to his feet, waited a moment until I'd got my breath back and then, without a word, held out his open hand to me. I knew what he wanted and, after a brief pause, I took it and we shook hands. He was letting me know that he understood, respected me for what I'd done, and from then on our relationship changed for the better, was once again sealed in mutual love and respect.

I know Gary, thank God, will not remember witnessing that scene – he was so young at the time – but I was so ashamed that it had happened in front of him. I truly was. I couldn't believe I'd reacted so violently, but I had. And had it not been for Alice starting to cry and stepping between me and Bill and shouting, 'Stop it, Julie. Stop it!' I don't know how it would have ended.

I'm inclined to think that incident was the culmination of everything awful that had happened to me up to that point in my life; but the one thing I know for sure is that what triggered it off was little Gary, jumping up and down with excitement, yelling, 'Hit her again, Grandad. Hit her again!'

I vowed before I fell into an exhausted sleep that night that I was never going to take *any* more crap from *any* man, and that vow has stood me in good stead ever since. It didn't really make that much of a difference to my emotional life, though. There are many kinds of abuse, mental, emotional and spiritual as well as physical, and over the years I've been subjected to my share of the first three. Relationships, for me, have always been a bit of a challenge.

Bill and I, though, understood that we had reached a mutual understanding that night, and, thereafter, because I knew in my heart of hearts that he adored my mother and Gary, I adored him back. I could see things from both their points of view, and I don't find that in any way extraordinary. I've always seen things that way; always understood why people behave as they do, and, as a result, I have been able to forgive. I don't bear grudges, don't do resentment, and I consider bitterness a waste of time and emotion.

When I meet somebody new, or even somebody I know, it is with a completely open mind, even though I have often been disappointed, shocked, surprised or even betrayed. I have also realized that while it is lovely to remain open-hearted, I can make – and have made – the mistake of thinking that everybody is endowed with the same way of thinking as me. But, having said that, when I look at the alternative approaches, which so often entail becoming bitter and twisted, I am glad I have always taken the route of risking the slings and arrows. If I can help someone, I will; if I can't, I certainly won't look to do them any harm. I'll just accept the damage and then walk away.

In 1963, three years after twenty-seven-year-old Ray left for Australia, leaving me holding our three-year-old son, I divorced him on the grounds of desertion. Because I was still under twenty-one, Alice had to come to court with me to sign the papers. It was the last contact I was destined to have with him. He had disappeared out of our lives without a backward glance, and Gary never received a letter, birthday or Christmas card, or gift from his father. Despite all that, though, it felt good to be free again. That painful chapter of my life now had what Americans call closure and I could truly start to move on.

I was only too aware as a single mother, however, that much as I tried to protect Gary there would be times when he would suffer very deeply from not having a dad like the other children he knew in the street where we lived, and at school. I can recall one particularly heartbreaking moment when I asked him what he was saving up for in his little piggy bank.

'A dad,' was his innocent reply.

That moment cut me to the quick in a way that perhaps only other single mums could truly understand. And I could understand *why* he wanted a dad. Yes, he'd got a fabulous granddad, but he wanted his own father. He was called Gary Sutcliffe and I was called Julie Goodyear. He must have wondered why? That must have been tough, and he must also have found it difficult at school when the other kids would say, as kids do, 'Ooh, I'll set me dad on you, Gary Sutcliffe,' or 'I'll get me dad to get you.' Gary would always be the one who was left saying, 'Tough! Wait till I tell me mam. Me mam'll get you.'

I never ever, though, regretted having Gary, and I can only hope that he has never regretted me bringing him into the world. Certainly we have always had a totally honest relationship. I truly believe that the greatest gift you can give a child is its freedom. For instance, if you hold a butterfly tightly in your hand, you crush its wings. You must let a child go and that can be very hard. I've always tried to do this with my son. He always knows exactly where I am at any given time. As a mother, I've always prayed that I'll be there when he needs me, and that I'll catch him if he falls. I've never been a perfect, stereotype mum, but I know I have always done the best I can. I also know that there are some things in each of our loved ones' lives that, however much we may long to kiss and make better, we can't. They have to be borne by the person concerned.

When Gary was growing up, it was very difficult sometimes. When he was about ten I remember wanting him to understand what I did as an actress, but he didn't want to watch *Coronation Street*. Of course he didn't. Quite right! So I got him a portable television for his room and he watched *Star Trek* instead. I understood that. It's embarrassing for a young boy when his mam is on television, and I know he took a lot of stick for that at school. I also know he got seriously bullied when the other boys saw me in *Coronation Street* on TV, but he learned to cope with it. I'm sure, even as a small boy, he would have protected my honour when he needed to, but that wasn't something he would have told me about.

Before the *Corrie* days came along, however, I took on all sorts of other jobs on top of being a typist. One of these was going round what we called on the knocker, selling washers and vacuum cleaners. I also worked at Earl's Court in London, selling speedboats. I was always good at selling things and putting people at ease, and I once worked in a nightclub as a hostess showing customers to their tables and making everyone feel settled, comfortable and ready to spend their money! Several shall we say business girls worked in the clubs then, and once, when we had a boss who for some reason didn't pay my wages, all the girls, knowing that I was a hard-working single mam, had a whip-round, gave the money to me and just made a joke of it. They were so good to me, they really were.

★

One evening in 1962 when I was at a dance at the Carlton with a girlfriend, Norma, I met a young man and, *bingo*, just when I was least wanting or expecting it, I fell in love. After just a couple of dances, my heart was skipping beats and there were feelings I'd never experienced before within my body. It was all very new and unfamiliar for me. I hadn't actually had what is called penetrative sex since I conceived Gary. When you go through the kind of hell I went through giving birth, and are left with a third-degree tear, you are not in a hurry to risk having sex again.

This time was different. I so wanted to please him. It really was the first time I'd ever been in love. And I didn't know then that it would also be the last time I would ever fall in love, in that way.

I'm not going to name this person because he still lives in the Manchester area, and I have no wish whatsoever to embarrass him. The son of a local businessman, he came from a well-to-do family, but that didn't matter to me at the time. When I fell in love, that was it – he could have been a rich man, poor man, beggarman or a thief. We were both just twenty years old. He wasn't particularly attractive physically, but he had presence. I thought we'd be best friends, soulmates and lovers for life, that this was *it*, what the poets and romantics wrote about, and that our love would last forever!

Wrong! But he didn't end it, and I didn't either. His father ended it. When his father found out about our relationship, after about a year, he told his son I was not good enough; that 'nobody else's bastard' was going to take over his family firm, not even over his dead body! The love of my young life phoned me at the Bay Horse Hotel to tell me that his father had gone 'berserk' and was now insisting that they come round to our pub for a 'showdown'.

'He's found out we are seeing each other,' he mumbled, distraught and very close to tears. Then, not pulling any punches, he sobbed out, 'He says you're soiled goods.'

Soiled goods! It was another of those 'your sort of girl' moments, a moment when I didn't even know for sure if I was still breathing. Everything had just ground to a halt, and I felt sick as the walls of the room closed in and started spinning.

'He's calling me now – we're coming round to the pub now. Please don't let me down. Don't say anything,' were the last desperate words I heard during that phone call.

Soon it was time for my father to call me. They were here. Dear God, let me be strong. At that moment I was upstairs, slumped on my bed, numb with shock, holding Gary for comfort while below the pub was very busy. I came downstairs shaking with fear, still holding Gary close to me.

I don't remember the exact words that were spoken when we all, including Alice and Bill, came face to face, but I do recall the love of my life cowering, ashen-faced, behind his father as he, face and neck flushed bright red, made it very clear that my relationship with his son was not going to continue. Nobody else's bastard was going to take over the family firm. I was shocked to the very core of my soul. I bit my lip till it bled and said nothing – my lover's eyes were begging me not to. I was made to feel like dirt – less than dirt – and in front of a packed pub. Jesus, this couldn't be happening.

I kept expecting – hoping – that my lover would say something, would tell his father where to get off, but he said nowt. Later, I realized that he was terrified of being disinherited, and that he hadn't the confidence or courage to appreciate he could make it through life on his own; that he didn't need his father's money. For me it was total loss, humiliation, an embarrassment in front of everybody, particularly Alice and Bill. I felt stripped of any dignity – naked. The pub, for once, had gone deathly quiet. My father struggled with himself for a bit, then said to the other father, 'Is that it, then? Is that it? Right, well you've said your piece, now *get out!*'

And, with no more ado, they both crept off. My father then turned his attention to me and said, 'Right! You, get upstairs and take Gary with you.' So I carried Gary back upstairs and slumped once again on the bed. I was distraught and shaking with shame and fear.

I hadn't been lying there for very long when the phone went. It was him, my lover, saying sorry one moment and thanks the next, followed by things like 'It's not fair. This is not the end. We'll let things blow over, then we'll meet each other again – soon.' But I needed him there and then – so needed somebody to hold me, reassure me, comfort me, and tell me that me and my precious son weren't just pieces of shit to be spoken to like that. We'd done nothing wrong!

Later, Alice put her head around the door. I looked up expectantly. 'Now look what you've done' was her anguished cry of despair, but then softly, 'It'll be all right, luv.'

We did meet again, in secret, many times, but only when it was dark. Love like that does not die easily. I carried on loving him until, without telling me, he married someone else. Presumably this was somebody who met with his daddy's approval. Word went round that she was pregnant with his baby – so he married her. If there'd been a table in my room in the pub for me to climb under the day I heard he'd got married, I would have. As it was, although I was still in love with him and my heart was breaking, I never shed a tear. I just drew back into myself.

What was my little mam's reaction to all of this? 'Eh, Julie, luv – will you ever get it right?'

I didn't answer back, wouldn't have dreamed of doing so. I loved my mother with a love that would eventually survive her death and go beyond the grave. That kind of love does exist sometimes in life, a love that will, and does, survive anything; and that is how I loved Alice. Sometimes, too, there is a pain that's so deep it goes beyond tears, and that is how I loved him.

There's a poignant PS to this story. Many years later I bumped into the man's father in the post office of all places. He apologized for his behaviour all those years ago and said, 'My son never stopped loving you, you know.'

THREE

In and Out of the Woods

I so wish I could have fallen madly and passionately in love again after that, if only for Gary's sake. But I am a perfectionist and perfectionists do not find it easy to compromise! The next man who became besotted with me – and to whom I owe so much, more than I can ever say – was Geoff Cassidy. I'd moved on from Avro and met this kind person when I was doing secretarial work in the solicitors' offices where he was the senior partner. To my astonishment, he soon invited me out.

Geoff was a truly lovely human being, a nurturing man who would have done anything to please me. But, although I did eventually become engaged to him, I just didn't feel the same way about him as he felt about me. All he ever wanted was for me to say I loved him, that I wanted to share each and every day with him. That's all he asked. But sadly for both of us, it was too much for me. It was a tragedy, but what could I do? You cannot, however much you may want to, manufacture such feelings and just make that kind of love happen. I was very good, though, at weakening and getting engaged, but not so good at seeing things through as far as the altar and the wedding day.

I so wanted something good to come out of my relationship with Geoff, though, because he truly was a very important influence on my young life. Before him, I was really naive – unworldly, unsophisticated – and he showed me a different way to live. He was the perfect man for the job. By the time we met I was in my early twenties and Geoff was a polished, middle-class, cultured, worldly-wise solicitor. Our meeting was, he told me, a case of 'true love at first sight'. I only wish it had been for me.

Alice and Bill, of course, would have been over the moon if I'd married him. Generous to a fault, Geoff lavished presents on me, even bought me a two-seater Triumph Spitfire sports car. My father wasn't too pleased about that, though, was livid in fact. I couldn't even drive then, and he was obviously convinced I would wrap it round a tree and kill myself!

The girl who gave me my driving lessons was full of advice when the time came for me to go for my test. 'If you get so-and-so,' she said, deadly serious, indicating the man she meant, 'break down in tears and go for the sympathy vote. But if you get you-know-who,' indicating who she meant, 'just hitch your skirt up a little bit higher. Either way, you'll pass.'

I got the latter examiner, unfortunately, but she was right. Having followed her advice, I passed my test first time. I did absolutely everything wrong, but he still passed me. Bill was furious. He knew I couldn't drive for toffee and thought I would be a danger to myself and others. I promised him, however, that I would learn to drive properly, and I did.

Although Geoff truly loved me and would have given anything to make me and Gary happy, I had too much respect for him to cheat and pretend I could love him back in the way that he wanted. There were many times when I wanted to believe that I *could* marry him and make him happy, but I knew, given how I felt, that, although doing that would make life much easier for me and Gary, it would be totally unfair on him. And, in the end, it would be doomed to failure.

Geoff, who was thirty-four and educated at Bury Grammar School and Manchester University, had been married before and had a son, Nicky, but he was now divorced. This was another reason why it seemed like a perfect match, but having been in love once I now knew the difference. Because I was always honest with him from day one, though, we remained good friends throughout the rest of his life.

To this day, I remember the first truly posh meal that Geoff took me out for. Yes, I felt in awe of the surroundings – the confusion of knives, forks and spoons, the waiters in their tuxedos, the other diners in their splendid up-market clothes and the beautifully presented food – but I absolutely loved every second of that evening.

As we were eating our starters, Geoff said conversationally, 'Have you ever had scampi, Julie?'

'No,' I said, looking suitably horrified, 'but I did have measles.'

Dear God! I'd confused scampi, which I'd never heard of, with scabies! I really thought scampi must be an illness of some sort. But he wasn't in the least bit superior. He just thought that was adorable! He was such a patient man, so happy to explain everything on the complex menu that night. 'What about lobster thermidor?' he asked me at one point.

'Hm?' I muttered nervously. 'What's that, Geoff?'

'Go on, I dare you to try it,' he challenged.

I did and, oh, it was food to die for. When it was time for a pudding, I ignored the list of goodies and said to Geoff, 'Can I have the lobster thermidor again, please?'

Neither Geoff nor the waiter batted an eyelid, and another portion of the delicious, mouth-watering dish soon arrived at the table. I was so sick later. What a fool! I'd spoiled the great treat by being greedy and not wanting the lobster experience to end.

Geoff, then, was my mentor. Totally. He introduced me to a whole new world, opened doors I wouldn't have dreamed of passing through without his arm to lean on. It was another world and I loved it. He also loved showing it to me. He was twelve years older than I was, and wanted to teach me *everything*. He took such pleasure in my pleasure. Everything I now know about fine food, wine, champagne, waiters and maître d's is down to him.

As a member of the Round Table and many other professional bodies, Geoff took me to lots of posh functions. Some of the wives were snooty and just plain snobbish. I didn't know where they were coming from and they certainly didn't know where I was coming from. It was a case of ne'er the twain shall meet! I was not 'a lady who lunched', a lady who had nothing better to do than consult her social diary and make yet another lunch date, and I didn't want to be.

At first, I tried to be pleasant, attempted the laugh-a-minute-girl approach to win them over, but I didn't have much in common with them. Some were just ill-mannered, and others made it very obvious that they looked down their noses at me. But Geoff didn't care about them and urged me not to care either. He was a natural-born gentleman and that kind of behaviour was beneath him, beyond his comprehension. He wouldn't even dignify it by noticing.

Our relationship came to an end because unfortunately he started to drink very heavily. I think this was related to the fact that I was always very honest about not feeling the same way about him as he felt towards me. My parents were so disappointed. They were so thrilled when we got engaged and so wanted me to marry him. That was only natural. Mums and dads always want to see their children happy and settled with the right partner, and that's just what I wished for my son. I waited until after we'd been on a week's holiday to Majorca — with Gary as well of course — and then I broke off our engagement. I didn't want to do it before the holiday because I knew Geoff had been working very hard and overdoing the alcohol, and needed a good rest.

Soon after that, Geoff went out on the binge one evening and met a woman who was less scrupulous than I was; who didn't mind getting married without being in love. I had insisted on giving him back the engagement ring — the huge diamond solitaire — he had given me. It was, I learned later, still in his breast pocket that night when he had too much to drink, and was very soon planted on that woman's finger.

They got married, but he and I remained good friends until he died. I had no regrets. I knew I'd done the right thing by Geoff in not marrying him. When I went to see him in the chapel of rest to say my goodbyes, it was so very sad. Nobody but me, apparently, had put their head round the door. 'Goodbye, lovely man,' I whispered. 'And thank you — *bless you* — for everything. Sleep the sleep of angels.' I laid a red rose in his coffin and my grief for him went very deep.

Throughout my relationship with Geoff, my self-confidence had grown by leaps and bounds, and I decided that the next time an opportunity presented itself, I would enter a beauty contest. Never slow to miss an opportunity that would further my dream of becoming an actress, I'd realized that if you were lucky enough to win a beauty title, you got your picture in the papers and the resulting publicity could be very helpful in at least getting you modelling jobs. This didn't mean that I'd given up on my aspirations to act; I was simply taking things one step at a time.

The other way I decided to give my hoped-for career a boost was to spend the twenty-five pounds I'd saved up at the Manchester branch of Lucy Clayton, the modelling and deportment school. It trained girls like me with ambitions to be models. So, in the early 1960s, still in my twenties and full of trepidation, I arrived for my audition sporting a beehive hairdo, my face plastered with make-up and wearing a tight short skirt and red stilettos. As far as I was concerned, I was there to have some of the rough edges knocked off me and, according to Pam Holt (who ran the northern branch), I proved to be a fast learner. She didn't pull her punches, though. She told me I wasn't the more 'usual elegant mannequin model type'; I was just a 'girl with a good figure'. She also informed me I wasn't really tall enough for a model – I am only five feet four inches – but, she added, I had 'great legs' and was a 'useful shoe size' (I am only size four). My small feet, apparently, also made me look a bit taller. She then added, looking rather doubtful, I thought, that I had 'personality'.

I ended up not really sure if any of what she had said was good news or bad, if I was a hopeless case or in with a chance! But, being me, I was more than ready to persevere with the four-week course and, if necessary, prove her wrong. 'Okay,' I said under my breath, 'maybe I'm not a classic beauty who will ever grace the cover of that snooty fashion mag *Vogue*. But that's not the be-all and end-all of modelling. And where there's life, cocker, there's hope!'

With that boost to my batteries, I threw myself body, heart and soul into the course. I never missed the keep-fit class in the morning, attended all the lectures in deportment – yes, I *did* strut about with books perched on my head – and listened intently to all the make-up, hair and show-work advice. For the catwalk, I learned how to take my coat off, model with an umbrella – much more difficult than it sounds if you don't want to trip over your own feet, however small – how to take a hat and gloves off, and how to use my hands elegantly.

In between, I worked at proving I could be a real trouper, a laugh-a-minute girl if that was required, willing to work my socks off and be trusted to be sent anywhere and arrive on time. I so wanted to be perfect and never let anybody, least of all myself, down. I must have done something right as, despite all my doubts and fears that my best would never be good enough, I was sent for photographic assignments to model my hands in gloves, and feet in shoes and stockings. At other times I worked at exhibitions and events as a promotions girl, and modelled wholesale clothes on catwalks in front of professional buyers.

Sometimes, too, I modelled second-hand furs at local auctions, where the man in charge used to say over and over again, like a mantra, 'When you are walking towards the customers, pull the coat tight around you, so that it hugs your body. When you are walking away from them, push the coat back so that it fans out. This'll make it look as if there is more fur in the garment.' I used to hear that in my sleep!

One firm where I was fortunate enough to become a firm favourite and found myself regularly booked was Eastex, which specialized in clothes for short women and paid their models five pounds a day. Their clothes were known to be good quality, but they were not my idea of high fashion! They were conservative, tweedy and frumpy rather than elegant. But, although I arrived in clothes that were much more to my young taste – a crocheted minidress (which incidentally nearly gave Bill a heart attack when he saw it) and white plastic knee-length boots – I always did my best for Eastex. And Pam Holt was kind enough to tell me that I had boosted the company's sales.

In the early 1960s ladies rarely used four-letter words, but I'm sorry to say my language deteriorated and became littered with expletives during those early modelling days. It went with the territory somehow, and, when you are young, you fall so easily into the trap of imitating others and do a lot of daft things to be accepted and loved. I like to think looking back that my well-groomed appearance gave the lie to moments when I joined in the racy conversations and talked like a navvy!

As a whole, I really enjoyed my modelling days, but there was one assignment that I failed to reach on the day. This was because, on my way there, I had a near-death experience. A fellow model, Val Martin, was driving us both in her nippy little Mini Cooper S when a car stopped without warning in front of us. It was midday and the motorway wet and slippery. As Val slammed on the brakes, our car went into a skid and crashed into a metal road sign which came straight through the windscreen, missing us by a hair's breadth. An inch to the left or right and either of us would have had serious head injuries and doubtless died on the spot. At the very least we would have been scarred for life.

As it was, we were only left with whiplash, a few cuts and bruises and suffering from shock. The other car, however, rolled over and over and, although we were dazed, we had to drag the driver out. Two cars passed but neither stopped to help us. Having got the driver out we collapsed on the kerbside, shivering and shaking like jellies. We must have been very dazed because neither Val nor I had any idea how we got to the casualty department of the nearest hospital, and all I could remember later was that I'd been wearing black tights, which had ended up full of ladders and holes. Some time after, Val received a bill for the road sign! We had, though, had a very lucky escape, and we knew it.

I must add that I wouldn't have missed my time at Lucy Clayton and my early modelling days for the world. Apart from the fact that I was bringing in a good income, it really was a period when I was fine-tuning myself, both physically and mentally, and all my rough edges were being smoothed out. Lucy Clayton and the modelling assignments gave me the kind of confidence that stood me in good stead many times later in life. I learned how to sit properly, walk correctly, speak a little differently (despite the swearing), dress more conservatively and use less make-up. It really was an invaluable time for me. Also, I have to add that I was mixing with Manchester models who were not from my background or class. They were all there because Mummy or Daddy had wanted and arranged it, but I met some really fabulous girls; and one, with a particularly large plum in her mouth that never ceased to crease me up, became a good friend, who was soon to accompany me on what was meant to be 'the trip of a lifetime'. What a joke that turned out to be!

At that time there was great excitement buzzing around the world of beauty contestants and models. Britvic, the pub fruit-juice manufacturers, were looking for a person to represent their product, somebody with the right image for juices; and they were holding competitions throughout the United Kingdom. Lucy Clayton's on King Street, Manchester, was just one venue they visited and, miracle of miracles, having entered the contest along with fifty other girls from all over the country, I was awarded the Miss Britvic title.

Looking back I can see that I was a very healthy, curvy girl. I had a bit more meat on my bones than most of the others, who were all very tall, lanky and skinny. I just happened to fit the bill with bumps in all the right places. The contest took place in July 1965, when I was twenty-three, and I could hardly believe my luck when I won. My 'glittering prize' was a week of frivolity and fun in Blackpool (yes, my old seaside friend), about £100 in cash, an evening dress and being the VIP guest of honour at a late-night ball. As I was allowed to take a guest with me, I asked Plummy if she'd like to come along and share my prize.

'You bet, sweetie,' she said. 'You know me – game for anything, especially a laugh.'

The Blackpool week we went on just happened to coincide with 'Scots week'. Now, I'm very fond of Jocks, but you can imagine the atmosphere! Whisky-laden and manic. And on top of that all my childhood memories of Blackpool came flooding back. I was not, to say the least, absolutely certain about this part of the prize, but I brushed off my doubts and went with Plummy accompanied by a couple of Britvic 'suits' who were supposed to be there to tell me how to behave, where to go, what to do, etcetera. Hmm.

It turned into a complete and utter fiasco. Dressed only in a crown, white swimsuit, sash and six-inch stilettos when the weather was absolutely foul and blowing a force eight gale, I was made to parade up and down the Golden Mile promenade on a float with a huge plastic pineapple on it. Within minutes, I had goosebumps the size of table-tennis balls! Every so often the float would judder to a halt and I had to get off and go into whatever bar or pub we'd parked outside, mingle with the customers and drink Britvic fruit juices. In no time at all, I'd been obliged to down so many of these that I was feeling decidedly queasy and was starting to develop an upset tummy to beat all upset tummies. Despite all this, I managed to grit my teeth and paint a broad smile on my face, but, believe me, it was *not* easy.

The highlight – after eighteen or so of these stops along a front bursting with hairy-legged Scots in kilts, and English blokes fulfilling the seaside image of braces and knotted handkerchiefs – was a visit to the top of the 518-foot Blackpool Tower. Having had the obligatory fruit juice at every single stop, I was violently sick and had to throw up off the top. By now, even my goosebumps were a lighter shade of green! All I wanted was to get out of the white swimsuit and stilettos and put on the largest, thickest sweater and comfortable pants I could find; but I had to soldier on, knowing that a week of this was my prize.

I know Blackpool is deservedly renowned for its first-class hotels and countless boarding houses, but the boarding house we had been booked into for the duration was not one of the better ones. By the time Plummy and I had got through the shoddy, flock-wallpapered reception area, with its minuscule bar and aspidistra in the corner, to go up to our room, I'd got two very nasty love bites on my neck, and she had several impressive fingerprints and bruises on her bum. The male punters had certainly had their one over the eight, were nigh-on legless, delighted to be on holiday, having a great time, and feeling very, very frisky! As far as they were concerned, they were not being offensive and just regarded us – me, in particular – as a holiday perk.

'Jesus, Mary and Joseph, darling gal!' was Plummy's back-to-her-upper-class-Irish-roots response when we closed and firmly locked the door. It didn't get any better.

It was past midnight when, having more than done my duty as VIP guest of honour at the late-night ball, I was allowed to leave and get out of the other bit of my prize, the white Grecian-style Tricel evening gown, but there were several more shocks to come. And come they did, after Plummy and I had dragged our weary bones and my gurgling fruit-juice tummy back to the worst boarding house in Blackpool.

The room we were sharing was not en suite, and the WC, as the owner called it, was a communal cubbyhole down the landing. Okay. But he omitted to tell us that the landing was guarded overnight by a large, fierce Alsatian that was happy enough to let us into our room, but bared its huge yellow canine teeth when we tried to open the door and come out again to pay a visit to the WC. As if that wasn't misery enough – God knows, we were both bursting – the two Britvic suits were in the next room to ours and kept tapping on the wall, pleading with us to let them come in and keep them company throughout 'the wee small hours'. No way! Nasty little runts.

After a miserable hour or so of trying to control my Britvic-laden bladder and lull it into believing that all it needed was a good night's sleep, I'd no choice but to surrender to the call of nature. Tiptoeing across the dark room to the washbasin in the corner, I drew up a chair, stood on it, suspended myself in the appropriate position over the basin and was, as they say, relieved. My companion, the usually unshakeable, kindly, posh Plummy, who heard what was going on, was shocked to her very core.

'How *could* you, d–a–r–l–i–n–g?' she drawled, utterly disgusted.

'Easily! Sorry, I had no choice,' I replied sheepishly. 'It was that or bust!'

'Oh, *r–e–a–l–l–y*, sweetie.'

She was much sneakier than I was, and very soon had to put aside her disgust and surrender. She obviously waited until she thought I was asleep, then unable to contain herself a second longer, she slipped out of bed, tiptoed over to the basin, climbed onto the chair as I had done, and set about peeing in the sink. But . . . idiot! Instead of suspending herself over the chipped porcelain basin, she sat on it. Unable to support her weight, it came away from the wall and fell to the floor with an almighty crash with her still perched on it. As it hit the sparsely carpeted boards below, its porcelain splintered and made bloody ribbons of her backside!

I kid you not. Her bum was seriously lacerated and bloodied, and, having leapt out of bed to examine it, I'd no choice but to risk opening our door a crack and braving the Alsatian, which greeted me frothing at the mouth. Peering out into the dark corridor, I stood there screaming, '*Help, help.*' Interestingly, the suits in the next room, who had been so active tapping on the partition wall, didn't emerge. They probably thought their worst nightmare had come true, that I was screaming attempted rape, and there would be hell to pay when they returned home to their wives on police report.

Poor injured Plummy! With me in tow, she was rushed off to the casualty department of the Victoria Hospital, stitched up and sent home to Mummy and Daddy. Lucky devil! Honestly, it would have been worth a bloody bum to get out of there. But, ever the professional, I stayed to finish the week alone, minus even a washbasin in the room. At least the suits didn't tap on the wall again.

Needless to say when, at last, I returned home, Alice's first eager question was, 'Well? Did you meet anybody?'

'Mother, no! Nobody special,' I replied, deciding to keep mum about some of the close-shave incidents.

'Well,' she sniffed, disgusted, 'you must be doing summat wrong.'

Oh Mam!

My heroics, though – getting through that week and surviving the fruit juice – had their reward. I received a good write-up, accompanied by photos, in our local paper, the *Heywood Advertiser*, and the publicity did, as I'd hoped, help my dream of modelling start to materialize. Having been lucky enough to win the crown, sash and sceptre for Miss Britvic, I followed up this success by becoming Miss Astral, Miss Langley Football Club and Miss Aeronautical Society!

Before I leave this Blackpool saga, I can't resist adding a much later *Coronation Street* anecdote from 1990, when I was thrilled to be asked, along with Roy Barraclough (who played Alec Gilroy when we were landlord and landlady of the Rovers Return), to switch on the Blackpool lights. Once again, this had its black-comedy moments.

The mayor of Blackpool was there with his wife. A truly short fella, he never once looked me in the eyes, but spent the entire evening talking to my knockers! 'Oooh,' he said, 'it's so luuvely to have you here.' And, to add insult to injury, he called me Bet all night.

'It's such an honour to have you here,' he kept repeating, his eyes at chest level. 'I can't tell you how much we've been looking forward to it.'

Please *don't* tell me, I kept thinking. Honest to God, there was never any eye contact.

'I were so excited when I knew it were going to be you. It was just too much, *marvellous*. As soon as I found out I said to the wife here, "There, luv, didn't I tell you Bet Lynch would be even better than Red Rum," because, you know, we had the Grand National winner here doing the lights last year.'

I was *so* glad that Newton and Ridley, as the crew on *Coronation Street* had respectfully christened my boobs, matched up to Red Rum's arse! Newton and Ridley was the name of the fictional brewery on *Corrie*. On the set, for example, if I'd got my shoulders too far back and the camera crew needed a shot across my chest, they'd call out, 'Julie, Newton and Ridley are a bit high.' It was a daily event, and a very nice way of referring to my assets!

But back to Red Rum. Blackpool's then-mayor was not the only person who had the pleasure of meeting that magnificent horse. I did, too, in 1994, and I also met Red Rum's owner, Ginger McCain, and his wife, who were absolutely lovely people. Rummy, as his friends called him, was such a character and the sauciest flirt you could ever meet. In the space of one heartbeat, we fell in love with each other. He was truly a gorgeous aristocrat of a horse. As he was led away from me in the cobbled stable yard, he did something that took all our breaths away. He glanced back over his glossy red shoulder, looked straight at me and *winked*. Then he proudly tossed his head and mane and, swinging his body most seductively, walked on. Vicki Claffey, my PA who had accompanied me on that visit, and Ginger McCain just fell around the cobbles, laughing their heads off.

'He winked, he bloody winked,' I kept repeating in astonishment.

'Yes, well, he's got *very* good taste,' Ginger replied.

I wasn't feeling great that day, was feeling pretty poorly, in fact, but Rummy was just the tonic I needed!

To sum up this phase of my life I must add that by the time I'd finished the Lucy Clayton course and begun modelling regularly, I'd started to appreciate that what Miss Holt had unintentionally convinced me might prove to be serious disadvantages could, on the contrary, be used to advantage! Many models are tall and have big ungainly hands and feet, whereas I have small hands and feet. Say no more! When jobs required hands and feet, I proved to be their girl. I cleaned up all the hands-and-feet modelling work in Manchester, London – everywhere. I'd found something I'd got and was putting it to good use and making money. The pounds, shillings and pence came flying in.

I didn't mind where I was sent. Alice and Bill were, as always, only too happy to look after Gary when I was working, and suddenly I always seemed to have a job on the go. This didn't mean, however, that I was out of the woods and feeling financially secure. I would be in and out of those for quite some time to come – and I don't just mean financially! My earnings were still, in the scheme of things, irregular and no great shakes, and that is not a comfortable thought to fall asleep with when you have a child to support. But change was coming – a big change – something that would, one day very soon, allow me to sleep more easily at night. And, even more important, set me on the road to fulfilling my long-cherished aspirations and dreams.

Above. Me in something knitted in Blackpool.

Right. My beloved grandma, Elizabeth Ann Duckworth.

My mam and me – looking a bit posh!

Above. Dad, Mam and Tom behind
the bar in the Bay Horse.

Left. Me, aged fifteen, in the school play,
We Must Kill Toni.

Below. Sixties ladettes:
me and three friends — Norma far left.

Aged sixteen, and the start
of my leopard-skin life.

Above. Me in the back streets, outside the Bay Horse, dreaming of making it one day.

Left. Miss Britvic in her white dress.

Below. Me on my float in Blackpool – what a trip.

Above. My first wedding.
Me, aged seventeen, terrified
but trying to smile.

Left. Me and Ray
– my shotgun wedding.

My mam, Gary
and me, in the
backyard of
the Bay Horse.

Gary with his
bucket and spade,
and a boat to sail.

Above. Me with Fred and all the crew from the boatworks in Heywood.

Left. Gary, me and my Dad.

Below. Me, mam and a friend of mine on holiday.

Me in *Nearest and Dearest*.

Above. Taking a break from cooking to read a *Corrie* script with Mam.

Left. Me with Tony Warren.

FOUR

The Wind Beneath My Wings

The very first time the Lucy Clayton agency sent me to Granada Studios was for an appearance on a news programme called *Scene* which went out at 6.30 p.m. This programme occasionally used models as extras for segments. I was really excited, saw being an extra as a way in. I would have played the back legs of a donkey if I thought it would help me get to where I wanted. Getting in was a passion for me, was what made me tick. It wasn't a sudden whim. As I've said, from childhood onwards I'd wanted to act, and I'd never lost sight of my dreams. But I hadn't been to drama school, had no training in the dramatic arts and, as a single mum, couldn't afford to stop and get some now. I hadn't, in truth, got much going for me.

In those days at Granada, in the early 1960s, it was a young Michael Parkinson, Mike Cox and Bob Greaves who appeared in the *Scene* slots; they were the first people I met in television. But, before I continue with my fledgling television career, I want to go back to the desperate financial situation my parents were in at the Bay Horse Hotel. By 1966 Alice and Bill were almost penniless. My mother had either drunk the takings or given it away to the poor and needy. If someone said they

87

couldn't afford to pay for a drink, she'd say, 'Then have one on the house, luv.' We came out of that business, which had been such a hard slog for thirteen years, with bugger all. And that was the case for so many backstreet pub landlords after TV arrived and drinking cans of beer in front of it became the new rage.

I was left with an inheritance, though, but not a financial one. What would stand me in such good stead was the experience I'd gained from living in and over a pub, but I never knew that at the time of our troubles. My inheritance was the fruit of standing in the margins and people-watching – observing and absorbing human behaviour and all its foibles. This became second nature for me and was perfect training for my later acting career. Like Bill, though, I didn't like pub life, even though it suited Mam down to the ground and she adored it. So did Gary. He found the chit-chat and antics of drink-sodden adults endlessly fascinating. The fruit machine and jukebox were also big toys for a little lad.

My reason for not liking it was because it was so *not* compatible with family life, especially for a thirteen-year-old girl whose room was over the Gents! As it happened, I was never accosted by any of the drunks. If they had ever tried to make their way upstairs to our living accommodation, it would not have been a fair contest. They were so pissed it would have been easy to push them back down again. Nevertheless, I learned not to sleep too heavily during that period and, to this day, I do not sleep well. I didn't have a lock on my bedroom door; it was never considered necessary. Locals got to know I would have killed for me and my Gary.

I remember sitting on the top stair, looking down and watching everything going on below. I would see them singing and laughing and making merry until closing time and long after

– when it became known as Billy's Night Club. It was as good as any television. Without knowing it, I absorbed a lot about human nature, both good and bad.

Alice was devastated when we had to leave the pub and move into another terraced house not very far away, in fact back into Gregge Street, just another number. By then, because of her anorexia, she was like a stick insect, all skin and bones. And Bill was out of work and stony broke. I physically carried my little mam out of that pub and she cried cos she didn't want to leave.

In addition to supporting Gary, I now found myself needing to support my parents, and that is when my cousin Irene, who I had been close to in early childhood, came back into my life. She'd been living and working in Blackpool, which was eventually to become a firm favourite in my life after I'd switched the lights on. She didn't, she told me, want to go home to her abusive father, so could I ask Bill if she could come and live with us as a lodger? She did, and was such good fun to share a bedroom with. We soon became close again, and I am glad to say we are still very close today. She's happily married, thank God, and is a grandma now. Back then, though, we used to have a race and wrestle every night to determine which one of us would get the comfortable bed – one was a real bed, the other one of those horrible camp beds. Neither Irene nor I were into any kind of camp then, didn't even know what it meant, so getting the real bed was a life-and-death tussle. But we were a family and I was so happy in that little house. We got a mortgage for £200.

Although I found working as a model a total laugh and was so grateful for the money I was earning, my real ambition never left me and I so wanted to appear on television. As Lucy Clayton often provided the local TV station with extras, Pam, who was aware of my dreams, started to send me along on a regular basis.

As a result, in addition to appearing in *Scene* and in a short satirical drama, playing actress Pearl White, fearless heroine of the silent screen, I was also spotted as a magician's assistant in *The Good Old Days*, a reconstruction of the Victorian music hall for television. I also had parts in the drama series *Family at War*, and the comedy *Nearest and Dearest* as lead actor Jimmy Jewel's girlfriend. The actress Hilda Baker, who was also in this production, hated me because I was so young! Then, thank the Lord, I was talent-spotted, apparently as a 'stunning blonde with a personality to match', and chosen for a bit part in Granada's young soap opera *Coronation Street*, where I was to play Bet Lynch for six weeks, a typical Lancashire lass who worked in Elliston's raincoat factory.

By then *Coronation Street* had been going for six years and on 2 June 1966, I received some exposure in the *Heywood Advertiser*, which ran the headline CORONATION STREET ROLE FOR JULIE. The copy read:

> The popular Granada TV serial *Coronation Street* is currently being given a face lift and one of the new parts has been given to Heywood girl Julie Goodyear of the Bay Horse Hotel, Torrington Street.
>
> Julie aged 22 [I was actually 24] has been working as a model for some time, but has also been on the files at Granada. When it was decided to inject more life into the series, she was offered the part of Bet, a typical Lancashire mill girl, who will be working at the new factory which is opening in 'the Street'.
>
> This is Julie's first speaking part on television, although she had previously had walk-on parts in programmes includ-

ing *Pardon the Expression*. She made her first appearance as
Bet last week and she is likely to stay with the series for
some time.

The broad Lancashire accent which she uses is authentic,
and as she says: 'There is no difficulty with the accent. I'm
from the North so it's natural to me.'

I made it a little broader for the *Street*, and I'm proud to still
have it.

You can only imagine how I felt when my first lucky break
came along and Lucy Clayton sent me for that bit part. Bit! I
would have jumped at any teeny-weeny morsel to get an airing
on television, let alone *that* series, which was the one that everybody was beginning to watch and talk about!

The first episode of what was to become Britain's most successful
and best-loved drama serial, bursting its seams with romance,
tragedy, intrigue and humour, was shown at 7.00 p.m. on Friday
9 December 1960, and, of course, it was in black and white.
From the beginning it enthralled those who watched it, including unlikely people like the poet Sir John Betjeman, who
described it as 'the best writing and acting I could wish to see.
And, thank God, at seven tonight I shall be in paradise!' A little
later he added, 'The secret of the *Street* is that it never plays a
false note. The sets are perfect, the interiors, both as to colour
and furniture, true to life: the awful browns and oranges and the
things displayed in the corner shop – everything spot-on.'

He was so right! It was the very concern – respect – for
detail that placed the *Street* head and shoulders above all other
programmes, and made it one of the most watched serials in the
world. That and, of course, its strong women. Other fans of it

round about that time included two British prime ministers: Harold Wilson (and his wife Mary) and Jim Callaghan. Even Mrs Thatcher sent a message of congratulations when the *Street* eventually celebrated its two thousandth edition.

I'd watched, on an old black-and-white telly, some of the early episodes and I am not kidding, I knew at once that this was the one for me. I just knew that it belonged to me, was mine. That, after all, was exactly how we lived. So, it couldn't be that difficult to be in, could it? But, oh yes, when the time came it was.

I gave birth to my son in April 1960 and Tony Warren, bless him, *Coronation Street*'s creator, celebrated the first showing of his drama that December, so they will both be the same age, forty-six, in December 2006, by which time this book will be published. Only a gay man could have created the phenomenon that was and is *Coronation Street*, and the only people who influenced the characters of Ena Sharples, Annie Walker and the rest of us were the real-life characters of the Northern backstreets that Tony observed and put down on paper. I absolutely adore Tony, have total respect for him as a man and a writer. I always remember him saying, 'Granada's licence to transmit in the North of England required it to provide employment for people in the North and to reflect the region, and this was at a time when the accent was totally unfashionable. I was thrilled about all that because I knew there were great burning talents hanging around in the North who just didn't happen to talk posh.' Since then, *Coronation Street* has created viewing records, been heaped with awards and has also been seen in Holland (where some children learned to speak English with a Lancashire accent), Hong Kong (where it was subtitled, with Chinese characters displayed vertically down the left-hand edge of the screen),

Australia, Canada, New Zealand, Nigeria, Singapore, Gibraltar, Greece, Belgium, Finland, Denmark, Sierra Leone and Thailand. And it's always been among Granada's top-ten-selling programmes.

When Tony was awarded his MBE, I was very touched when he asked me if I would accompany him to the Palace, and, later in life, I tried desperately hard to fill the huge gap in his life left by the death of Pat Phoenix, who was then married to Anthony Booth, but I couldn't. Nobody could have done that for Tony, but we have always remained good friends.

When I told my parents I'd got work playing a character named Bet Lynch in *Coronation Street* they looked at each other, and said, 'Oh, yeah, Julie, pull the other one,' and fell about laughing because they didn't believe me. It must have sounded far-fetched at that time and in our situation.

'Honestly,' I said. 'Honest, I'm not joking. I've been offered the part of Bet Lynch who works in a factory.'

When they finally accepted that I was not fantasizing, that this was a true bit of good news, they were chuffed and very proud of me. By then, Bill was getting bits and pieces of building work and I was also proud of him. When he got hold of the little terraced house after we had to get out of the pub, he made it into a miniature palace. And, even though Alice was not eating enough to keep a mouse alive and was so frail at this stage I didn't know how she was managing to keep going, we were so happy in that little house.

As I've mentioned, I *adored* Pat Phoenix, who took me under her wing almost as soon as she noticed me on the set. She was truly my mentor and role model. Our first meeting, though, wasn't so hot. This occurred on what was to be my very first day on *Coronation Street*. I was standing at the bus stop to go to the studios when I was lucky enough to be spotted by a mate of my dad's. Having pulled over, he said, 'Do you want a lift, Julie, luv?'

'Oh, please,' I said, knowing this would mean I could save on bus fares and buy a butty for my lunch.

'Get up into the cab then.'

He was driving a truck with a cement mixer on the back. I climbed up and off we drove in the direction of Manchester.

'Where are you going, luv?'

'Granada Studios,' I replied.

I don't know why, but I thought he'd drop me round the corner, not at the front door. He didn't and, come to think of it, why should he? But, horror of horrors, as he pulled up at reception, stopped and I was climbing out of the cab backwards, I realized that we had just parked bumper to bumper with Miss Phoenix in her vintage Rolls-Royce.

Having looked me up and down as though I were a piece of dog dirt on her shoe, she said, 'Don't you ever, ever dare to try and upstage me again, young lady.'

'No, Miss Phoenix,' I whispered.

I have to say, I didn't know what 'upstage' meant, but I was eager to find out, always eager to learn anything from and about Pat.

Having climbed out of her Rolls, she swept passed me, every inch the star. She looked fantastic. Her hair was squeaky clean and shining, her clothes immaculate, and there was I wanting the ground to open up and swallow me. I was determined to keep out of her way, everybody's way, so that they would let me stay.

I think there must have been something about me that Pat

felt sorry for, or wanted to nurture. I remember her saying to me, 'Always be kind to the kid in the next dressing room because it used to be you.' I never forgot that and I can honestly say, hand on heart, that whenever anybody new came into the series, I was always the first to show them where to find the coffee and tea machine, the loo and the rest.

None of the powers that be seemed particularly impressed then with my acting abilities, but that was not surprising: I was wet behind the ears! But I found an unexpected admirer in Pat Phoenix, the formidable *grande dame* of the show, who played the *Street*'s pin-up Elsie Tanner, and who, with her deep cleavage and just-got-out-of-bed looks, was often described as the 'working man's Raquel Welch'. At that time Pat was sending such shock waves through the nation's male population that she received at least four marriage proposals a week. I've always remembered Pat saying that when she auditioned for *Corrie*, she was so sure she wouldn't land the job that she was in a *very* arrogant mood. 'When the producer asked me to take my coat off,' she said, 'I said to him, "No! You'll just have to bloody well guess, won't you."'

Always renowned for having a fiery temper, she, bless her memory, spotted my raw talent and was happy to advise me on my craft. She was even overheard saying to Tony Warren, 'You've gotta meet this kid, Tony, she's the funniest thing on two legs. She'll slay you.' She was my great ally and I was star-struck and hung on her every word.

Having got into a mess with the tax man, which meant most of her *Corrie* salary went straight to him, she used to do a lot of personal appearances in order to get spending money. She had a really good contract with Mecca and the bingo halls and sometimes, just for company, she would take me along. I really enjoyed that. On one particular occasion, when she was booked to do a personal appearance in London, the managing director of Mecca arranged to take us out to dinner. That was the moment I found out Pat had a thing about wearing knickers. She hated panty lines showing under sheath dresses and, to avoid this, didn't wear any.

As we were putting on our full-length sheath dresses, she turned to me and said, 'Oh, you're not going to put knickers on, surely?'

'Yes . . . yes, I am,' I said meekly. After all, Alice had always told me to wear knickers and make sure they were clean ones – in case I got knocked down!

'Don't be daft,' Pat said. 'They'll show – look a mess.'

So, with great reluctance, I left them off.

Pat, you have to remember, was exactly the same age as my mam, but as we left the room together to meet the chaps from Mecca in the foyer of the White House Hotel, I thought she looked fantastic, the bee's knees, and there was nobody in the world I'd have rather been with that night. As she introduced me to the managing director, I stepped forward to shake hands with him, and, precisely at that moment, I felt the zip on the back of my dress pop and open from top to bottom. Before I could retrieve my hand, my dress had slipped right down to my ankles. It was bad enough having Newton and Ridley exposed, but I wasn't wearing any drawers either.

Pat looked bloody furious. 'You've done it again!' she said. 'What did I tell you that day in the car park when you parked the cement mixer next to my Rolls-Royce!'

I was too scarlet with embarrassment to make any kind of reply. And, as I fled back to the room, I could hear her screaming like a banshee after me, '*Never* upstage me again, d'you hear!' Once upstairs, I set about finding summat else to wear; summat very proper with a high neck and no zip, and back on went me knickers, never to be left off again. Once downstairs again, I apologized profusely to the waiting gentlemen, who pretended that nothing untoward had happened, and stayed very quiet for the rest of the evening.

Pat, however, really was furious. I honestly think she thought I'd done it on purpose. I was very hurt, didn't understand her reaction at all, but, soon after that, she began, slowly but surely, to give me the cold shoulder – freeze me out. I found that so painful and I missed her so much. Before this, I used to go and stay with her, and she was so comfortable having me around that she'd sit with me without any make-up on and without putting her false teeth in. That says summat, doesn't it? But then I always thought she looked even more beautiful without her make-up and her false teeth. She truly did, and I always felt so privileged that she was comfy enough to do that.

At that time, she had a wolf from Chester Zoo that someone had given to her. Called Blackie, it was a very handsome, beautiful, fearsome-looking creature. On one occasion when we were waiting for a car to collect us and take us to work, Blackie, who was roaming around, took Pat's false teeth off the top of the table. Having done that, it just buggered off with them into the garden – and there I was, charging around the shrubs like a lunatic, chasing the wolf, trying to retrieve Pat's teeth! If Pat hadn't been so distraught, it would have been hilarious!

'*Drop them, now drop!*' I kept yelling. It did eventually, but as Pat didn't laugh, I didn't dare.

That's how close we were before she froze me out. I can't remember now how many years I was in *Corrie* before Pat's attitude towards me started to change, and I've never been able to work out what happened. I only know that I longed to put whatever was wrong, right, but I couldn't, and she always remained aloof after that.

When she left *Coronation Street*, she gave me a mirror from her dressing room and I treasured it. I knew what she was saying: 'At the end of the day, you have to be able to look at yourself.' When I left *Corrie*, I gave that mirror to Sarah Lancashire, who didn't stay very long in the series. When I made my fateful return to the *Street* many years later, I asked where the mirror was, but nobody knew who it had been passed on to.

All these memories came flooding back the day of Pat's funeral. Pat died of lung cancer aged sixty-two on 17 September 1986. I remember one moment after the funeral that left me feeling so embarrassed I could hardly hold my head up. As I came out of the church, one of the hacks pointed at me and yelled, 'The queen is dead. Long live the queen.' A more fitting epitaph came from the *Guardian* journalist who said of Pat, 'Red-haired, resilient and remarkably stylish "Elsie" epitomized northern warmth.' I can vouch for that – she did, and I still miss her now.

I was totally convinced when I got work on *Corrie* that I would be there for the rest of my life. No question. I didn't think that, at the end of six weeks, I would be laid off. Why would I? *Coronation Street* was where I belonged. I was in heaven. So you can imagine it was a phenomenal shock when I was told, 'Thanks very much, Julie,' and *that*, despite my pathetic pleading, was *that*. My naivety at the time meant I didn't realize how short-term a TV job could be. I thought that as long as I impressed the producers and played the role to the best of my ability, then they'd keep writing me into the scripts. But it was a six-week job and then it was thank you and goodbye.

Totally devastated, I sat slumped in one of the dressing rooms, which always smelled of powder, scents and deodorants, thinking, 'What have I done? Have I upset somebody? Spoken out of turn?'

'Now *what* have you done?' I could hear Alice chiding. 'You could cause trouble in an empty house.'

It was then that a guardian angel, in the shape of my idol Pat Phoenix, stepped out of the wings with some very sound advice. 'You haven't had any theatrical training, done any rep,' she said thoughtfully. 'And I think this is the moment for you to do so. I know some people at Oldham Rep,' she added. 'I'll put in a good word for you.'

True to her promise, she did, and I was taken on as an ASM (assistant stage manager). I know that sounds rather a grand title, but it wasn't in the least a glamorous job! At Oldham Repertory Company I made the tea for the acting troupe and served out my apprenticeship in each and every part I was offered onstage. Not that there were many *on*stage offers; it was more cleaning it. On my first day there I heard later that Carl Paulson, who was producer/director, summoned Kenneth Alan Taylor, who later played the brewery boss Ces Newton in *Coronation Street*, and said, 'Come downstairs, Kenneth, I want you to see something.' He then pointed out the wonderful white shining Spitfire that had been given to me by Geoff Cassidy, which was parked next to Carl's battered old Mini in the theatre car park.

'That's the first bit,' Carl said. 'Now come with me.' And, going into the auditorium, he drew Kenneth's attention to a blonde girl wearing a short mink jacket, who was busy sweeping the stage with a huge broom that was almost bigger than her.

'Who the hell is *that*?' Kenneth asked.

'It's the new ASM,' Carl replied. 'And, hold your breath, that's *her* car in the car park!'

In Oldham in those days you didn't see white Spitfires. It was the equivalent of owning a Ferrari – and most ASMs wore overalls when they swept the stage!

While there, I arrived at 9 a.m., and didn't leave until after the evening performance at 11 p.m. or later, usually a fourteen-hour day; and my duties were about as glamorous as delivering coal! I was a dogsbody and didn't get much opportunity to act because I had to go out buying props, move all the furniture offstage and paint it once a week matt black, a job every ASM hated. If I was given a part, which was nowhere as often as I would have liked, I always seemed to be asked to play the old maid. It was a weekly rep, so the company staged a new play every seven days, and every six weeks 'Mr Paulson', as we all called him, chose six new plays and posted a list on the noticeboard. Desperate to get on, I was always plucking up courage and breaching company etiquette by saying, 'Is there anything in this for me, Mr Paulson? Can I be in this one?'

'No,' was his regular reply. My roles remained few and far between and I didn't get to play any big parts. I was, though, one of the slave girls, called Vibrata, in *A Funny Thing Happened on the Way to the Forum*, and I once played a bunny girl, wearing a black leotard with a white powder-puff tail, and succeeded in stealing the show as I hopped across the stage, saying my couple of precious lines. And I wore leopard skin in that!

Around this time I went out for a short while with twenty-seven-year-old 'Diddy' David Hamilton, who was living in Manchester and working as an announcer for ABS television as well as compèring a pop music show for BBC radio called

The Beat Show. He was already a heart-throb, with scores of women chasing after him. The story that was put around, though, by an unscrupulous writer later in my life was totally untrue. This piece of nonsense claimed that somebody said to me, 'How did you get on with Diddy?' and that, to entertain them, I replied, 'Oh, all right. We went to a club, then he drove me to his mum's. I was in the mood for a fag rather than anything else and, having got my lighter out, I said, "Before we go any further, let's have a look at it then." When he obliged, I lit my lighter, peeked, then said, "Now I know why they call you Diddy."'

What can I say? We are defenceless when hacks publish such lies and, honest to God, none of it was true!

So, my work at Oldham Rep, which had promised so much, just consisted of sweeping the stage, cleaning the auditorium and other parts of the theatre, going out to buy props and, yes, cleaning the lavatories, my most hated job. But I was not downhearted. I had set myself the target of twelve months in the job and during that time I saw other ASMs come and go at a rate of knots. That was not surprising. It was tough work and Carl Paulson was a very forbidding and frightening man. A stickler for discipline, training and respect, he took no prisoners.

I remember when I was a minute late one morning, on one of my long days, that he made me stand in the auditorium in front of the stage while the rest of the troupe, which included Barbara Knox, who later played Rita Fairclough in *Corrie*, and Roy Barraclough, were taken up to the gods. He then shone a single spotlight full on me and made me project my voice to carry an abject apology up to the gods. I felt so small and he kept shouting, 'Louder – we can't hear you.'

Oldham Rep felt a very lonely place to be that day, but I was never late again. Peter Dudley, who played Bert Tisley in the *Street*, was also a member of the company and before I arrived Dora Bryant had also been there. The rep, then, had chucked up some really good actors, but there were times when I despaired of ever being one of them.

One stage manager was an absolute pig, which was one of the reasons why ASMs kept coming and going. He had it in for me, and he wanted me out. Although I'd stood up to him, I was scared of him because I needed the job, needed that training in rep, and I was determined, come what may, to see it through. I'd saved damn hard even to be able to consider going to Oldham Rep, and I wasn't going to let him snatch my prize away. It was a real financial struggle that year because I'd only got a few quid behind me, and I couldn't do my secretarial work while in rep because of the hours. I never got home until well after eleven o'clock at night – knackered – then kissed Gary and went to bed.

One night he cornered me in one of the dressing rooms when everybody else had left the theatre and we got into an almighty argument. Things got very heated and I gave as good as I got.

'You're fired, you fucking mad bitch,' he yelled.

A little later that night, when I'd calmed down a bit, I phoned Geoff Cassidy and asked him for help. 'I've worked so hard and I haven't got much longer to do to complete my twelve months,' I mumbled, obviously deeply distressed. I have no idea what Geoff, who really was a brilliant solicitor, said to Carl Paulson when he telephoned him, but I was, bless him, reinstated. After that night the stage manager kept well out of my way, and I made absolutely sure that I kept out of his. As a result I managed to finish my twelve months.

Many years later I met Carl Paulson at a party; he was dying, terminally ill with cancer. I was still afraid of him, but he beckoned me over. 'Oh my God, he's going to shout at me again! What have I done now?' I thought, trembling. But by then I was in the *Street*, and those thoughts didn't make sense. So, as bidden, I went towards him.

'How are you, Julie?' he asked gently.

'I'm fine, thank you, Mr Paulson,' I replied deferentially.

'Was I *very* hard on you?' he added.

'Yes, you were,' I replied truthfully.

'You always wanted to go on the stage, didn't you?'

'Yes, I did. Desperately.'

'But we couldn't teach you anything. You had it all. The only thing you lacked was discipline, and I tried to teach you that, didn't I?'

And, my God, he did! And terrified the life out of me in the process. I kissed his cheek, he smiled and I went home.

When I finished my year at the rep, I went straight back to the front desk of Granada. 'Who are you?' the security guard asked.

I kept my cool, but soon learned he was not the only one who had forgotten me. They had all forgotten me. Totally.

'I've done my twelve months at rep,' I kept repeating desperately to anybody who would listen. 'I've done rep now, so I've come back for me job.'

'What job?' was the baffled reply.

Oh dear! It was heartbreak time again, a case of back to the drawing board. I had really been under the illusion, had convinced myself, that there would be a job waiting for me – my job. But then that's the sort of naive fool I was then – and still am. I had no choice but to get a job in a Manchester-based firm of solicitors situated in Deansgate. There I specialized in conveyancing and common law, which I became quite good at, but it was a tough period. I was lost. All I wanted was to be an actress. I had to wait until the birth of the 1970s, 5 May 1970 to be exact, three more long years, for that, and even then it only came about by chance. But never mind – for some it never comes.

I'd got a very small cameo part in a drama series called *Family at War*, the ninth episode. This series was directed by June Howson, a very sensitive and talented director. I did my part and, as we finished that particular scene, she came into the studio and said, 'That was marvellous, Julie. It really was.'

'Thank you very much,' I said, blushing to the roots of my hair, quite overcome by the unexpected praise.

'I wonder,' she said thoughtfully, 'would you ever consider becoming a regular member of the cast of *Coronation Street*?'

'Yeah, right!' I said, thinking she was now spoiling things, going too far and having me on. I started to walk away. I had to get the bus home. Sometimes when a dream comes true you just can't believe it, especially when you want it *so* badly. She couldn't possibly have meant what she just said, was my attitude, but she did. Unbeknown to me, she was about to take over as producer of *Coronation Street*.

I could still hardly believe it, even when I learned that fact. But, my God, she must have seen something in the performance I'd given in *Family at War* because she got in touch again, via Granada Television, and the contract duly arrived at the house – for six whole months at fifty pounds an episode, two episodes a week. That was £100 a week. Christ, we'd won the bloody lottery! Clutching the contract to my bosom, I grabbed Irene, my cousin, ran for my 'gogomobile', which used to make Mam crease up and laugh every time she saw it, and off we went to Vintage Wine in the centre of Heywood to buy a bottle of cheap champagne. The gogomobile was a bright yellow bubble car which the blokes at the boatworks in Heywood had fibre-glassed for me. Down one side in large black letters it said 'Groovy baby', and on the rear end were two big eyes winking at you. You could walk faster but I had more fun in that car than I did when, many years later, I owned a Rolls-Royce.

'Gary,' I murmured that night, 'we're really going places at last.'

I had the wind under my wings. Nothing, but *nothing* could stop me flying now!

FIVE

Magic in the Making

Once back at Granada Studios, I reminded the powers that be that I'd been in the series before; had played Bet Lynch, a worker in a raincoat factory. Although nobody seemed to show much interest in this piece of information at first, somebody (doubtless June Howson) listened because I was again cast as Bet Lynch, who was now a launderette manageress but destined to work behind the bar in the Rovers. Annie Walker, the storyline went, would be absolutely horrified when her son Billy employed Bet as a barmaid. For Annie's prim and proper taste, Bet was far too popular with the menfolk and also had a bit of a reputation. Annie, though, wasn't the only one to disapprove of my character. Betty Turpin had been used to being the centre of attention behind the Rovers bar and her nose was also out of joint. Annie, however, softened her attitude when she realized that Bet, with her blonde hair, personality and quickfire banter, pulled in the customers.

It took me a while to believe that I was going to be in the series six months and not six weeks this time. This was just as well, as signing the contract had meant chucking in my secure job at the solicitors.

At home, both Alice and Bill were on their mettle and had warned, 'Don't let this go to your head, young lady.'

Earlier, when I'd returned to the house, rushed in and told Bill my good news, he had been sitting in his armchair, reading the newspaper. I remember rushing across the room, saying, 'Dad, guess what! I'm going to be a regular member of the cast of *Coronation Street*.'

'Go and put the kettle on, luv,' he replied. 'I've been dying for a cup of tea.'

And, of course, I did.

But that is the Northern way. We believe in keeping everybody's feet planted firmly on the ground. Bill's response might sound like a cruel put-down, but it wasn't. It was done to protect me from being hurt – 'the higher you rise, the harder you fall' syndrome. Alice, though, reacted differently and in a very un-Northern manner. She was absolutely thrilled when I told her, positively hugged herself – and me.

This was my big chance and, from the moment I got the job, I was determined that Bet Lynch would be a great character, and that, with the help of make-up and costume, and of course the scriptwriters, I would put my body, heart and soul into establishing her place in the series. They were not gonna get rid of me again, not ever!

When Bet first appeared in *Coronation Street* in 1966, she was a factory girl and dressed like one. When I went back in the seventies, though, she quickly became a barmaid and I realized at once that she needed to have a certain authentic look. Again, I was truly blessed. Lois Richardson, who worked in the make-up department at Granada Television, lived in Rochdale just up the road from me in Heywood. That was perfect because it meant the pair of us could trawl the local markets, looking for things for Bet. Lois had her ideas, I had mine, but between the two of us we came up with a look that gelled with the times and, in a funny kind of way, a look that turned out to be timeless. That wasn't something we did on purpose, though. Fashion has this habit of going round in circles, and although Bet's clothes may have been a bit ahead of their time to begin with, that look came in and out and back again during the twenty-five years I had the pleasure of playing her.

I'd always liked leopard skin. In those days it was considered a bit naughty, racy, *very* sexy, but I thought Eartha Kitt looked fantastic when I saw her in cabaret in Manchester, singing 'Just an Old-Fashioned Girl', wearing a leopard-skin jumpsuit. I'd also got a leopard-skin bikini, the one I'd worn for the pin-up girl photo at Avro, so leopard skin was always going to be part of the Bet look. Another bonus was that leopard skin was not expensive, quite the contrary. It could be picked up very reasonably in markets and from catalogues. I was always very careful with Bet's character. I wanted to know how much she would have earned, how much she would have spent. And I made sure we stayed within that budget, true to her. I did that assiduously, to make her totally believable and credible. To see an actress playing a character dressed in something she couldn't afford just doesn't do it for me.

Lois Richardson was also brilliant with Bet's make-up and hair. The beehive style was very fashionable and my own hair was quite long at the time so, initially, Lois used to backcomb it into Bet's beehive and lacquer it. This continued for many years, until I felt brave enough to ask for a hairpiece. If I hadn't done that, all the backcombing, which leaves your hair with an almost candyfloss texture, would have made me completely bald. When

I got the hairpiece that, too, was backcombed, lacquered and set, and then perched on a block. As well as preventing me from becoming hairless, it saved a huge amount of time because it could be prepared in advance by the hair and make-up department.

The way Bet's appearance evolved was a fascinating process. There was a very formidable woman in the costume department called May and, one day, I actually dredged up enough courage to go into her den and say, 'Could I possibly have a pair of tights for Bet, please?'

'Tights?' she snarled. '*T-i-g-h-t-s!*' Then, with a loud sniff, she added incongruously, 'It's not easy living on your own in a caravan, you know.'

'I'm sure it's not,' I answered, meek as a lamb, turning tail and leaving without the tights.

May obviously thought that having spoken those few words she had given me the potted history of her life. She was a *very* angry woman. Nobody messed with her and, as a result, very few things were requested from the costume department.

Human nature has always fascinated me and I found experiences like that very intriguing. I also understood the value of a pair of tights! When I couldn't afford them, I used to dab gravy browning on my legs to make them look tanned, just as if I were wearing tights. I promise you that wearing gravy browning and a pair of white stilettos was not a pretty sight if it started to rain when you were standing at the bus stop. You looked for all the world as if you had had a very nasty accident down your leg which had gone into your shoes. It would also mean a journey back home to wash the shoes and redo the gravy browning.

When Gary was very young and there was never enough money to go round, myself and a local girl called Norma, who I am still friends with, often only had one pair of tights between us, which we shared. This was very much a make do and mend period, and we were lucky that Edna Barlow, who lived opposite the Bay Horse Hotel, was a wizard with a sewing machine, absolutely brilliant at knocking up a frock or skirt. Norma had two kids and I had Gary, but occasionally we would manage to have a night out together at the Carlton in Rochdale. I thought this was a magical place. It had a big dance hall and balcony, a glitter ball that went round, rock 'n' roll and jiving – all that stuff. We might not have had much money, but we sure knew how to enjoy ourselves.

But back to Lois, who was absolutely invaluable during the creation of Bet. She was also a tall, stunningly beautiful girl, who wore huge round glasses, and had long dark hair and a slim figure to die for. She really should have been on my side of the camera because she was every inch the star. But, there I was, a jobbing actress at last – and she was my mate.

Granada, I learned, had been looking for a sex symbol for the character of Bet. The company had this habit, I soon found out, of replacing existing actresses as they got older with some-body younger and sexier, which I thought was quite cruel really. They still do this. As people who have given their all get older, past their sell-by date, a younger version is brought in. I never thought of Bet as just being a 'tart with a heart', with a sexpot, man-eating image and a gift for raunchy banter. I thought she had a very wide appeal, more to offer than 'If you've got it, flaunt it,' and I was determined that she would be a three-dimensional character.

For example, I couldn't understand at first, really didn't know why, but I discovered that a huge chunk of Bet's fans were little girls – still young children. The more I thought about it, however, the more I understood. Those girls were just at the age when they were becoming interested in make-up and starting to experiment, as little girls often do. I have to say I was never one of those little girls, but I know many are! Bet's earrings, which were always eye-catching, fascinated them. To my surprise, they started to send in cheap plastic, junk-type earrings by the bucketload, then the shedload, which they bought with their own pocket money for their 'Auntie Bet' to wear. I was so touched by that, I really was.

I always had to get permission to wear the things that were sent in and I dutifully asked the costume department, the directors, the producers, when I did. There were boxes of the stuff, and sometimes the children who sent things couldn't even do joined-up writing. Little notes, however, always accompanied the presents. If I knew a child was ill, I would bring their earrings forward because I knew how much it would mean to them to see them on the telly. And I know it did mean a lot because they would always write and tell me so. It was very much a two-way love affair. Much later I sent them off to be auctioned for charity – so love continued to go round.

The most important thing about Bet, though, was, as I mentioned earlier, that everything she wore had to be the sort of thing a barmaid could afford, and something about her appearance always had to clash. I decided right at the start, that for Bet either the lipstick wouldn't match, or the nail varnish, or the earrings. Something would stand out as wrong. If it didn't, it wasn't right and wouldn't be true to character.

Every single time I was due on set, I had to look in a full-length mirror as I left my dressing room. Head up, shoulders back, hands on hips and I'd say, 'Go for it, girl.' The transformation was complete.

Yes, of course Bet was busty, raunchy, voluptuous, a woman who knew how to flirt and manipulate, and give as good as she got. But she was also vulnerable. Unlucky in love, she could cry; rejected by those who got nearest to her, she could hurt. It was that mix that the viewers were hooked on. The ready wit, the clever put-down, the brittle manner, are all part of Bet.

In the early days I never stopped researching the character of Bet on the streets of Salford with Tony Warren, and every time we went out, we would see a Bet at the market shopping, and either Tony or I would say, 'Look at that silver mac/hairdo/earrings.' You could see Bets everywhere and we took inspiration from each of them. Bet was based on the women we saw in real life. As time went by, some people said 'too much', 'too over-the-top even for Bet', but Tony and I always knew it wasn't, and Bet's fan mail proved us right.

It has always been difficult for me to describe Bet's character, and particularly how hers differs from mine. Certainly I have never confused her with me, but I am aware that many do, and that some actors confuse themselves with their character. I have often been asked how I avoided doing this, what my secret was, why I did not. I can only answer truthfully that I knew, without an atom of a doubt, that I was *not* Bet. I was just Julie! When I finished work, I washed my face, changed my clothes and went home. I know that sounds simplistic, but that is how it was for me, and it is God's honest truth. I didn't know any other way to do it. I used to take the scripts home to learn the next day's lines, and I always took it as a tremendous compliment when people thought I made the character so completely credible.

Perhaps, though, I am just too close to the character of Bet — and to my own character, of course — to make a good job of describing her (and me!). It's probably better for me to let the very few people who know me best try. Bet, they have said, is 'brassy and loud; you are not'. She is often 'outrageous, you are not'. She dresses in a 'cheap, common-as-muck way, you do not'. It's all true. I am much more conservative in the clothes I choose to wear and couldn't even walk in Bet's stilettos. We both have quite feisty personalities, though, have both learned through some very hard knocks how to fight our corner; we are both survivors and, from experience, somewhat wary of men; we both get our teeth into things and, when forced, will give as good as we get.

Although Bet was always being hurt, she was actually only married once. I gave marriage a go three times and got engaged on several other occasions. But that wasn't because I was particularly impetuous, prone to making rash decisions, jumping in feet first and chasing after men. On the contrary, the men I married, or became engaged to, did the choosing and chasing, and ran after me! They also persuaded me that getting engaged or married was the right thing to do. Of course I always wanted a happy ending, and I went into all my relationships with the best intentions. But finding the right person isn't quite as easy as some books or scripts make it sound. 'And they all lived happily ever after.' Yeah, right.

I take after my mother, who was always a *very* shy, reticent person underneath the surface bravado, but only a couple of people have ever realized that about me. Most have not really looked beyond the surface appearances I have adopted to help me cope with life. In truth, it was only when I put on Bet's make-up and clothes – and became her – that I felt the wind beneath my wings. When I removed the make-up and clothes, I was just Julie again: shy, reticent, over-sensitive, often awkward and uncomfortable, and certainly vulnerable.

Without that side of my character, though, without that vulnerability, I don't think I would ever have been able to portray Bet in the way that I did; just as without the capacity to laugh at myself and some of the situations I have found myself in I wouldn't be here now. I love comedy and have an especially soft spot for black humour. Laughter and the ability not to take yourself too seriously are great blessings and healers.

Bet is vulnerable, too, of course, but she is certainly not shy. In truth, I really do not like people running away with the idea that we are one and the same. *We are not.* But I also take it as a compliment that I made Bet so believable.

When I first joined the cast of *Coronation Street*, the other members of the cast weren't particularly welcoming apart from Pat Phoenix and Betty Driver, who played barmaid Betty Turpin. It was not the done thing, then, to be familiar with others. It was all 'Miss Carson', who played Ena Sharples, and 'Miss Speed', who played Annie Walker, and all that. I was very much a newcomer and expected to know my place. I totally understood and respected that. I accepted that I had to earn my stripes before I would even be able to enter into a conversation. It was very much a speak when spoken to situation, working your way up and woe betide any newcomer who, even without knowing it, sat in an established cast member's chair. As time went by, my motto was 'Kick one and we all limp.' I totally believed in teamwork, closing ranks, protecting each other, all of that – and I still do.

Betty Driver, bless her, took me under her wing and became my workaday mam. A one-time singer who had worked with bandleader Henry Hall and travelled the world entertaining the troops, she had never had any children herself, but she should have done. She would have made a fabulous mam. Later on, when I'd been in the *Street* for about six years, I remember getting a letter from one of my old employers, offering me my secretarial job back at more money than I was on at Granada. When I showed the letter to Betty, she tut-tutted and said, 'Well, how much are you on here?' and when I told her what I was earning, she spluttered, 'I've never heard of anything so ridiculous. Now, you take that letter up to them in the office and get 'em to do summat about you.'

'Oh, I daren't, Betty,' I replied.

'Yes, you do. You take it up there, d'you hear, and show 'em.'

'Oh, Betty . . .'

'Take it – *now*!'

So, in fear and trembling, spurred on by Betty, I took the letter up to the offices and said what she had told me to say:

'I've had a wonderful time working here,' I began, 'but, as a single mum, I can't turn down the kind of money mentioned here in this letter. So it's with tremendous regret . . .'

My salary, which had been the same for the past six years, was doubled. What an eye-opener that was! I came out of the office walking on air, and as I passed Betty she gave me a nod and a wink. I never had to complain again. After that, my salary went up on a regular basis. On one occasion, though, I remember saying, 'I'm not bothered about a salary increase; I just want somewhere to park me bloody car.' By then I was thoroughly fed up with having to rush out to feed meters, or having to bribe somebody to do it for me. When I got the parking space, I was absolutely thrilled. Eventually I got a dressing room of my own, too. Prior to that – depending on who I was sharing a room with, or if they had visitors – I used to change in the Ladies' loos.

For the first six months I was in *Corrie*, I was so desperate to be recognized as one of the cast that I used to walk up and down Manchester's main street, Deansgate, hoping that someone would recognize me. Eventually a well-dressed businessman approached and offered me some money for my services. He'd obviously seen me parading up and down every bloody day and thought that I was plying my trade. I ran all the way back to Granada Studios and was never tempted to do that again.

Also around this time, during a scene with Lucille Hewitt, played by Jennifer Moss, I became aware that she had a serious drink problem. This was nothing to do with me, of course, but Jenny was so drunk she couldn't get her lines right. She was sacked on the spot. Permanently. Out.

I was, to say the least, very distressed on Jenny's behalf. She had been in *Corrie* for quite a few years and was by then pretty fragile. Foolishly I rushed to her defence, tried to stand up for her, and pleaded for her to be given another chance.

'*Shut up*,' I was told by the producer, who had come down from the office into the studio. 'Shut up or leave with her.'

I shut up.

That was a lesson I didn't need to learn twice. You do not interfere in cast politics and, whatever the circumstances and however justified it may seem at the time, you don't drink when working. *Absolutely no alcohol*. Fortunately, though, that was never a problem for me. Yes, I like a social tipple but, thank God, I've never been a heavy drinker or had a drink problem.

I remember the very first time I saw Margot Bryant, who played Minnie Caldwell. I'd only ever seen her on screen in the very early days and I was transfixed when she came into the studio. She was a tiny demure-looking woman, dressed in a mac and a little hat, and she glided around just like she was on casters. Especially when she was quite near to me, I used to flatten myself against the wall and shrink into the shadows. Then, unseen, I could watch scenes I wasn't in and learn. I was hungry to learn every aspect of work in a TV studio, and I always did this when I could. One day, though, I realized that Margot Bryant, who always looked as if butter wouldn't melt in her mouth, had spotted me. So, trying not to look flustered, I said, 'Good morning, Miss Bryant.' Having stared at me for a moment, she then looked straight ahead and muttered, 'They're all *cunts*.'

I was shocked. That's impossible. She's so demure, she can't have said that. I must have imagined it.

But she had said it and, as I found out later, was prone to saying such things, despite appearances. If my father had heard that word being used on set, he would have frog-marched me out of there on the spot. No kidding! There was Margot Bryant, a doctor's daughter, whose characterization of Minnie Caldwell was absolutely brilliant, coming out with words like that!

I must have been in the cast about six months before Doris Speed asked me to go to her dressing room. Absolutely convinced I was going to get a telling-off, I was very frightened, and racked my brains: 'What have I done wrong? How can I put it right? How can I apologize?'

Having knocked on her door, I waited until I heard Miss Speed say, 'Come in.' Then I entered, *very* nervously.

'Sit down, dear,' she said, 'and close the door.'

Oh God! I sank into the chair and said, 'Miss Speed, I'm so—'

'Just a moment . . .' she said, raising her hand imperiously. 'I've been thinking, dear, thinking, yes,' and her face broke into the most beautiful smile, 'and I've decided you can call me Doris.'

Before I could recover and say anything in reply she raised her hand again and, wafting it in the direction of the door, added, 'Yes, you may leave me now.'

I stood up and left. I could hardly wait to tell mam *this* news. It surely meant that I'd been accepted, had got my stripes. When I did tell Alice, she said doubtfully, 'Hm, I wouldn't say it very often, if I were you. Don't use her name every other word.' Then she paused and, scrutinizing my face, added, 'Are you sure you're not making this up?'

'No! Honest, Mam! I'm not making it up.'

'Well, don't say it too often,' she cautioned. And, as it didn't trip that easily off my tongue, I didn't.

As the years went by, however, I came to adore Doris, and she, luckily, adored me back. I would be the one behind the set doing up her suspenders and helping her with her hearing aid, and letting her know if she hadn't heard when we had a 'clear' or were going for another take. I was like a Labrador puppy around her, a guide dog. There was nothing I wouldn't have done for that woman. Doris had had a long career before she came into *Coronation Street*; lived until she was about ninety-two and died in a nursing home. After that, I always said that I wouldn't want to go straight from *Coronation Street* into a nursing home. I really didn't want that.

There were no real windows on the set or in the studio, so

we never saw natural light or knew what the weather was up to outside. The only way I could find that out, or ask what I should wear, was to phone the switchboard, and say, 'What's it doing out there? Do I need a coat or a brolly?' Yes, I definitely wanted to see daylight and watch the seasons change after all those years spent in a TV studio.

I first met Bill Tarmey when I was already behind the bar, but he was still working as an extra on *Corrie*. I always used to chat to all the extras, having been one myself, and Bill and I hit it off immediately. I very quickly learned that Bill had a fabulous voice and used to sing in the local Manchester clubs. I was delighted when he was offered the part of Jack Duckworth, and that this meant he'd be a regular in *Coronation Street*. Producers and writers at this time, towards the end of 1979, were looking for a married couple with a very similar relationship to that of Stan and Hilda Ogden.

Bill's very first lengthy scene in studio, however, was with Bet and he was really shitting himself with nerves. Because I knew that, I did something which is virtually unheard of in a studio situation – I took the floor manager to one side and asked him not to use the words 'It's a take', so that Bill would think it was just another rehearsal. The floor manager very kindly agreed but said, 'Only on this one occasion', as under normal circumstances this was a very unprofessional thing to do.

We then went for what Bill thought was just another rehearsal, the scene went like a dream and much to Bill's amazement he was given the clear. Bill had completed his very first lengthy scene with me and he never even knew it! From then he could fly too, and he did. Bill Tarmey is one of the nicest human beings, both as an actor and a singer, that you could ever wish to meet. He and his wife Ali remain close friends to this day.

The more I got into playing Bet, the better the writers wrote for me. It was like a fantastic game of table tennis. They served 'balls' to me, and I returned them, always trying to add something extra to a scene. Sometimes this was a certain smile or look, or for no apparent reason I would place some knitting needles and a ball of wool in Bet's hands and set her off knitting. Why not! It was just something extra, a few additional touches and flourishes always true to Bet that I knew the writers and cameras would pick up on; and, my God, they did and it served her and me so well. Plus it was great fun.

I only ever saw the scriptwriters once a year, at the anniversary party, and I was always very much in awe of them and their craft. Sadly, I never enjoyed the anniversary party. It always came at the end of a very long day's filming, and we'd have to get changed, put all the gear and make-up on and try to be the belles of the ball for the press calls. Once I'd done that duty, all I ever wanted to do was go home, kick off my stilettos, put my feet up and talk to Gary. I used to stay as long as I could bear it, though, but towards the end of my time in the series, there was always an undercurrent of jealousy if it was thought there was a bigger picture of me than anybody else in the papers the day after; and I never thought it was worth the aggro.

Seeing my picture in the papers, however, always gave Alice a thrill. She thought that was wonderful. There was her daughter, the apple of her eye. And, at the end of the day, that was all I was really doing it for, saying, 'Love me, Mummy. *Please love me, Mummy.*'

Of course she loved me. But can the small child who always

lives within you ever get enough of a mother's love? Mentally, I always kept Alice and just a few of her friends in mind when I was performing. I kept the number I was actually acting for very small. I just knew I would never be able to cope with the idea of the twenty million viewers that I was told were watching what we were doing.

Often, in those days, because I was always studying the scripts, I found myself thinking back to my schooldays, and some of the comments teachers had written about me on my school reports. I'd had many of the usual that read: 'Julie could do better'; 'Julie does not pay attention'; 'Julie sits staring out of windows'. All that was true until Miss Parker, a truly inspiring English teacher who I vividly remember wearing a brown tweed suit with brogues and knitted stockings, took me for English language and literature. One day, without even knowing it, she ignited something within me that lit up the whole world by suddenly making sense, for the first time, of a piece of poetry. I have never forgotten it:

> Full many a gem of purist ray serene,
> The dark unfathomed caves of ocean bear:
> Full many a flower is born to blush unseen,
> And waste its sweetness on the desert air.

Right, I thought. Now I understand. It is not just me or the here and now. It has all happened before. It must have done for Thomas Gray to have written *that* in the eighteenth century. And I understood those lines to the very depths of my being and decided there and then that I was not going to be that gem that nobody could see, that flower that would 'blush unseen'.

It was a shaft of light – a breakthrough – that I would never forget, and it kick-started my love of poetry, as well as reading and delight in all kinds of books. I even remember reading the Bible back then because, apart from those on herbs and potions, that was one of the few books my grandma had in the house. This joy in reading, though, faded after a while to the point of being virtually gone. Why? Because whatever I read in those days, I automatically learned by heart, even what was on a menu or the back of a tin or packet, *anything*. If I saw a written word, I would learn it, and it took me quite a long time after leaving the *Street*, twenty-five years later, to rediscover the joy of reading.

But, looking back, I don't think I was blessed with a photographic memory. For me, it was more the repetition, going over and over each scene. I always had to get the rhythm and feel of each episode, and Mam and I would read all the scenes through, so that I would know how to pitch – almost like an orchestration – my voice and actions for the part that I was doing. I needed to know what went before and after the lines I was to speak, whether it was happy or sad, a high or low moment, so that I would know exactly how to pitch my voice and play my scene. I wanted any filming of Bet to glide effortlessly from the scene before and into the scene that followed, just like turning the pages of a good book. I think – hope – that this approach was a great help to the directors.

Learning scripts was not, I discovered, hard work for those lucky actors who did have a photographic memory. Ann Kirkbride, for example, who played Deirdre Barlow, had one.

When I joined the cast, aged twenty-eight, in 1970, there were two episodes a week of *Coronation Street*, going out in black and white, on Monday and Wednesday evenings. Just about everybody was talking about it, waiting eagerly for the next episode, and God help anybody who phoned just when it was about to start or during mid-drama! Colour didn't arrive until 1972, a moment that was marked in the series itself by the Ogdens hiring a colour TV as a status symbol. When the TV man came to repossess the set because of lack of payments he kindly agreed to take it out through the back way so the neighbours wouldn't notice. Mentioning the Ogdens reminds me of a very caustic bit of dialogue in the series when Hilda Ogden said, 'Bet Lynch's place is behind a bar, wearing a pair of daft earrings and very little else.' The advent of colour meant that viewers got to see Bet in all her glory, but it caused extra work for a lot of the crew because the sets that had looked so right in black and white suddenly looked too good in colour.

We used to get the scripts the week before, and soon learning scripts became virtually second nature for me. Also, because my little mam was so thrilled when I got the job on *Corrie*, she found it an absolute joy to sit and have a drink together, and I would let her read every other part in the script, apart from mine. For her, it was like party time, and I loved having her sitting there alongside me. She was over the moon, so proud that at one stage she had a badge made with the words 'I'm Bet's mam' on it. That rather upset me. I wanted it to say 'I'm Julie's mam'! Still, if it made her happy then I was happy.

Alice, bless her, also used to sit with me and watch the scenes she'd helped me learn. Sometimes, as she watched, she'd break her heart. I'd look in amazement at the tears running down her cheeks then say, 'Mam, for God's sake! It's not real you know. You know that because you've been through this scene with me. It's only pretend.' 'Sshh,' she'd say, frightened she'd miss something. I used to use the same lines on set to relax the mood.

I got into the *Corrie* routine very quickly. I normally got up about 5 a.m. and, because I was always first in make-up, I earned the nickname 'first in last out'. But there was method in my madness. Because I would have the first make-up call, around seven, that gave me plenty of time to do all the normal things like go to the loo, have a bit of toast and make sure I'd got everything ready. When I first joined, it was a question of sharing a dressing room. I didn't get my own until much later. The working day, with a one-hour break for lunch, continued until 6.30 p.m., but I never seemed to do much hanging around. Bet was in great demand! One thing I discovered, though, was that the powerful studio lights affect your eyes.

When I got the job, it was an ambition of mine to say 'Same again, luv' in the first episode and 'Last orders' in the second episode, but it never happened. Just as well! A positive response to that kind of special request would have created jealousy, which I never understood. There were always other members of the cast, though, who would have liked more scenes, more good storylines, and, to begin with, that also puzzled me. 'But it's the same money, isn't it,' I used to say tentatively. 'It's just that some weeks, some of us are doing more and earning it for everybody else.' Well, that reasoning made sense to me!

It wasn't until I'd been given a proper contract on *Coronation Street* that I began to feel anything like financially secure. And one of the reasons why I was so glad when I got the more permanent job with the series was because I was now in a position to pay for Alice to have private treatment for her anorexia. But they never got to the bottom of her illness, never really established why she could no longer eat (didn't even give it a name) but I know the treatment extended her life.

At that time, the work was well paid. As I've said, it was fifty pounds an episode, with two episodes going out a week, which totalled one hundred smackers, a lot of money back then. It would have taken me three or possibly four jobs a week to earn that kind of money in any other way, and I was getting £100 for one job in one place. It also meant, joy of joys, that with my first week's wages I could buy Gary (then aged ten) his first bike. That was just fantastic. The two of us went to the bike shop in the centre of Heywood and got a racing bike, complete with gears and drop handlebars. I bought it on condition that I could have the first ride. And he let me!

The second task I set myself, as soon as I could get enough money together, was to buy a family plot at Heywood Cemetery. My grandma was buried there and I wanted somewhere to place a headstone and some nice pots. She would have liked that. My third task was to buy some land from the local council in Heywood to give to Bill, my father, so that he could start work again and get his self-respect back. The plot had to be big enough for him to build at least three pairs of semi-detached houses on it. My only proviso was that we would move into one of them as a family.

He was thrilled, absolutely tickled pink, and did a fantastic job. The piece of land I purchased was opposite the bowling green and there was enough room for each house to have a garden. We were going to occupy the end one, which was a dream come true. I could hardly believe that, after years of living in terraced houses, we were actually going to have a *semi-detached*! My God! Any spare minute I'd got, I was down

there with Bill. My father was known locally to be a perfectionist, and the footings that he dug were exactly the right depth. I
knew more about sand-and-cement mixes – and everything else
to do with building – than almost anything else. I bought the
bricks and the window frames. Ever since Bill and I had shaken
hands, all those years before, we had shared a mutual respect.
Getting that plot of land put him back on his feet and helped
him financially. He was able to support my mother again and
hold his head up high, as he deserved to. We were a real family
once more.

I scrimped and saved and I was able to take Alice to Wharf
Mill, Heywood, where they had everything for the home –
carpets, curtains, suites – and the joy that gave me was beyond
measure. We had everything new. It was a total dream come
true. They had their bedroom, I had mine, and Gary had his, all
with fitted carpets no less. We also had a garage. We really were
on the up.

I kept on saving, which really wasn't that difficult because I
didn't have that many needs. When I arrived at the studios I'd
take off whatever I was wearing, put on somebody else's clothes
and become Bet Lynch. As a result, I was more than happy as
Julie Goodyear to wear jeans and a sweatshirt or T-shirt and
trainers. It didn't matter as long as I was squeaky clean, which I
always was. I adored having two baths a day then, and still do
now. Because of the way in which my grandma died, though, I
have always been afraid of being out of my depth in water. But
a candlelit bath, with lovely smelly things added, and thick fluffy
white towels waiting, is absolute heaven for me, a glorious
luxury to this day, especially after growing up with only a tin
bath in front of the fire.

I have just remembered that, while we were still living in

that semi-detached house that Bill built, I bought Gary a second-hand car as soon as he was old enough to drive. For some time, however, I made him pay me back so much a week before deciding enough was enough and letting him off the rest of the debt. I was so afraid of spoiling him, so wanted him to know the value of money, really thought this was an essential lesson for his later life. He called that car his silver skateboard.

So during the 1970s I was a *very* happy, fulfilled girl, who often needed to pinch herself. Slowly but surely, I'd worked my way up from waiting at the bus stop in all weathers to modelling assignments then Granada Television. A bit later still, I was able (thanks to my dream job as an actor) to buy a Rolls-Royce, but that turned out to be a real pain in the proverbial because, unbelievably, it kept breaking down! There was one time when I was driving to work and was stopped at the lights in Cheetham Hill. A car pulled up alongside and as I pressed the electric window switch, turning my head to smile and show off to the bloke next to me, the bloody window fell out and smashed on the road. He pissed himself laughing and drove off. The story of my life!

But, oh boy, did that sleek machine feel good to run around in. Gold, with a gold lady perched on the front and personalized number plates. I know! But hard-working lasses who've risen from nowt have to spoil themselves sometimes.

SIX

Someone to Share My Life

Being Bet, inevitably I suppose, brought out the dirty old men – the mucky mac brigade. That, I guess, went with the territory. Other members of the cast used to wait with great anticipation for my mailbag, which just grew and grew! I also got stalked, which was very unpleasant and frightening. During that time, which was a good few months, I even had to stop driving myself because this particular nutter would suddenly tear up out of the blue, point his car in my direction and then head straight at me. So, for a while, Bill drove me to and from work. We learned some time later that the man had served a prison sentence, had been diagnosed as a schizophrenic, but discharged from Her Majesty's prisons before his treatment had been completed. He was, in fact, a very dangerous character and I didn't sleep at all easily while he was on the loose. In the end I was told it had all been sorted locally, and that he wouldn't trouble me again. He didn't, thank God.

There were also really lovely fans. One, a very young boy called Jimmy, loved collecting autographs, and still sends me birthday and Christmas cards, and I send them to him and his family every year. He's a married man now, with children and grandchildren of his own, but he still keeps in touch. In those days, though, Jimmy was always waiting at the studio gate along with lots of other people, and it was always a pleasure to stop and have a natter with the fans before I set off back to Heywood and home.

My life, in some ways, has been a series of incredible surprises, moments when I look over my shoulder and say, 'What on earth's going on now?' I remember being in a hotel room in Hong Kong in 1981 getting ready for a dinner, and hearing the theme tune for *Coronation Street* coming out of the TV set. It was surreal. I turned round, looked at the TV and saw myself as Bet Lynch, the lines dubbed into Chinese, with English subtitles at the bottom of the screen, saying, 'A pint of bitter, luv?' I could not believe it, and I immediately asked to meet the girl who had dubbed my voice. So, with my producer's help, the person was tracked down and, to my astonishment, it wasn't a girl. It was a boy, with what was considered a suitably deep husky voice for Bet. My voice, incidentally, used to be a little bit higher when I was young but, since then, ciggies have played a role in making it deep and husky. Or maybe, just maybe, my balls have dropped!

Another surprise was when I was dressed in a full-length evening dress after a Royal Variety Performance, and Tina Turner, the star performer that night in 1989, asked if she could see my legs. Taken aback for only a second and without batting an eyelid, I lifted up my skirts, thinking, 'Aye, aye, it's one of those nights!' and showed her. There was a pregnant pause, then she drawled, 'H-o-n-e-y, just as I expected. You should n-e-v-e-r cover those up.'

This incident took place backstage at the Palladium and, after Tina had told me she was an ardent fan of *Coronation Street*, especially Bet Lynch, we found ourselves jamming around, arms entwined, singing her famous, never-to-be-beaten number, 'Simply the Best'. I could hardly believe this was happening. I was a tremendous fan of Tina's and especially that song, which I often sang in low moments to boost my self-confidence and put the wind under my wings. I thought she was absolutely fantastic, and I was totally in awe of her talent. Later I was astonished to read in a newspaper that she had told a reporter that she thought I had the 'best legs in showbiz'.

'H-o-n-e-y,' I drawled silently under my breath, blowing her a kiss, 'that's some compliment from a lady who's renowned for having the best legs in the business.'

You couldn't buy such moments; they are absolutely priceless. And there were so many of them as my twenty-five years as Bet ticked by.

Because Lois was so good at her job and probably because she was also such a stunner to look at, she came in for an awful lot of jealousy within her department. But jealousy has always had to be explained to me – still does. It is not something I have ever suffered from and I have never really understood it. Don't get me wrong. This doesn't mean I never think, 'Oh, she looks great in that,' or 'He was absolutely fabulous in that,' or 'That's a house to die for,' or 'So-and-so is so talented,' whatever. It is just that I have always known that if I worked hard enough at something, I could achieve it, go there, buy it or do it myself. My philosophy has always been that there is nothing that cannot be achieved by getting up earlier and working harder.' Often when I was puzzled or bewildered by somebody's behaviour, my mother used to say to me, 'She's just jealous, Julie,' and I'd say, 'Oh, no, not that again? What shall I do? What *can* I do?'

'There's nothing you can do, except try and understand it,' Alice would reply. 'And rise above it.'

But I never quite succeeded in doing that.

Lois was so good at make-up that Granada was about to put her on a production that had Laurence Olivier (before he was knighted) in it. It was a case of 'Wow-ee' and the place was agog. Laurence Olivier, who was a god, an actor's actor, was coming to Granada to work! 'Lois,' I said, beside myself with excitement, 'just to be able to breathe the same air as this man will be an honour.'

I thought, 'Just maybe, if I'm really quiet, I'll be able to put me head round the door and get a glimpse of him working. After all, I know all the crews.' And I did – they were my real friends in the studio: 'cameras, lights, action', sparks, prop men, switchboard, reception and cleaners. They were the ones I could identify with. I always knew where they were coming from, and they knew what made me tick.

I didn't have to worry, though. Lois got in touch and said, 'Julie, you are never going to believe this.'

'What?'

'He's such a fan of Bet's, it just isn't true!'

'No! You're joking. Are you winding me up?'

'No, Julie. He's just said he would give his back teeth to be in *Corrie* – maybe as an old tramp – just to have you throw him out of the Rovers.'

'What are you on, Lois? Don't wind me up,' I said, gob-smacked.

'I'm not, and it gets better. He's thought of a way that I can make him and you up at the same time.'

'No! Now, Lois, I know that you've got two hands, but that's ridiculous.'

'He's insisting,' she said.

Well, I was absolutely blown away.

The first time I saw Olivier he was wearing a pair of white gloves (I don't know why). I didn't know whether to curtsey, bow, salute, flatten myself against the wall or prostrate myself on the floor. I'd no idea what to do, but I needn't have worried. He smiled, the kind of smile that lights up the whole universe, and was absolutely charming – *so* charming it wasn't true. I can't remember what he said or, for that matter, what I said. Probably nothing. I was completely tongue-tied. But I did, as suggested, go into make-up the following morning at 7 a.m., the time he usually arrived.

I was in the make-up chair, letting Lois perform her magic, listening to Doris Speed in the next chair, who was always saying to the girl who made her up, 'Glenda, there are eyes in there somewhere, and it's your job to find them, dear.' Sitting there, I sensed a presence and, as I opened my eyes, which were closed because Lois had been doing my eyes, there he was.

'Can I get you a coffee, darling?' he asked. 'I am just going to get mine.'

Olivier offering to get me a coffee! Had the excitement been too much for me? Had I finally lost the plot? But that was only the beginning of our make-up-session relationship. On that first morning he went to the canteen, got two coffees – one for him, one for me – and came back. And from then on, while he was working at Granada, we took the coffee-fetching in turns. If he was in the chair, I got the coffees; if I was in the chair, he did the honours; and we laughed so much together.

He used to have posh wicker hampers from Harrods flown into Manchester Airport and brought to Granada Studios, and, blimey, I was *so* impressed by that. Then we started to send each other silly still photographs that had been taken on set, each of us trying to outdo the other with the daftest picture. A friendship, a bond, very quickly formed between us and, at his invitation, I was allowed when I wasn't working to go on the set and watch him from the sidelines. How lucky was that! To be able to watch the great thespian, the master, at work; to be able to study the way he used his eyes and all the detailed movements he made. How well he knew the cameras, and how outrageous he could be at times during a performance and yet get away with all the risks that he took. The man was a genius and I marvelled at his talent.

During one particular scene he was required to retch and then be sick, and how he approached and did this, fascinated me. 'Watch, learn,' I told myself. 'You too may be called upon to be sick on cue one day.'

But how the hell did he do it? I had to wait, of course, until he had finished filming, then I asked him and he told me: took the trouble to explain all the technicalities involved in retching and vomiting in a way that I would never forget. In fact, whenever I asked him anything, he was happy to explain. He became my teacher; and I was able to observe him in minute detail, both in make-up and on set.

As it turned out, many years later in 1986, when we were doing the Rovers-on-fire scene for an episode of *Corrie*, that lesson came in very handy. It wasn't in the script but, as I crawled through all that smoke, I knew it was time to do my Olivier retch and vomit. And, my God, it worked to perfection, so I silently blessed and thanked him for that.

But the pleasure of being with him was not to last. Unbeknown to me, there were spoilers at work behind the scenes. Although our friendship was totally innocent and harmless, I received a message that somebody wanted to speak to me in the offices above. That always meant trouble. Actors were never invited up there unless there was some bother. It was never good news. And, oh Lord, I'd been summoned.

Up I went in the lift, perplexed, my knees knocking, and David Plowright, Joan Plowright's brother, told me he thought maybe I should 'cool it with Olivier'. At this time Larry was married to Joan and David added, 'It is *not* going down well.' Bloody hell! Why not? I'd done absolutely nowt to be ashamed of, and neither had Larry, as I was, by then, allowed to call him. Nevertheless, it was with a very heavy heart and leaden feet that I left the office. I knew my friendship with Olivier, which I'd so enjoyed and valued beyond measure, was over.

I never had the good fortune to meet Joan Plowright, whose acting I also admired, but, there again, was it a question of jealousy? Surely not. What had that great lady to be jealous about? Me? No! Impossible.

I know Olivier didn't understand why – and I certainly never attempted to tell him – but I did 'cool it' as suggested. I just melted away, avoided all contact with him after that. I got the impression that this hurt him very much at the time. My silly photos were removed from his dressing room, but he refused to go on set until they were returned. It was just terribly painful, and so sad. It was a case of 'Girl from backstreets meets Laurence Olivier' and now I'm just so thankful that I got the chance to spend some time with such a great man.

Remembering that period has brought to mind another learning curve. When Bet got the news that the son she had given up for adoption at birth had been killed in Ireland, I was working with a director called June Wyndham-Davies and became very interested in the editing process and was allowed to visit the editing suite. This came about because when we had finished a scene that felt okay to me, but I was waiting for a clear, June came down to the studio and said, 'Will you do me another take?'

'Course,' I said. 'But why? Tell me what to do differently – what else I can give you.'

'Make it smaller,' she replied simply. 'Just give me a take that's smaller than before, if you will. What you have given me is incredible but, after the retake, I would like you to come into editing and you choose – you choose which one you think we should run.'

'Really! That would be fantastic,' I exclaimed.

'Okay, then, are you ready?'

So I did the retake, trying to take on board what she had said, and arrangements were then made for me to go to editing. 'We'll watch both, then you choose,' June said.

Guess what? The winner was, as she had put it, the 'smaller' take. It was no contest. I learned so much from her that day. Minimalism was so much more effective on screen. In fact, there were times when it hurt, was almost too painful to watch! The fact that June had been so willing to share her knowledge with me helped me to fly higher. I never forget moments like that; I'm always wishing I could spend more time with such teachers.

I was lucky. I really did work with some very creative people as I was climbing the ladder. On yet another occasion I was allowed into the director's box, which initially nearly finished off both me and my career. I was stunned, watching the director at work, but it taught me so much. I just sat there quietly mopping it all up, and it helped me to take a big step back and learn to respect everybody else's job and what they hoped to achieve. The final result – the end product, the complete picture – became all that mattered to me.

Doing my homework, then, ferreting my way into other aspects of the work, allowed me to help my colleagues: to know when to get out of frame, take a step back, move in, clear a shot so that it could move seamlessly on to the next scene. I never treated the camera as a lover, though, despite hearing that many actors did. What I do remember is saying to a cameraman, who brought the 'lover' far too close for my comfort one day, 'Oi, not that close! That's rape! Back off, buggerlugs!'

Doris Speed, I noted, was brilliant at camera angles. The monitors were placed up in the ceiling, and she would look up at them, which gave Annie Walker that air of superiority that was so important to her character. In this instance, though, Doris looked up to prevent her make-up cracking and creasing, and her neck look longer and wrinkle-free. Clever lady!

I can't resist adding another story about May – she of 'It's not easy living in a caravan' fame. In the 1974 storyline Bet had won a 'Spot the Ball' contest, which had the prize of a week's holiday in Majorca, and she was taking eight of her pals – the majority of the women in the cast – with her. This plot, however, created blind panic in me! Having had a baby, I'd been left with terrible stretch marks. As a result, I hated anybody seeing me with no clothes on, and was much too shy and embarrassed to change in front of other people. As I got older, of course, my attitude to this changed to, Who gives a damn? By then I just thought, 'Bodies are bodies, just a shell.' At the time of the Majorca plot, though, it was a different matter.

'Oh my God,' I thought, 'what will they put me in for the sun and sand shots? Knowing Bet's taste in clothes, it will be something really sexy and skimpy.' So, in a panic, I plucked up all my courage and went to see May in the costume department, who I knew was just as intimidating as ever.

'Could I possibly have a private word with you, May?' I asked meekly, keeping my voice low.

It wasn't going to prove easy, but then nothing ever did where May was concerned. 'When I've a minute,' she replied in her usual huff.

'Yes, all right, May, any time,' I said obligingly. 'It's just that—'

'Are you deaf and blind? I'm busy.'

'Yes, of course. Sorry, May.'

When she eventually came round to my dressing room, I said, 'You know I've had a baby — a baby son?'

'Yes?'

'Well, you know I've got this filming to do in Majorca?'

'Yes, c'mon, c'mon.'

'Well, I wondered what I would be wearing?'

'Wearing? Christ! Don't you think I've got enough on my mind with the current episode?'

'Well, it's just that I've . . . I've got some marks and it's *very* embarrassing.'

'Why? What have you done to yourself?'

'Nothing. It happens during pregnancy and childbirth.'

'Well, let's have a look, then.' So, with fear and trepidation I unzipped my jeans and dropped them to my knees. As God is my witness, this woman looked, reeled back, then said, 'Oh, my God! Leave it with me.' And, on that note, she ran out of the dressing room.

'That's it. I'm done for!' I thought. 'She'll grass on me and Granada will put me in hospital and tell me it's a job for a plastic surgeon.' Nothing of the kind happened. May came up trumps and organized a virtually non-see-through net bikini for me, which had three fig leaves – one placed at the bottom – and a completely non-see-through little net jacket. Not a single stretch mark could be seen.

That so-called week in the sun, I remember, was organized by Susie Hush, a new producer who arrived in 1974 to take over from Eric Prytherch, who had done the job since 1972. One reason I've never forgotten Susie Hush was the accommodation provided for us. I couldn't believe it when I learned that the crew were in five-star hotels while all us actors were in two-star accommodation along with genuine holidaymakers who really did not want their R & R disrupted by us! To make matters worse, two poor girls had to do make-up in a room that was over an open sewer. The smell was absolutely disgusting. We were not sorry to return to the set at Granada! But as we always say as jobbing actors in situations like that, 'We only joined for the glamour.' Yeah, right!

Just after the Majorca drama, Peter Dobbs took over in the costume department and we became life-long friends. He was an absolutely brilliant costume designer, who always came up with the goods whether it was something for Bet, or for me for the anniversary party. It didn't make any difference to Peter. He was always there for me – and not just for me, for everybody who sought his help. He was so creative, so obliging and a genuinely nice person. I was also very fond of his mum.

At one stage, however, a complaint was made. Let's just say that someone felt that he was putting extra time into Bet's character and my personal costumes. He was called into the office and given a warning. That incident really hurt him. He was so depressed because he never showed favouritism; always made a point of looking after everybody. But I have to say there was a lot of backbiting and internal politics then.

When it came to Bet's marriage to Alec Gilroy, played by Roy Barraclough, everybody in the costume department got involved and made part of her dress, and that was lovely. It was a real team effort but the cream dress, which had a crinoline, although marvellous to look at was hell to walk in. The filming of that scene in the church was another of those magic moments. But the first time Alec put Bet's wedding ring on her finger, I couldn't believe what he did!

'It's the wrong fuckin' finger.' I laughed, knowing the cameras would have to stop rolling anyway, for it to be redone.

The director, I can tell you, was not best pleased with me for using that word and she was quite right. I apologized profusely. We were, after all, in a church, but when you are filming, it's so easy to forget where you are. I can only hope the real vicar wasn't hiding behind a column somewhere and listening in.

In the normal course of events, I never had any problems with directors because I always tried to give them exactly what they wanted. Likewise with the cameramen. When the make-up department changed and was going through a state of flux, with a lot of new trainees coming in, I always grabbed one of these because that meant I could keep her for six months or, if my luck was in, until she qualified. I gladly gave up my lunch hour for trainee make-up girls to practise on me.

In all, I shared in the ups and downs of *Coronation Street* for twenty-five years and, d'you know what, I have absolutely no regrets and would be happy to go back and do it all over again. I really mean that. The writers gave Bet some truly memorable scenes and lines over the years and it was a great honour for me to be part of its history. Some of the lines I am remembering now are: 'Me behind a bar, I'm in my element. I'm like Santa in his grotto.' And to Fred Gee: 'There are only two sorts of women, propositionable and dead!' And to Bet's lover Mike Baldwin, when he tells her his wife is about to visit: 'Right, what do I do? Borrow Hilda's rollers and make like I'm a char?' And, last but by no means least: 'Hope keeps people like me going. You hope that one day there'll be someone who won't cheat or lie or pretend they care about you when all they really want is a willing tart.'

There's a lot of women around who will understand that. I know I do.

Talking about cheating and lying, I had only been in *Coronation Street* for two years when, in 1972, I had the misfortune to meet Tony Rudman; this was when I know Gary, aged twelve, was really missing having a dad. I also knew the fact he was called Gary Sutcliffe and I was called Julie Goodyear was particularly troubling him.

Around this time when I talked to Alice, she would often say, 'It *is* time, luv. You can't keep having boyfriends come and go, none of them amounting to much; and I think it is something you should think about. Because, as you know, I'd love to see you settled . . .' And off she would go again, just as I did with my son later! Alice and I often had nights out together, and sometimes we'd go to the Norbreck Hydro, which was posh then, for the weekend, or fly off to Majorca or Portugal. I always had more fun with my mam than anybody else because she had this fabulous sense of humour. The only drawback was that she was always trying to get me off with someone!

One evening we went to the White Hart, then a local poshish

restaurant-cum-bar, not far from Heywood. The people who ran it were a very nice couple called Margaret and Fred, and quite a nice class of customer used to call in there. It was there that Alice and I first set eyes on Tony Rudman. I remember my mam pointing him out, discreetly of course, and saying, 'Look, luv. You can tell by the cut of his suit and shoes and everything, that that's the sort of man you should be looking at. I'm really surprised you've not met anybody like that at Granada.'

'Mother, I've told you before,' I said wearily, 'they're either all married or gay.'

'Oh, don't talk daft,' she replied. 'You're just putting things off. Look at that group there, the one he's with, they look nice fellas.'

'Yes, and they're probably married too.'

'How d'you know? Are you tellin' me you've got a crystal ball?'

'I'm just saying . . .'

And so it would go on as her eye never stopped roving around, looking for 'talent' on my behalf.

The next time we went into the White Hart, the same group happened to be there and eventually Alice, ever determined, got chatting to Tony Rudman.

'Are you married?' she asked eventually.

'Actually, I'm divorced,' he replied.

'Oh, that's ideal – *ideal*. Julie here is divorced, too.'

'Mother, for God's sake, stop it.'

Once again, he turned out to be a quiet man, came across as an absolute gentleman. He was *very* quiet, I learned later when he invited me out to have a drink; he was, in fact, a very softly spoken accountant with a pleasant lilt in his voice, and everything you'd have thought would make good dad material for

141

Gary. As far as I was concerned, it wasn't love at first sight, certainly not fireworks or anything remotely resembling those, but, spurred on by Mam and his obvious interest in me, I began to go out with him on a regular basis. Would I have dared defy Alice! The fact that he never made the usual randy leg-over propositions or tried to jump on me encouraged me to keep him filed in the gentleman category.

In later years, my solicitor Roger Harper said, 'If you *ever* again tell me you've met a gentleman because you've not been pounced on, you and I will have a serious falling-out. Don't always think, Miss Goodyear, that men who don't jump on women are gentlemen. There are other reasons why they do not do that.' Roger remains a good friend to this day.

Okay, y-e-s. By then, I knew that! But I didn't know it when I met Tony Rudman.

So when the courtship began, my mam was delighted, and Gary was thrilled too. Especially important to him was the fact that we would all have the same name. He would no longer be Gary Sutcliffe, he would be Gary Rudman; Tony would be Tony Rudman and I would be Julie Rudman. Boys always need fathers and security in their lives, but Gary was just at that stage in adolescence where the need for these is especially intense.

Because, later, I had a complete nervous breakdown when my relationship with Tony Rudman came to a very abrupt and dramatic end, my memory is a bit shaky on some of the details. But I do remember that his mother was still alive then, that she lived in Bamford (which was considered a very posh area locally), and Tony Rudman's little bungalow, which I thought was so charming, was not very far away in a little place called Jericho, near Bury. That bungalow was such a sweet place that we would often meet there before going out for meals together,

or taking Gary out. Rudman was still being a hands-off gentleman then, so we were not having an affair, just enjoying one
another's company and getting to know each other. Looking
very intense and determined one evening, he asked me to marry
him and I said yes. I was saying yes for Gary to have a father
figure as much as anything, and I hoped this would finally mean
having some stability in our lives.

Because he owned the bungalow, I thought it was only right
and proper that I should put half the amount it had been valued
at into it; I also put my bank account into our joint names too.
I'd live to regret that later, but that's just me. Granada's press
office knew about the wedding coming up and were absolutely
delighted. Then they took over, of course. But that was fairly
normal procedure for *Corrie*'s press office and publicity department and I really didn't mind at the time.

I need to backtrack a little here before I write about the so-
called big day – the wedding. I'd gone to Belfast in 1972, much
to my mam's dismay and alarm, with Granada's press office to
do a morale-boosting visit to our troops. With Vera Lynn's
Second World War efforts very much in mind, I was proud
and honoured to be asked. I truly was. It is quite something to
stand up and be counted in front of a veritable sea of men in
uniform.

This visit, though, had an impact on the day of my wedding
to Tony Rudman, when several Saracen tanks emerged from
the midst of hundreds of fans who had turned out and, to my
amazement, rolled forward, before stopping at our feet. But then
we have to remember that Bet was these soldiers' pin-up; they
used to have a picture of her stuck to the inside of their tanks.
If that picture ever became loose, I was told, and fell off, that

particular tank was grounded and not allowed to go out on manoeuvres. The soldiers were very superstitious about that and didn't feel easy in their minds until Bet was safely restored. They really were fabulous guys, and that's how some of them, plus their tanks, came to be at my wedding day. Another piece of icing on the cake was that Gary, whose voice hadn't broken yet, was in the choir at Bury parish church where the wedding ceremony was to take place.

All seemed well then, very exciting – thrilling – and I'd even bought Tony's mum and my mam lovely new suits for the occasion. I was really pleased about this, especially so because my first wedding had been so downbeat and I really wanted this one to be right – perfect in every detail. Norman Frisby, who was in charge of Granada's press office and had accompanied me to Belfast, was there and so was Leita Donn, who looked after the *Coronation Street* press. Lots of members of the cast were in attendance, including Doris Speed and Pat Phoenix, plus Tony Warren. It really was a big occasion. Jennifer Moss and my cousin Irene were bridesmaids, and I was in a magnificent gold dress. The reception was to be held at the White Hart after the church service.

As we were about to leave for the church, I remember Bill suddenly turning to me and saying in a very intense voice, 'You don't have to go through with this, you know, not if you don't want to, luv.'

'You *are* joking,' I said.

'No,' he replied, 'I'm deadly serious.'

I thought it was a very strange thing for him to say at that moment when all the arrangements had been made and everyone was waiting in the church, so I just laughed it off. I just thought he was letting me know that he suspected I was not head over heels in love and might possibly be getting married so that Gary could have the father he craved. That was only partly true. I wasn't head over heels, but I'd become very fond of Tony, who had still not attempted to consummate our relationship. I respected him for that, thought he was being a kind, considerate, thoughtful gentleman who wanted to set everything off on the right foot.

However, things on the day got off to a bad start because the vintage car that was taking me and my father to the church in Bury broke down, and, as if that wasn't enough to create a feeling of foreboding, I discovered that my magnificent bouquet had been left on the bed in the bungalow. I know it is a bride's prerogative to be late, but I am not a late person and, anyway, there is late and late, and this was becoming ridiculous. All else aside, when you know you have almost the entire cast of *Coronation Street* waiting plus God knows how many fans, you do not exactly feel relaxed about being late!

Somebody was sent back to the bungalow for the bouquet, and the car was somehow sorted. When I finally arrived, a bit shaky after all this, I just couldn't believe the crowds. There were so many people there it was like a state or royal occasion, and knowing my son was about to sing with the choir while his mother was getting married was just so special it brought a lump in my throat.

Without further ado, the Saracen tanks (which I must admit looked a bit out of place) were parked up, the soldiers and other guests filed into the church and I walked down the aisle, my arm threaded through Bill's, to the traditional strains of 'Here Comes the Bride'. The service then progressed without a hitch to further ruffle my nerves, the vows and rings were exchanged and, to my great pride, I could hear Gary's sweet tones rising above the voices of the other choirboys.

As we made our way back outside the church, my arm now threaded through my new husband's arm, the crowds parted with a deafening roar and the Saracen tanks rumbled through. Dear God! I was now able to take in that some of the soldiers there had suffered terrible injuries since I'd met them in Ireland. One had lost an eye, several had limbs missing. It was a terrible shock. My heart went out to them and I felt I just had to stop and have a special word with one or two of them.

That was the moment when I felt Tony's hand tighten like a vice on my arm, and tighten so firmly it really hurt. I was shocked to the core. This was a side to Tony I'd never seen before and I couldn't believe it was happening. The next moment, I felt his hand move from my arm to the small of my back, followed by a discreet but hefty shove, which once again hurt me. 'Get in the car,' he hissed through clenched teeth. This was a face I didn't recognize, wearing a vicious expression I'd never seen, but I still thought I was imagining things and must have misheard what he said. Wrong! As I looked up at him, bewildered, he repeated in another frenetic hiss, '*Get in the damn car.*'

I was stunned. I had no idea what had happened to upset him and I couldn't bear the idea of any of our guests becoming aware that we were having a tiff. Was it the service? The tanks? The presence of the soldiers? The cast of *Coronation Street*? The fans? I just didn't know, couldn't guess, but I knew there was something seriously wrong and my first instinct was to cover up, get through the post-ceremony motions double quick so that nobody else would know.

'Please, Tony,' I pleaded, whispering. '*Please* try to smile. There are so many people here, watching, taking photographs, including our own photographer.'

Forget it! He just indicated to the best man that we were about to move, then he waved all the photographers aside and beckoned the car, with its streamers of white ribbons, forward and hustled me into it. I got in, a smile painted on my face as if nothing untoward had happened, but inside I was beginning to react, to seethe even, about being handled so roughly and having that part of our day ruined.

What did he have to say for himself on the short journey to the reception? *Nothing.* He wasn't speaking to me; was just slumped in the far corner of the car, his face set like granite, his eyes staring unseeingly straight ahead. Although I was seething, I had one last try. 'What, in the name of God, is wrong, Tony?' The best man, noting the extreme distress in my voice, shifted in the front seat and glanced over his shoulder, but Tony remained totally silent.

The moment we got to the White Hart, Tony leaped out of the car and, leaving me totally on my own, disappeared inside the building. When I entered, smile still painted on my face for the benefit of the waiting staff and a few people with cameras, he was nowhere to be seen. A little later I realized his mother had also disappeared.

Too late, then, I began to have suspicions. Maybe he wasn't just being a gentleman when he made no attempt to nudge our relationship on to a more intimate basis. Perhaps he was now suffering agonies, terrified of consummating the wedding night? Maybe he was impotent but hadn't had the courage to tell me? Maybe, but surely no, he didn't like women. But why ask me to marry him? Why pursue me and go through with the wedding service? Why, why, why? So many whys and so few answers.

I was in such a state of shock I couldn't even take it in, believe it had happened, and I kept expecting him to reappear. He didn't.

I think I gave one of the best performances I have ever given in my life that day. Although I can't remember all the details because of what happened later, excuses – good, convincing ones – were obviously made for my missing bridegroom, the best man and his mother, because I'm sure nobody knew at that stage that there had been a major incident. Tony Warren, though, told me a story, much later, which I am sure is true. He had apparently come looking for me at one point and eventually found me in an isolated Ladies' loo, with several cigarette burns in my veil. I had just looked up at him and said, 'All fellas are bastards.'

Nothing could prepare anyone for something like that. What do you do? What do you tell people? I was there and I still don't know. The important thing, it seemed to me, was damage limitation, to just get through the reception without any further humiliation. I retreated to a far-off place, and the next thing I remember with any clarity is being back, still in my gold wedding dress, at the little bungalow.

When I arrived I was absolutely convinced that he'd be there, waiting for me, feeling very sorry and sheepish, ready to put it all down to wedding-day nerves, but he wasn't. So, sitting at the kitchen table, my head in my hands, my headdress askew, I thought, 'There's only one other place he can be – his mum's. It's all been too much for him. After all, in all fairness to him, it was a bit OTT, too much even for me, let alone him, and I'm used to show business.'

The big treat, which I'd booked and paid for myself, was a week's honeymoon in Paris, the city of lovers and romance. We were due to go the next morning and I'd arranged for a car to collect us from the bungalow and drive us to the airport. I said to myself, 'When we get to Paris in the morning, everything will be fine. So I'm just gonna get the Mini out of the garage and go round to his mum's to see if he's there. That's what I'm going to do. It isn't far from here, and everything will be sorted. We'll kiss and make up. Of course we will. It's our wedding night for God's sake. And he wanted this, he asked me to marry him! What's happened must be all my fault. All that showbiz stuff was just too much for him. Surely I can understand that; surely we can both forgive and forget.'

At that stage I so wanted to put things right, I was more than ready to make endless excuses for his behaviour, make everything better. But, far from getting better, things were about to get worse. I did what I said I would do. I levered myself up from the kitchen table, scooped up my gold dress so I wouldn't trip over it, went out to the garage, got into the car and drove round to his mother's house. I was still in the head-dress and veil, too. I parked the car, went up the steps, and knocked on the door. It opened. There she was, his little mum who I'd grown so fond of, still wearing the suit I'd bought her for the wedding.

'Yes, what is it?' she barked, nothing like the woman I'd met so many times before.

'Is Tony in?' I asked, feeling for all the world like a small child, wanting a mate to come out to play.

'Yes, he is. And I've only just managed to get him off to sleep,' she replied and slammed the door in my face.

Dazed, I turned around, walked carefully back down the

steps, got into my Mini, arranged the dress and drove back to the bungalow. Having let myself in, I closed the door and returned to my slump at the kitchen table.

It was a long, long night, the longest I have lived through – and that's saying something. I poured myself a brandy and added soda to it from his siphon; then I poured myself another, and another, and another. The next thing I remember was the doorbell shattering the silence in the kitchen. When I opened the door, blinking, I was still dressed as I had been the day before. It was the car to take me and my husband to the airport. It was only then that I remembered I'd arranged a week off work; had booked one of my holiday weeks – and, God knows, we didn't get many.

Tilting my head and looking over the top of the driver's head – I couldn't bear to meet his eyes – I said, 'I'm *terribly* sorry, Miss Goodyear won't be able to make it. I'm just the cleaner.'

As he shook his head, baffled, and started to retreat, I closed the door. I stayed at that kitchen table in the bungalow for most of the week, only getting up to go to the loo. I was too ashamed to speak to anybody, couldn't go out. I was too embarrassed, didn't want anybody to know that I'd made one of the worst mistakes of my life. Tony Rudman was no gentleman! Our marriage, like our so-called courtship, was never to be consum-mated! He'd married me under false pretences for a reason I'd never really know. But he certainly benefited financially from the arrangement: kept my half of the value of the bungalow and enjoyed using our joint bank account for a time. In fact, he got half of it.

Later on, rumours reached me that the first 'marriage' of my husband of a few hours had been annulled – struck off the register, as if it never happened. My heart went out to that poor girl. All this, though, was hearsay. He never attempted to communicate with me after our wedding day, never gave any reason, never bothered to make any excuses. *Nothing.* And, as I have now heard that he died some years ago, he won't do so now.

At the end of the week's 'holiday', I went back to work. I couldn't wait to be Bet again. It was so much easier than being Julie!

Throughout all this, Gary, who had been staying with Alice and Bill, thought I was away on honeymoon. And when Alice and Bill found out what the situation really was, Alice said, 'Oh, it'll get sorted, luv. Of course it will. You must have done summat wrong. What did you do? What did you say?'

What could I say to Alice, or anybody else for that matter? By then, I didn't really believe it was my fault. I was just bewildered, didn't understand. As a person who has always, to my subsequent cost on several occasions, taken people at face value, I never, ever think that anybody has a hidden agenda, or a different motivation to mine.

Once I went back to work, it was a case of getting on with it amid all the usual post-wedding nudge nudge, wink wink jokes of 'Good honeymoon, was it? Get any sleep? Eh . . .' I played along with it, all smiles. I was now doing a daily per-formance within a performance. I couldn't have done anything else. It was just so important to me that nobody should find out, not yet anyway. Not for a long time and preferably never. Because, somehow, I was still thinking it *would* get sorted. He would come round, wouldn't he? Marriages just didn't end on the day of the wedding, before the reception. That was *imposs-ible*. Unheard of. It was, no other words for it, total humiliation. I was still living at the bungalow, and when I got back from the studios, it was brandy and soda time. I'd never drunk so much alcohol in my entire life. But I couldn't eat anything. Was I becoming like Alice? Did I care?

All I wanted was to get through another night and return as quickly as possible to being Bet, back to what I so loved doing. As soon as the costume and the make-up went on, everything else was completely blanked out. I didn't want to know about anything else. The viewers might have thought that Bet was having a bad time in the series but, dear God, Julie Goodyear was only ever happy being her. It was when I went back to my dressing room and washed off the make-up that Julie Goodyear returned and all hell kicked in again. I'd tried so hard to do the right thing by Gary because he so needed a dad; by Alice, who was always trying to fix me up with somebody; and by Bill, who worried about me and wanted to see me happy and settled, too; and this living hell was my reward.

Often, in the past, when I'd been creased up with laughter about this or that, Alice used to say, 'Just you remember, young lady, there'll be tears before bedtime,' and she was often right. But then mothers usually are because they speak from experi-ence. She wasn't spoiling the moment, she was preparing me for the lows after the highs. Another thing I understood immediately was when somebody said, 'Perpetual sunshine creates a desert.' Of course it does. If it didn't rain, we'd never have flowers. If we didn't have tears, we'd never know laughter.

These sayings that I collected along the way used to make

me smile and helped me. But now, sitting at that kitchen table, they were circling around at an ever-increasing speed in my mind. Why was it a tears before bedtime time, especially as I was somebody who didn't know how to cry, who couldn't cry? Why was I living in a perpetual desert? What had I done wrong?

Yet another Northern expression that I heard regularly when I was growing up and indulging in a bit of showing off, was, 'Who does she think she is? Queen of the muck heap?' Well, I must have done something wrong. I sure as hell had my own muck heap now. And hadn't Alice said often enough to me, 'D'you know, Julie luv, you could cause trouble in an empty house!' She was right. Once again, when I was least expecting it, trouble had found me. I was living a lie, and my brain felt as if it was about to explode. Everybody at work thought I was happily married, but the truth was that I was just like Humpty-Dumpty in that first moment when he fell off the wall and realized there was no way he could get up, no way he could put himself back together again. I was in bits like a smashed glass.

One day when I wasn't needed at the studios, I spent it alone in the little bungalow with thoughts circling endlessly around my tortured mind. Then, suddenly, it all came to a head: something like a Catherine wheel went off, there was a white-out followed by red mist, and everything went manic and began swimming before my eyes, then everything blanked. It was just as if somebody had swung a lever and switched me off.

The next thing I remember was being barefoot, with bloody feet and dressed in a bloodied nightie in the street, somehow knowing that I had to get to the nearest hospital. It took some time before I got there, though, because I kept thinking I was a child, running away from Rochdale and going back to my grandma's in Heywood. Everything had become jumbled, like an ill-assorted jigsaw, with no pieces in the right place, and I was terrified.

Many years later, when I was used to people coming up to me and saying, 'Do you remember me?' because I had once signed their autograph book, a drag queen approached me in a gay pub. 'Do you remember me?' he asked, smiling broadly.

'Sorry?'

'I met you the night you had your nervous breakdown,' he said. 'I was the porter at the hospital who half carried you, half dragged you into casualty when you stumbled, screaming with terror, through the gates, all on your own.'

'Oh, my God!' I exclaimed. 'But you wouldn't have been dressed like that then, would you?'

'No, I wasn't.' He laughed unabashed, straightening out his skirt and touching his long blond wig.

'Then how could I possibly be expected to remember you?' I laughed.

'I know, Julie, luv,' he said, his voice dropping several notes with emotion. 'You were so poorly that night. I didn't think they'd ever get you back. I don't think any of them did.'

'But they did!'

'Yes, praise the Lord,' he said.

'And the staff and the psychiatrist,' I added. 'I'll never forget them, never be able to thank them enough.'

As I said in the Prologue of this book, I was admitted to an NHS hospital first, the nearest one to where I was living. Then Granada got involved, and I was moved from there to Cheadle Royal, a private clinic that specialized in mental health problems.

In the first hospital they gave me some electric shock treatment (ECT), and the most extraordinary thing was that the song 'Please Release Me, Let Me Go' was always playing while they prepared the electrodes and attached them to me. Somebody there must have had a black sense of humour!

I don't know how many ECT shocks I was given. My mind, a delicate mechanism at the best of times, had completely shut down by then. I know what caused that shutdown to happen, though. I am basically a very straight, honest person and I was living a lie on a daily basis. And I couldn't sustain the pretence any longer. Everybody thought I was all right, but I knew I was disintegrating and that something was seriously wrong with me. I didn't want to feel the way I felt. I wanted somebody to see what was happening to me and put me back together again. I was looking through a shattered mirror and I couldn't see myself, couldn't see anything any more.

Once in hospital, I wasn't allowed to see Alice, Bill, Gary or anybody from Granada, but my ever-loving father was eventually asked to come and collect me by car from the first hospital and take me to the next. I remember that journey as a very long silent one, and as we reached our destination and went up the long drive, I started to scream again and couldn't stop. The next thing I recall is being half carried into a dazzling all-white room that had steel bars at its windows. Christ, was I in prison?

There really were moments when I felt like an extra in that film, *One Flew Over the Cuckoo's Nest*. Like most of the other patients, I thought I was all right, behaving normally, but apparently I was roaming about in a full-length evening dress and a white fox stole for much of the time. I obviously thought I should dress for the occasion. It was, after all, a very grand place I'd found myself in, or so it seemed at the time. We all had very pleasant separate rooms, complete with alarms and bars at the windows. The worst aspect was the pain in my head. That was absolutely excruciating, and there are no words to describe it or do it justice. The nearest I can come to it is a constant high-pitched screeching sound, like a fingernail being dragged along a blackboard. It was truly terrible.

After several sessions with Dr Mailey, the psychiatrist – some in which I remained totally silent, some in which I was unusually vocal – he asked Sister Tudor, another member of staff, to arrange for Tony Rudman to pay us a visit in the hospital. Rudman was considered key to my breakdown and, therefore, necessary to the treatment.

In our second session, largely devoted to the therapy of talking, Dr Mailey consistently returned to the subject of drug-taking and kept asking me what drugs I'd been on before I came into hospital.

'None,' I kept replying in lucid moments. 'I have never done drugs. Never in my life.' And that was God's honest truth. I've never even been tempted to go down that path and chase any dragon. My ciggies were my only vice. The doctor, though, was obviously convinced my state of mind had not been helped by drug-taking and might even have been drug-induced. To my astonishment, some blood tests that he had requested revealed some substances in my system. '*No!*' I kept saying, thinking I was losing my mind again. 'No, I don't believe it. I wouldn't try to hide it. I would put up my hand if this were true.'

'The evidence is unmistakable,' he replied gently.

I was totally baffled. Frustrated.

Then, very gently, he told me more about the state of mind

I was in just before I left the bungalow and ended up in hospital. 'I know you remember nothing of this,' he said at one moment, 'but you trashed and smashed everything in the bungalow. There was practically nothing left whole or undamaged.'

'No!' I said, shaken rigid. 'I don't understand. That is *not* me. I'm the sort of person who treasures things, who knows the value of money and what everything costs. I would never do that in my right mind, not ever.'

'But you were not in your right mind,' he reminded me gently. 'You were having a complete nervous breakdown.'

It wasn't until later, after someone from the hospital had obviously been back to the bungalow to see the extent of the damage I had caused, that the mystery of the drugs in my system was resolved. Having examined a soda siphon, which I freely admitted I'd used regularly during that time for my brandy and soda, they found illegal substances inside it. That siphon belonged to Tony, so I can only guess that it had been spiked by him. He was the only other person who had a key to get in – but *why*?

So the mystery of the substances in my blood sample was solved, but to this day I don't know exactly what had been added to the soda siphon. I was so relieved because I honestly felt they didn't believe me at first when I denied all knowledge of drug use. I was, though, very shocked by the soda siphon discovery because I'd no idea why Tony Rudman would have wanted to drug me. He certainly knew that my favourite tipple was a brandy and soda when I arrived home at the end of a day's work. However, the discovery was important because, once they were able to eliminate drug abuse from my problems, we could move on.

I could have told them, though, that I didn't need alcohol

or drugs for kicks; I just needed someone dependable in my life! If Tony Rudman had been that sort of person, the man I believed he was, I would have been married to him for life. I would never have been unfaithful to him, either.

As I recovered, a large part of my heartbreak was knowing that Gary would be gutted by what had happened. He had hated being Gary Sutcliffe while I was Julie Goodyear, and now he was Gary Rudman at a time when I could hardly wait to revert to being Julie Goodyear. Many years later, completely off his own bat and without telling me at first, he changed his surname by deed poll to Goodyear. I was so touched when he did that! We had the same name at last.

Anyway, a meeting was arranged with Tony Rudman and I was absolutely terrified, full of dread at the thought of seeing him again. When I walked into the room there were three chairs, one behind the desk, two in front. Tony was already seated and Dr Mailey was on the other side of the desk. As soon as I sat down, wearing a name label – which were all over everything in there – bearing his surname, of course, the conversation began.

I was horrified. I felt as if I was listening to people talking about a complete stranger. Tony Rudman was saying terrible things; no one was defending me, and I was so shocked I couldn't speak. The psychiatrist seemed to be aiding, abetting and encouraging him to talk, and the pack of lies seemed to be going on for ever. All of a sudden, in a moment of blind terror I realized that Tony Rudman was trying to ensure that they kept me incarcerated in that place for the rest of my life. I'd never felt so frightened, and I was convinced that he was achieving his heart's desire. He was certainly telling a very convincing story, outlining my so-called bizarre behaviour. He was making things up and it seemed to me that the psychiatrist was having the wool pulled over his eyes – that he believed everything Tony Rudman was telling him. I wanted to scream, 'No! Stop! None of this is true. He is lying,' but I was rendered incapable by shock, and just sat there utterly speechless.

I don't know how long this continued but then Tony Rudman started to complain in greater detail about how I'd smashed up our home. This felt like the final nail in my coffin, but suddenly the psychiatrist's attitude changed and, as I sat, my hands clenched, looking down at the floor, I heard him say, 'Oh, come on, Mr Rudman. Julie never actually broke anything that was yours, did she?'

'Oh my God! Am I in with a chance?' I thought, hope springing suddenly in my breast. 'Does he actually understand what is going on here?'

'Well, I suppose not, but even so . . .' Tony Rudman replied, his voice trailing off.

'No, let's have it right, shall we?' the psychiatrist interjected in a voice that brooked no argument. And, believe me, he totally changed his approach then and wiped the floor with Tony Rudman.

Oh, the relief! Dr Mailey had completely seen through Rudman; had only bided his time to draw him out, get to the truth and to the bottom of his character; and Tony Rudman didn't like *that* one little bit. Slowly but surely, he began to show more and more of his true colours. But I didn't really care any more. Dr Mailey had sussed him, seen through him, and was even tackling him about the substance in the soda siphon.

'You have got off lightly, Mr Rudman,' he said at one point.

I didn't know how I could ever thank him. But I knew he wasn't seeking any thanks. He was just doing his job, and thank God he was there for me when I needed it most.

During my life, one man has saved my sanity, one has saved my life when I found out I had cancer, and one has cleared my good name. And these are the three things that are so important for all of us: your sanity, your life, your good name. What have you got without them? And I was destined, at one time or another, to be sorely tested on every single one of them.

I was Dr Mailey's last patient before he left to go to Canada to take up a new post. I wished him everything he could possibly wish himself and more, and I thought his departure was a great loss to this country. Some years later when I was making guest appearances in Canada promoting *Coronation Street*, I was lucky enough to catch a glimpse of him in a crowd of fans and onlookers. I would have recognized him anywhere! He smiled, such a gentle smile full of approval, waved and disappeared back into the throng.

It was exactly the way he would have behaved, would have wanted it to be. Psychiatrists have a code of ethics which includes not keeping in touch with their patients. He had, though, turned up to catch a glimpse of me from afar, must have seen my appearance advertised somewhere. And he smiled because he knew that my biggest fear the last time he had seen me was that I would become a regular in-patient at the clinic, just like so many of the other patients there. 'You won't,' he had kept repeating. 'You won't.' And I'd found that so healing and reassuring. Nevertheless, it's rather like a broken glass. You know the glass can be glued back together again, but you feel it's never going to be quite the same, quite as safe as it was before, that any pressure could cause it to crack again. I still feel that these days. And when it happens I just take some healing time on my own.

But, there he was, a face in the crowd, giving me the thumbs-up, and I was well, happy and working. It was a lovely moment for both of us, and he was truly a lovely man.

When Tony Rudman visited the hospital was the last time I ever set eyes on him. One of Alice's sayings was, 'If you can't wish a person well, wish them *nowt*.' I think that's very wise and I applied it to Tony Rudman, my husband of less than an hour.

SEVEN

Cry Me a River

When my grandma was found drowned in the canal, I didn't cry. This lack of tears was noted by people at the time of her death and funeral, and was considered a bit odd, especially given everyone knew I adored her. Crying was something I just never did after her death. And that is how things remained for a very long time, even though for comfort over the years I often played Ella Fitzgerald's heart-rending classic song, 'Cry Me a River'.

Any pain, shocks or traumas I suffered seemed to run so deep that they were beyond tears. It was as if the tears rained backwards, became frozen into droplets somewhere inside me. And that's how things remained until Dr Mailey started to locate the tip of the iceberg while I was in the clinic, and then helped me to understand that, for any true healing to take place, I had to begin to 'melt', dissolve some of that solid matter and learn how to cry. This was not put in so many words, but that was certainly the gist of what he meant. I found the first tears I shed in the hospital, however, very difficult and incredibly painful. Crying hurt so much, because all the grief had been held on to for so long. It felt like blood coming out of my eyes.

The remarkable thing about my non-crying time is that I

found it so easy, when asked, to cry as Bet. Unlike most actors, I could even do it without any glycerol being dropped into my eyes, without any kind of external help whatsoever, and without the camera ever needing to be stopped until I was ready. I could cry in five seconds flat as Bet, but I couldn't cry as Julie. The pain was just too deep.

One evening in the hospital, shortly after another bout of screaming had subsided, and I was lying in bed in a calmer frame of mind, I fancied I could hear a voice I recognized, saying, 'Just remember, luv, nothing's gonna hurt you, not while I'm here . . .' Straining my ears, I soon without a shadow of a doubt recognized the voice. It was my grandma – and that, almost word for word, was what she used to say whenever I was upset, frightened or needed reassurance. Protecting me from every-thing, and everyone, was the function she'd always fulfilled in my life. And that was why I had always felt so safe from harm and hurt when she was alive. She was like a glorious guardian angel, capable of destroying any monster or demon on my behalf.

That was the night my room filled with the scent of lavender and I stopped screaming and started to get better, the night when I was restored to my rightful mind.

The next morning all the staff looked sunny side up and smiled at me, and each of those smiles, which was like a tender kiss, said, in its own individual way, 'The worst is over, Julie. There's been a change in you.'

And there had. I'd survived and was on the road to recovery.

I have so many memories of my four weeks in that hospital. I remember a nurse giving me a Scrabble board as part of my therapy, but I couldn't bear it near me because my mind was all over the place and I couldn't make any recognizable words, couldn't make any of the pieces fit. So I picked it up and threw the whole lot up in the air, then just sat there humming and rocking. Luckily, the nurses always seemed to know what to do at such moments, and for a long time there was a nurse posted at my door during the night, obviously part of the hospital's suicide watch and security system. Not that I needed a suicide watch. I never contemplated killing myself. I think I was too disturbed then, even for that. And, anyway, I would never have left my precious son with that memory for the rest of his life.

I met such characters in the hospital: some spaced out, some tragic, some just strange and some really funny. I remember one of the more tormented patients, a woman, sidling up to me and saying, 'Have you got a Silk Cut?'

'Yeah, course,' I said, easing a cigarette out of the packet and giving it to her.

Having lit it, she started stabbing the lighted end into her arm. There was an instant smell of burning flesh, then somebody must have spotted what was happening. The alarm sounded, as it did so often in there; nurses rushed in and I found myself taken aside and give a stern reprimand. 'Couldn't you see?' a nurse said angrily. 'Are you blind? Her arms are all covered in cigarette burns. She self-mutilates. Never, ever give her cigarettes or matches or anything that she can harm herself with. Understand?'

'Right!' I said meekly and continued blowing smoke-rings and watching them swirl through the air.

There was a very young girl in there who, I learned, belonged to a strict religious sect. She walked around, all day and all night if allowed, holding a Bible up to some imaginary threat and repeating the same prayers over and over again. There was a boy who always created a fuss when it was time for him to get out of the bath, and who was forever getting back in and submerging himself. He, poor fella, could see germs crawling all over him all the time. His own skin was virtually falling off. Another chap was forever peering intently through the window and repeating earnestly, 'Can you see them? They'll be here any moment now. Look, over there! They're coming. Can you see them?'

On one particular night in the clinic, I became aware that somebody else was in my room with me. When I sat up and switched on the light, there was a pretty young girl standing next to my bed. 'D'you want to look at some photos?' she asked, obviously totally unaware that it was the middle of the night.

'Okay,' I replied, wondering where my nurse had gone from outside the door, but not particularly worried by the girl's presence.

She handed me some dog-eared photographs, one by one, and the first thing I noticed was that in every picture the head of one person had been cut or torn off. I didn't mention this to her because she was only in the room for a very short time until my nurse, who had only popped to the loo, came back, sounded the alarm and had her removed. I found out later, though, that showing me those pictures had been a breakthrough for both the girl and the nursing staff. The person whose head she had cut or torn off in all the photographs was her brother, who had raped her then killed himself. That was why she had gone mad and was in there. Dear God. I was discovering people in the clinic who were far worse off than I was, and my heart went out to that girl.

Something that surprised me was that there were so many male patients. I was under the illusion that things like nervous breakdowns only happened to women, but there were men in there who were in a terrible state. I'd grown up thinking that men were not victims, but there were plenty of male victims in there, and from all different age groups.

The other patients' behaviour only disturbed or scared me for a short time. Then I began to take it in my stride; I very quickly became institutionalized. I know this was the case because after four weeks I was much more frightened of coming out than staying in. By that time I was already used to being institutionalized in a different way. I'd been on the set of *Coronation Street* so long – where I rarely saw the outside world – that I couldn't be anything other than that.

During the four weeks I was locked up, a contract was brought in from Granada for me to sign up for another year. I grabbed it with both hands and hugged it close to my chest. I so wanted that contract. It was a great comfort; represented security – another year's work. My marriage to Tony Rudman had virtually cleaned me out financially, and I needed to start earning money again. He might have got half of everything that was mine, but at least I'd kept my integrity and dignity, and had walked away from him with some pounds, shillings and pence. I always paid for my own divorces – that used to annoy my solicitor.

I have never been a person who suffers from headaches, but reliving that period for the benefit of this autobiography has been rather like being back in the mental institution, and I have had a constant pain in my head. But it was my choice to do this and, in my heart of hearts, I know the time is right.

Towards the end of my stay in the hospital, I was allowed a visitor – my son. Oh God! The thought of him coming to see me in there very nearly cracked me up all over again. It was also, as it transpired, to be the first time I was allowed out of the place. And where did they send me with Gary? Manchester Airport of all places, to have a cup of tea before going back!

I suppose they chose that venue because everything was within a compact area, and somebody could be present, unknown to us, ensuring all was well. I was still wearing a lot of labels and my hands were shaking so much I couldn't even hold a cup or saucer. I remember Gary, this young lad, holding the cup and lifting it to my lips. It must have been a nightmare for him to see me like that and be thrown in at the deep end. I so loved being with him again, but I was so relieved to set him free and get back into the hospital. I'd found the whole outing a terrible strain, absolutely terrifying. It was clever of them, though. They obviously knew that I would need to face the outside world one day soon and that I would hold myself together during that first outing for Gary's sake. They were, in fact, preparing me for going home.

During my remaining time there, they gave me a job washing old people's hair and that really helped me. 'They don't think I'm crazy,' I thought, 'and they know I would never harm another soul. They must know this or they wouldn't let me do what I'm doing now – shampooing this patient's hair.' I did it with love and very gently.

Part of the final treatment was to take me back to the bungalow where I had first had the brainstorm. I was horrified. I'd smashed everything to bits, including the windows, and even damaged the doors. It had been some brainstorm! I was absolutely devastated by what I saw that day because I really am a person who looks after and values the things I have.

By the time Bill and Alice collected me from the hospital,

though, the bungalow had been put back to rights, and Bill, bless him, had used his building skills to sort out the worst of the damage. So, unbelievably on one level, I went back to live there while Gary stayed on with his nan and granddad. That was much the best thing. There was much more stability for him there, and although I wanted and needed him by my side, I wouldn't have dreamed of moving him. He needed them and they needed him; and he could visit me any time.

It was very important that I got back to work at once. Having fortunately signed another contract while I was still in hospital, I knew I could do just that. Knowing I was coming out to a job and that I could begin to pay off the bills that had mounted up during my time away was a big help. I couldn't wait to get the marriage annulled so that I could breathe more freely again and make a fresh start; try once again to turn negative into positive.

My chief fear at the time was that I would become a regular patient. This took root as soon as I began to realize that many of the patients had been in there before. I wanted to get well, didn't want to come back again – not ever. Touch wood, thank God, I haven't. It was a very fine line I walked, though, on some occasions; and that was certainly the case, many years later, when having left the *Street* after twenty-five years of playing Bet, I was persuaded to go back for a twelve-month contract which nearly finished me off. But more of that later.

One of the last questions Dr Mailey asked me in the clinic was, I thought, a very surprising one. 'Have you, by any chance, ever had a relationship with a woman, Julie?'

'What do you mean?' I replied, genuinely puzzled.

'A sexual relationship,' he answered.

'Good God, no!' I replied, truly shocked.

'Do you know,' he added, 'I am rather surprised by that.'

'Why?' I asked, baffled.

'No particular reason. But I am surprised.'

That exchange stayed in my mind and raised many questions. Why had he asked me that? What on earth had he picked up? Was it anything to do with my relationship with my mam? Did he think I was overprotective where she was concerned? Loved her too much? What had put that idea into his head, and now into mine?

Don't get me wrong; Dr Mailey did not labour the point that day. It was just that what he said stayed with me. I was soon to discover that Dr Mailey hadn't put the idea into my head; he just made me think about it. My next relationship, after Tony Rudman, was with a woman. I thought it was worth a try.

EIGHT

Looked at Love from Both Sides Now

Never at any time while I was growing up did I have a crush – or anything resembling those kinds of feelings – for a member of my own sex. And if anybody had asked me during my twenties, in fact into my thirties, I would have said I was 100 per cent heterosexual. Not all gay women are born gay – some are driven to it. Even though I worked in television, and had several lovely gay men as good friends, I didn't know any gay women. At the time we're talking about here, such things hadn't even crossed my mind. Anyway, I couldn't see how two women could make love. What on earth did they do?

When I returned to work, my troubles with Tony Rudman and the nervous breakdown were never referred to by other members of the cast or crew. I was very relieved about that, and grateful too. I didn't want to regurgitate any of that pain for anybody, however well intentioned they might have been in asking. As it was, I needn't have worried. They were all just pleased to see me. It was as if I'd never been away and I could just get back to being Bet. That was exactly what I wanted to do. Bet was my best friend, my soulmate. She let me fly far away from Julie, and she paid the bills. Once again, I couldn't wait to step into her leopard-skin life.

I never actually did the choosing or made the running in any of my relationships, heterosexual or gay. The people concerned always chose me and did the initiating and the running. And, if I didn't recognize the early signs of a bloke finding me attractive and sexually desirable, how could I possibly have recognized what was going on in a woman?

I really was the last person to think that someone, male or female, was interested in me in that way, so they needed to do the running if I was ever to wake up! Mostly, though, I was too busy working and too insecure, too vulnerable, too lacking in self worth. I didn't look in the mirror and see what Alice was always claiming others saw. I really didn't value myself or my looks. It was, therefore, always a surprise when someone came on to me. Alice always used to say, 'You just don't know what you've got, do you?' Then she used to break into that song: 'A, you're adorable; B, you're so beautiful; C, you're a cutie full of charms; D, you're a darling and E, you're exciting and F, you're a feather in my arms . . .'

'Oh, don't be daft, Mam,' I used to say, laughing. She really was an incredibly supportive mother.

What I did know, then and now, is that people come into our lives for a reason, even if, at the time, we are unaware of what the reason might be. Whether it is to teach us something – perhaps tolerance or a better understanding – I'm not sure. But I'm convinced that people who come along and touch our lives in some way, especially intimately, do so for a specific reason, even if they don't stay around very long. Even though it can be very painful, traumatic even, there are, I believe, lessons each of us has to learn along the way; and how we deal with what is dished out is all-important. What sort of person we become as a result of this determines whether we emerge wanting to pass our pain on to somebody else, or want to be a better, wiser person who, as a result of our own experiences, develops compassion for others.

I hope it has been the latter result for me. I really do. After all, if we become bitter and twisted, it is not only physically, mentally and emotionally draining; we are the losers in the end, left at the mercy of the deadly sins – jealousy, greed, anger and suchlike – that so often surround us. Although it's been my experience along the way that people often mistake kindness for weakness, kindness is a tremendous strength, but we need to be aware that many will try to abuse it. These days, I try to recharge my batteries by remembering what peace there is in silence, and that it is empty vessels that make the most noise. I also find great solace in nature. I remember Tony Warren once saying to me, 'I'm the sort of person who, if I run out of pavement, runs out of life.' I didn't understand at that time, but I now know that I'm the sort of person who, if I run out of grass and fields, I run out of life.

I suspect, at this moment, I am using delaying tactics to avoid introducing the person I will call No Name in this book. This is a device necessary to protect her present position in life, which is quite an elevated one professionally. I will hang back no longer. I met the woman who became my first same-sex partner in 1976 when two gay boys who were great friends of mine thought I needed cheering up and invited me out for the evening. The occasion began in a very jokey way, with one of the boys asking me, 'Have you ever, Julie, in any of your relationships, felt a genuine connection?'

I knew they would be disappointed if I just replied, 'Yes, in my relationship with Bet,' so I answered the question in another truthful way by saying, 'That's what I've tried to do in the past, but I don't think I've succeeded.'

'We must see what we can do about that,' one of the boys replied, giggling mischievously. 'Come with us. We're going to take you to one of our favourite watering holes, a gay club.' That night, then, began rather strangely, but it ended rather well.

In no time at all we were going up some steep stone stairs into one of the dimmest-lit clubs I have ever found myself in. I couldn't see a thing at first, could only sense that it was packed to the gills with shadowy people smooching around, dancing to a very slow tune coming from a record player behind the bar. By the end of the second song my eyes were becoming accustomed to the dark, and to my astonishment I saw that most of the people dancing were women, not gay boys. Bloody hell! That's different!

Although this did seem strange on one level, on another it also looked perfectly natural. I was confused. At one moment I even remember thinking, 'Ah, bless 'em.' When my two mates melted into the crowd, probably to have a chat with a friend they'd just spotted, I became very on edge. I was utterly alone and had been spotted by a group of five or so girls. As somebody who had never been seen there before, I was attracting a lot of unwanted interest that I was finding embarrassing.

'Get you!' one of the bolder butch-looking girls uttered, sidling up closer. 'You're a dark horse, Bet Lynch!'

'Julie Goodyear, actress,' I said formally.

'Wanna dance?' another enquired.

173

'Hm, thank you, no,' I answered politely, clearing my throat. 'I—'

'Come here often?' yet another enquired, giggling.

'Er, no. I'm with two gay friends of mine,' I said, pointedly I hoped.

They had obviously all had a drink or two, and I was getting very nervous about the attention, desperately trying to make eye contact with the boys. Suddenly, close up, from behind my left ear, I heard another voice, a voice that sounded sober and pleasantly friendly.

'When you're less busy,' a girl said gently, 'I'd love to buy you a drink.'

'Thank you,' I said, glancing down at my near-empty brandy and soda glass and thinking this offer sounded the most polite and least intrusive so far. 'That would be nice.'

A second later she had melted away and once again I was left fielding unwanted attention. Then, as another song began to play, the giggling girls grabbed their partners and drifted off. 'Where the hell are the boys?' I thought, wondering if I dared move from the table and risk moving around the club to find them. But, feeling too vulnerable for that, I decided to stay put.

'Brandy and soda?' said the voice I'd heard earlier. 'I hope I've got it right.'

'Thank you, yes.'

'May I?'

'Of course,' I said, indicating one of the empty chairs opposite me.

She was pleasantly boyish, had short, cropped dark hair that had been extremely well cut and, although wearing a white open-necked linen shirt and blue jeans, looked extraordinarily neat and tidy for someone so casually dressed. She was also quietly and pleasantly spoken, not predatory but very polite, and I got the impression she had been well brought up and probably came from a reasonably well-to-do family. I later found out I was right about that.

As the conversation continued and we skated across far too many topics too soon, I found myself thinking, 'She's nice. Yes, she's really very nice.'

'Shall we have a dance?' she asked at one point.

'Er . . .' I glanced around the dimly lit crowded dance floor, then, feeling suddenly adventurous, added, 'Yeah, why not.'

It felt a bit strange at first, but then the rhythm of the music took over. I love dancing and I'd just started to relax and enjoy myself when a beer bottle whistled past my head and smashed against the wall just behind us.

'*Jesus!*' I exclaimed, startled. 'What the hell was that?'

'Oh, nothing,' No Name replied, glancing in the direction of the bar but looking totally unconcerned. 'That sort of thing happens all the time. Nobody gets hurt.'

As she finished speaking, another beer bottle flew past us and crashed against the wall. Then, just seconds later, a third. By then, though, I was taking my cue from No Name and carried on dancing. At the time I thought this was some sort of strange custom, like the Greeks with plates. It wasn't until a week or so later that I discovered the girl who was launching the missiles at us from behind the bar was No Name's current lover!

When the dance ended and the boys eventually re-emerged from the gloom, No Name introduced herself to them and then, just before she left me in their care, turned back to me. 'I'd love to give you a ring some time and perhaps meet for a drink?' she said with a winning smile.

To my astonishment I took the notebook and biro she held out to me and, to my even greater astonishment, found myself jotting down my telephone number.

'Thanks,' she said. 'I'll give you a ring.' And the next moment she was gone.

'Well, get you!' said one of my mates.

'Better still, get your coat, you've pulled,' was the other's nudge nudge, wink wink remark.

'Don't be daft,' I said and, to cover my confusion, took a deep swig of my brandy and soda.

She phoned the next day. 'I so enjoyed meeting you last night,' she said. 'Can I take you out for a drink?'

'Let's take each other out for a drink,' I replied, nervous but pleased to hear from her.

'That sounds great to me!'

She was just as polite and charming as before and I actually found myself looking forward to meeting her again.

So it began, my first same-sex friendship that from the start felt different from any friendship I'd had with other girls. It was just like mates. Then came the visits to a variety of Manchester clubs where gays of both sexes met and whiled away the evenings, drinking, smoking, dancing, making eyes at each other. Soon the expression 'Get your coat, you've pulled' became familiar. It was fun, a laugh, and just what I needed after what I'd been through.

However much attention I attracted as a new kid on the block, I always kept close to – and made sure I left with – No Name. I guess we were going through a kind of courtship period, but I didn't think of it that way at the time. I was just glad we were friends who were getting to know each other and seemed to have so much in common. I knew she was longing to kiss me goodnight, but I dealt with that at the end of the evening by making sure I leapt out of the car the moment it came to a halt. 'See you,' I'd call over my shoulder as I let myself into the bungalow, alone. (When I eventually moved from there, when I could afford to pay off Tony, I discovered it can be just as hard leaving pain behind.)

I hadn't, however, reckoned on our first slow dance. Everything changed then. It was a Roberta Flack number, 'The First Time Ever I Saw Your Face' . . . No Name held me close, very close, but I didn't feel ill at ease or awkward. On the contrary, we felt so right together. She moved beautifully, always seemed to know when to draw me to her, when to cut me some slack and give me breathing space; and I loved dancing with her. And I kept coming back to that word – it felt *natural*.

What was happening to me? I asked the question, but I didn't really want to probe any deeper. I just wanted what was happening to happen. And, to my surprise, I also actually found myself wanting what by now seemed inevitable to happen, almost as much as she had made it clear, very clear by now, that she did!

Right! I have always been a person who feels better when I have some of the control. I still hadn't a clue about the technicalities of what women did in bed but, by then, I'd gleaned from some of the less savoury jokes I'd overheard in the gay clubs that it was possible to buy aids or gadgets. Yes, those were the words, and I wanted to be prepared, wanted whatever was to happen to be right and good. I wanted to please her!

So, at the twelfth hour, the day she was coming round for drinks and a sandwich at my home in the evening, I decided to visit the electrical department of Kendal's in Manchester to get, I hardly dared say it, a Pifco. Needless to say, I was in a right state. Marching boldly up to a counter, I collared a young male assistant and blurted out, 'You know what I want. A Pifco.'

'Sorry?' he queried blankly.

'Look,' I snapped. 'Don't come it with me, sonny. The thing that moves – women use it. *Get it*, and get it now, please.'

I was horrified with myself. I'd never been so short, so *rude*, to anyone in my life. But I was beside myself with embarrassment, feeling exactly as young men must do when they go into chemists and end up buying four items they don't want instead of their first packet of Durex.

The assistant, who had left for a minute, came back still looking confused. 'For God's sake . . .' I muttered grimly. 'Just get it. Don't show it to me, and make sure you wrap it up very carefully in brown paper.'

Having popped away again, he came back carrying a box. '*No!* Wrap it!' I hissed, glancing nervously all round me. 'Wrap it in brown paper like I said, and seal the edges with Sellotape.'

Trying very hard to retain his 'The customer's always right' expression, he withdrew again, then returned with the box duly wrapped. I was so relieved, I didn't even ask how much it was. I just thrust some notes into his hand and started to leave the store.

'It's too much,' I could hear him calling after me as I leapt on the escalator. 'You've given me too much money.' Bollocks. Who cared? Change was the last thing on my mind at that moment. I just had to get out of there and back to the safety of my Mini. Having reached my car, I put the box in the boot, covered it as best as I could with a rug, closed and locked the boot and, shaking like a leaf, sped off. I'd got it. What? I'd no bloody idea. But I'd got it.

Arriving home, I drove the Mini straight into the garage and locked the garage door. I would, I'd decided on the journey home, not carry the box into the house until after dark. Yes, I know I was behaving like a twat, but that's what some of us do on first-time, nerve-racking, never-before-experienced occasions!

As soon as night fell, I crept out of the house, unlocked the garage door, unlocked the boot, collected the box and shot back indoors. Once in, I made for my bedroom, stuffed it (still wrapped) into the wardrobe and locked the wardrobe door. Then, out of breath and still shaking, I started making other preparations for the evening. After all my horrible relationship experiences, it felt very important to get this one off to a good start.

I got myself ready, donned a pretty pale-blue dress, polished the crystal glasses until they squeaked in protest, made up the smoked-salmon sandwiches in brown bread, adding just the right amount of cracked black pepper and beautifully thin slices of cucumber, and put the champagne on ice. I did all this with my heart thumping and knees knocking, then waited for her to arrive.

Having composed myself – again – I lit some scented candles, put on a soft Lionel Richie cassette, and had just decided to have a little calming glass of champagne, when the bell rang. '*Oh my God!* She's here.'

Deep breath, pause to reassure myself with the thought that the mystery package – the box – was in the wardrobe, quick glance in the mirror, then I opened the front door, looking for all the world like I was perfectly in control.

'Hi. Come on in.'

And in she came, looking shiny, clean, very attractive, dressed in her usual white linen shirt and flares – which were in then. On her feet were those awful platform shoes, which meant that, until they came off, you never knew what height anyone really was.

'Glass of champagne?'

It was pink, of course. I hate the white; it's too gassy for me.

'Oh! Yes, thanks.'

'Sandwich?'

'Oh, yes, please.'

Let the evening begin!

It was great fun, lovely to have her there in my own space. We chatted, smiled, laughed, frequently avoided each other's eyes, just a little afraid to reveal too soon what we were sensing – feeling. She was as charming as ever. We got on like a house on fire.

Three or more hours later, she suddenly got up from where she had been lounging on the fitted carpet and said, 'Would you excuse me?'

'Yes, of course,' I replied, wondering why she suddenly looked strained and just a teeny bit nervous.

She went to the bathroom – oh, she must have needed to wee – and I fiddled around tidying up the sandwich crumbs and plates, all the while aware that she was being rather a long time. Then, shortly after this, I thought I heard a door open and then heard her call, 'Okay, Julie, you can come in now.'

Come in now – where? The bathroom. Why?

I crossed the room but on my way to the bathroom realized my bedroom door, which had been closed all evening, was now ajar. Walking in I was surprised to see she was lying on the bed.

Even more surprised when I took in that she had undressed and was naked as the day she was born.

'Oh! *Oh!*' I said, covered in confusion as she held out her arms to me. The penny dropped. This, she had obviously decided, was the moment. 'Just a minute,' I murmured, remembering the box and crossing to the wardrobe. After all, I'd made the effort to be prepared, so I had to show her the contents and let her know that I wanted to please her.

As she lowered her arms, surprised, I unlocked the wardrobe door, and got out the box. 'Whatever are you doing?' she queried, sounding, I thought, a little rattled.

'Here you are,' I replied triumphantly, crossing the room and perching at what I thought was a reasonably safe distance on the side of the bed.

'What is it?' she asked, perplexed. 'A present?'

'Open it,' I said, thinking, 'Don't ask me, luv. I haven't the foggiest idea.'

'Oh, all right,' she said, her eyes lighting up.

She opened the box. I couldn't actually see what was inside because I think, coward that I am, I'd closed my eyes! Also, I was on one side of the bed, fully clothed, still in my pretty pale-blue dress, while she was on the other side in her birthday suit. I was just sitting there. I saw her expression change, her lips pucker and forehead crease into a frown. 'Oh God! What now?' I thought. Was it the wrong size? Wrong shape? What?

'But, Julie,' she finally said, 'I haven't *got* arthritis.'

'No, I know *that*,' I said, keeping my cool and making the quickest recovery I'd ever made in my entire life. 'I know *you* haven't, but your mother has!' It was an arthritis massage kit – yes, a Pifco – especially recommended for painful, aching joints! 'Now, put your clothes back on,' I commanded in a serious but semi-jokey voice, 'and go home immediately. I think you are very forward. Very forward, indeed.'

And, although she fell about laughing, she did get dressed. I never told her the real story behind the box but, as she was leaving, I let her kiss me for the first time. But only a peck. Not long after that I discovered that gadgets weren't necessary when two women made love.

After she had left, I poured myself a very stiff brandy and added a bottle of soda. She probably had a stiff drink when she got home, too. No matter! We might not have got off the ground that night, but the relationship continued to deepen, develop and blossom, and, yes, we did eventually get our act together and enjoyed a very special intimate relationship for three or so years.

'This is *it*,' I often thought during those days. 'This is what was wrong. I'd got my sexual orientation all arse about face and had therefore made a number of mistakes which were my fault all along. That had to be the case because this felt so right. I must have been gay all the time; had to be because I felt so tender towards her and we cared so much for each other.

No Name, who had not really had a 'proper' job up to that time, came to work for me. This meant that she could move into the bungalow with me without raising eyebrows or too many questions. Our relationship became, in fact, like the marriage I'd never had, and I was forever delighting in the thought, which I expressed in words from that wonderful song that Joni Mitchell sang so well, that I had 'looked at love from both sides now' and had finally found someone who I wanted to spend the rest of my life with. What's more, No Name felt exactly the same as I did.

I met her parents. She met my parents and my son. And

Alice, being Alice, cottoned on to us at once. But Mam didn't seem that surprised or bothered. She just said, 'As long as you're happy, luv. God knows you deserve some happiness after what you've been through.'

Gary wasn't daft, either. When the gutter press started to poke their noses into this aspect of my life it didn't help matters, but he and I had always been very close and honest with each other, and nothing would alter that. As long as he was happy, that was always fine by me, and I know he felt the same about me. We both have that kind of love and caring for each other. It's real – absolutely priceless.

So, I could not have been happier during those years. I was happy in *Coronation Street*, getting some really brilliant scenes and lines, and happy that I'd finally found someone who loved me and who I loved back.

It was not to last! Trouble, big trouble, had crept into my life unnoticed.

NINE

Treat Me Like a Lady

Sex maniac? Sex kitten? Nympho? Someone who enjoys 'three-in-a-bed romps and orgies'? Diva? Me? *Never!* But, according to some of the press coverage I have received since I started to play Bet in *Coronation Street*, I am all of these things and more. So what is the truth – not about Bet – about Julie? The truth is, I've read interviews I have never given, with journalists I have never even met. But that doesn't deter the gutter press. They have imagination to surpass any reality and they put it to good use.

Yes, I can honestly say, hand on heart – sorry to disappoint those who would have it otherwise – that I was never, ever that sort of person. Yes, I've faced lots of dark alleyways, made crap decisions, taken wrong turns at life's crossroads, but it's always been done with the best of intentions, always been motivated by the search for love. The actual act of sex, however, has never been number one on my list of priorities, and I am not what hacks describe as 'highly sexed'. Maybe that resulted from my first, disastrous experience when I got pregnant at the age of seventeen. Whatever. Love is what motivates me and it is a trillion times more important to me than sex. So, when I heard or read lurid tales of what I was supposed to be getting into and up to, I was stunned. And whenever another of these stories broke all I could think was, 'My God, these journos have vivid warped imaginations; this crap surely says more about them than it does about me.'

Three in a bed? I don't think so. Piss off – not my scene.

There I was again, cutting up little squares of newspaper, threading string through the corners, and sending the bundles off to editors. That, apart from occasional wonderful journalists such as Jack Tinker and Margaret Forward in the 1980s and 1990s, who saw through it all, was the only defence I had. I was so grateful for reporters like them!

Many people – particularly members of the press – are in my experience very confused by the word 'diva'. Some of the confusion has doubtless come about because there is a very fine line between a diva and a perfectionist, which journalists, with very rare exceptions, do not seem to take into account.

The picture they've painted of me is of a very difficult, bolshie, demanding, bossy-to-a-fault person – and that is totally untrue. I remember reading, 'Her PA is always expected to light her cigarette'; and 'She demands pink champagne.' What utter rubbish! Of course, I am happy to light my own cigarettes, but, hang on a mo, I'm not going to push somebody's hand away when they are trying to light it for me, or say 'No, thank you very much' when pink champagne is on offer. I have never, though, demanded pink champagne in my entire life. In fact, between you and me, I am as at home with a bottle of Mateus Rosé as I am with a bottle of Cristal Rosé. But don't tell anybody who wants to give me a treat; the difference is only three hundred–plus quid!

To put it another way, it is always very nice to be treated

considerately and I like to be treated as a lady. But, because I enjoy being treated like that (along with the rest of the female population), does that make me a stroppy, demanding and bossy diva? I don't think so. 'Little Things Mean a Lot' – another of Alice's favourite songs.

We are back to warped imagination. And, where the press is concerned, if something is not nipped in the bud, it is given legs to run and starts popping up and getting repeated all over the place. For example, the first time I was described as a 'legend', I knew I was in for another pasting! Such labels always add fuel to the fire. If I am a legend, even a legend in my own lunchtime, I am not complaining about that, but it's the way it's said and the inferences that accompany it. Anyway, I thought all legends were dead and, as far as I was and am aware, I'm still here. I also thought, 'Hang on a minute. I bet they've already written my obituary; bet it's already on file.' I don't have any illusions about things like that. I'd just like to mention that if any editor wants an epitaph to put on my file, I'd like it to be, 'At least she tried.' That says it all. You can only do your best.

I would also like to add that creative people, by their very nature and the nature of the work they do – which is often demanding and stressful – are not the easiest people in the world to live with; and I am the very first to hold my hand up to that. People who spend any time with or around us do need the patience of a saint sometimes, a bit of compassion and under-standing; and they need to bear with us, give us some space in which to be creative. These things are important for any artist, writer or actor because they often inhabit a different dimension while honing their varying crafts. Be kind, be gentle with us, though, and we can be very rewarding companions and good friends.

So, treat me like a lady and you get a lady; treat me like an alleycat and you get one with claws; treat me like a tart and you get a tart, and it may not be a tart with a heart; it could be a whiplash tart! So stand well back before you light the blue touchpaper.

My mam, who was forever reassuring, was always saying to me, 'You can only do your best, luv.' I tried to remember that, but, as any perfectionist will tell you, your best is never quite good enough. You never quite feel satisfied. I am obsessed with attention to detail. If I am working a stage or a set, I prowl it for a minimum of an hour. I stand by practically every seat in the auditorium to look at the stage before I walk on to it. I want to know what the audience is seeing and be sure that people have as clear a view as possible. I want to welcome the studio and theatre ghosts and spirits. I'm like a boxer preparing for a prize fight. I want to feel it, smell it, sense it, know it. That's how I prepare. It's a form of self-preservation because I don't want to fall.

Tabloid journalists, however, take none of this into account. They have created a monster, somebody who doesn't exist except in their imaginations. I used to think, 'Why do they do this?' Do they get off on it? I certainly don't. I just want to do my job and maybe meet the right person one day to share my life with, and make my family happy. At the end of the day, when we close our front door we have to live with ourselves.

Alice knew it was all rubbish, that today's newspapers are tomorrow's fish and chips wrappers, but it was nevertheless awful, particularly for my son, and I used to find it very difficult to talk about. Not now, though. Enough is enough. I really am ready to stand up and be counted, to tackle the thorny issue of the tabloid press in my life, even if it does bring them all down on my head again. So be it – most of it's bullshit and, guess what, the readers can tell that now, anyway.

I could be forgiven, couldn't I, for thinking that I had enough real-life dramas for reporters to get their nicotine-stained teeth into without them making stories up, but *no*. Was I surprised? Not really. I always said that if the royal family, with all their power, influence and connections, could not protect Princess Diana and themselves, what hope had the rest of us?

I guess some goody-two-shoes who have never taken a risk in their entire lives, never put a foot wrong, would say, 'Getting pregnant at seventeen, married and divorced before twenty, entering a second marriage that didn't survive the wedding day, then changing her spots and having a same-sex relationship; don't you think she deserved everything she got?' But did I? Just because I played Bet Lynch on telly didn't mean that every Tom, Dick and Harry was entitled to dine out on portions of my private life, or that the press should be given carte blanche to write a pack of lies. Yes, I made mistakes, but then I am only human, and I paid a heavy price for the mistakes I made. I know that. I was there; got the T-shirt. And I honestly would not have minded some of the press coverage half as much if the tabloids had just kept to the facts.

Likewise, people were constantly coming into my life and then selling a story that could not have been further from the truth. There was Justin Fashanu, the footballer, for instance (God rest his soul), who was openly gay and who I met in a gay club when I was out with some friends. After our first meeting and just a couple of other occasions when we had a drink together he spoke to the press and pretended we had had a steamy love affair, but that he had ended it because I was too old for him. Later he sent me a bouquet of red roses to apologize for this pack of lies and say how terribly sorry he was. He didn't say why he had done it. I suspect that he needed the money the paper was prepared to pay for such rubbish. To my absolute horror, I heard some time later that he had killed himself. I felt so sorry for his brother and his adoptive parents.

Then there was the birthday party for Liz (Elizabeth) Dawn, who played Vera Duckworth. Just a private party for her and other members of the cast. 'I know what'll give her a giggle,' I thought. 'I'll get her a strippergram. She'll love that and it will give her a good laugh.' The next thing I knew was that the toy-boy strippergram lad, apparently on the advice of his agent, sold a story to the newspapers saying that he and I'd had a red-hot love affair. Then, when he killed himself a year later, the blame was laid at my door.

'Oh my God!' I remember crying aloud. 'Will this nightmare never end? He was somebody's son, for God's sake; I have a son. I can only begin to imagine how his family are feeling. And the story about him and me was all based on lies.'

The problem is the tabloids offer so much money for this kind of trash that some people are tempted to say anything. Don't the editors, who are often family people themselves, ever stop to think that they are damaging someone's reputation? True, this is only among those who do not know the person concerned, but it's still painful. Thankfully, though, your family and real friends know what's what. There has always been a thing in this country which goes, 'Build 'em up, knock 'em down.' Okay! But at least give me a break and put me back on the top shelf for a while. Even if it's only now and again.

I always managed to go back to work and hold my head up high, but I would be lying if I said it didn't get me down. My only comfort now is that I think people have lost trust in the newspapers, and often disbelieve the stories they read. They must do cos they're always smashing with me when I get to meet them.

No one explained to me why I was so often in the hot seat. After my early days as a beauty queen, when I used press coverage to help me get into acting, I sought journalists' attention. Having got the job I longed to get, I just played the game that was expected of me, did what Granada's press office asked me to do, but I never went out of my way to get coverage, and it's only on very rare occasions, when I am somebody's guest, that I'm seen at places that the paparazzi stake out. Maybe that's one of the reasons they do it. I'm a home bird at heart and always have been.

Another incident that happened much later was after I had left *Coronation Street*. At this time, 1995, there was a woman who worked for Granada, who I was led to believe had been unfairly sacked. We had always got on really well and, feeling very sorry for her, I asked if she would like to come and do some work with me. A divorced woman with a couple of kids, she was absolutely thrilled. It was a dream come true for her, but I think it cost me dearly. At the same time that she was taking money from me, I suspected she was selling me to the press behind my back – running, as they say, both with the hare and the hounds.

I began to wonder how the press knew where I was going to be and so many other personal details about my life. It took me a long time, however, to catch on to her, because she kept suggesting that it was someone else leaking the information. The various suspicions that her comments then aroused were unpleasant for me and others close to me. Meanwhile, she even leaked news of my forthcoming MBE, which could have meant me losing it. I found it all so embarrassing, because nobody knew who was doing it, and some people may have believed it was me. Never in a million years. I eventually learned that the same thing had happened at the press office at Granada. She had been the leak there, too. Once I'd absolute proof, I asked her to come round to my home so I could tell her face-to-face that the game was up. 'But what did you expect?' was her callous response. 'I've got a mortgage and two kids.'

I am very proud to say that, although I was tempted, I never laid a finger on her. But I did go outside, where her mother was waiting for her in the car, and said, 'You have my deepest sympathy, to have a daughter like this.' Her mother's eyes filled with tears – she knew. The last time I heard anything about her, she was working on the deli counter in a supermarket. What goes around, as they say, comes around.

On one occasion in 1986 a journalist accused me of taking unnecessary risks by refusing to allow a stunt man to stand in for me for the scene when an electrical fault in the cellar caused a fire at the Rovers. Other papers then published the same story, but there wasn't a word of truth in it. There was a fire, of course, when Bet was sleeping upstairs, but I wasn't offered a stunt man or, for that matter, a stunt woman. Gareth Morgan, the director, wanted to see real fear in my eyes, wanted the cameras to get really close up. They did and there was real fear all right. I was bloody petrified!

Alice, when she knew what I was going to do, was terrified. 'Don't be daft. Crawling about in a real fire. You can't do that,' she said. 'It's absolutely ridiculous. They have no right to put you through that. It's too dangerous.'

'It'll be fine,' I said, trying to reassure her, but, in truth, I shared her doubts and sentiments, and I was in fact *very* frightened.

The first time we did the scene, it didn't work because the fire got completely out of control. A retake was scheduled for the week after. That's when I knew real fear because the fire caught hold and, once it had swept up the staircase, proved very difficult to contain. There I was crawling on my hands and knees through all the smoke, and although Bet's nightdress had been flame-proofed, it caught fire. Gareth – we're talking about someone very creative here – said to the cameraman, 'Keep rolling, keep rolling.' He was getting 'magic' and, at that moment, it was all that mattered – he had not noticed my nightdress on fire!

The pyrotechnic experts and fire brigade were on standby that day, but it was John Friend Newman, our on-the-ball, fast-moving floor manager, who saved me. 'Cut. *Cut!*' he yelled, rushing forward.

Luckily, at times like that when a life's at stake, rank is forgotten. Had it not been for John's quick thinking, I would have been seriously burned, possibly cindered. Having dashed onto the set and beaten out the flames, John then grabbed hold of me, chucked me fireman-style over his shoulder and got me off. Gareth had been so intent on getting the close-up shots that he had just thought the fear in my eyes was a bit of brilliant acting.

I have to be honest here; the first thing I said after I'd stopped choking from all the smoke I'd inhaled into my lungs and thrown up, was, 'Give us a fag.'

I soon recovered. The Rovers, however, did not. It was completely gutted. When Bet saw it in the next episode, she was gutted too. 'When I came here to the Rovers, it was the first time in my life that I'd found a place where I finally belonged,' she stuttered, her voice cracking with emotion. 'Jobs came and went, fellas came and went. But at this old dump I felt that I'd found somewhere I could hang on to.' I had a good deal of sympathy with her sentiments.

So, there you go. Over the years they tried to burn me and then tried to drown me, but then that's what creative writers do: go for the maximum drama to keep actors on their toes and the rest of us glued to the screen!

The 1983 drowning scene was filmed in Tatton Park Lake. It consisted of Betty Driver, who played Betty Turpin, and Bet stranded in ice-cold water. And what did the costume department give us for below-the-waist protection? A black bin liner each, with two holes ripped in them for our legs to go through. We were waist-deep in freezing cold lake water, in the middle of winter, for two days' filming. They never even pulled us out for a tea break! Instead, Props (my mate Vinnie) came out in waders, to that bloody car parked in the middle of the lake, with a couple of paper cups of lukewarm tea, and *that* was it. Oh the glamour of it all – yet again.

The storyline for the scene was when Fred invites Bet out for a picnic and she, very wary of his lecherous intentions, invites Betty along. When, after a reasonably relaxing time together, the girls realize they're late for work, they rush to the car and get in while Fred tosses the picnic gear into the boot. Then, as Fred slams the boot of Mrs Walker's Rover, the car starts to roll forward down a slope, gathering speed all the way, until it careers nose first into the lake.

The car involved in the crash was actually sent down into the water on a hoist chain, but both Betty and I still got whiplash as it hit the water too fast. We had a cameraman clinging to the bonnet to get the shot and holes had been bored in the bodywork so that the car would sink more quickly. Time, I can confirm, goes very slowly when you're waist-deep in ice-cold water; and other problems soon come on apace. After what seemed like hours, with Betty in the back and me in the front (waiting for Fred to give us piggybacks), I remember Betty saying, 'Oh, God, Julie, I'm desperate to spend a penny.'

'Oh, I've already done that,' I replied casually.

'You haven't! You're joking!' she exclaimed, horrified. 'Oh, Julie, how *could* you? That's dreadful.'

'Betty,' I said wearily, 'there are sticklebacks, eels, frogspawn, tadpoles and God knows what else swimming around my waist and in my drawers. What difference is a drop of wee-wee gonna make?'

She was very quiet for some time after that. Whether she peed or not, I don't know. But, knowing Betty, probably not. Some swans kept sailing past the car, their feathers up and hissing, and that doubtless put her off. I'd no such inhibitions.

The sequence took two days in all to film, but the stuff they got was pure magic. Those sorts of scene were absolute classics and I knew they would make our viewers laugh till they cried, which is all I cared about.

By the end of the filming the car had been in the water for so long the crew said, 'It'll be knackered. Forget it!' It says an awful lot for Rover, though, because when I replied, after they had got Betty out and I was still sitting there in the lake, 'Can I just try it?' they said, 'Aw, go on, then.' I was always one of the lads to the crews and therefore allowed to turn the ignition key. I'm not trying to advertise Rover here, but d'you know what? That car started the first time, it really did, and I drove it out of the water.

Classic the scene may have been, but Betty and I were like two drowned rats; taken back to our dressing rooms at Granada, we were given very welcome tots of brandy. Were we ready for that! We could have done with more the day after, too, when we were back in the studio, doing the inside filming to match up with the crash in the lake. But, by God, the end result was well worth it.

'You know,' I used to say, after such dramatic scenes. 'This killer stuff doesn't work on a witch. We can't be burned, can't be drowned. You can't get rid of us – not white witches, anyway.' I've often been asked if I have a favourite scene, and I always give the same answer: 'No. After about two thousand six hundred performances, how could I possibly choose just one?' I did every scene to the best of my ability and with love.

Roots have always been important in my life. By the early 1980s, I could have chosen to live anywhere and followed in the footsteps of a lot of successful people from our part of the world who had headed for the softer landscape of Cheshire. But that wouldn't have been right for me, and London wouldn't have been right either.

Heywood is often called Monkey Town and I am an original Heywood Monkey. I know lots of people can't wait to leave after they've made it, and that's fine by me, but my love for the area runs very deep. It's a place that keeps me grounded. I love the people, the market, the local Morrisons. I love everything about it; it's my home. I am very proud of my roots and where I have come from, and I don't ever want to forget that.

Yes, of course there are problems, but there are problems everywhere. The basic goodness of people where I live shines through in everything they do. They might not have much, but they are honest, Northern, working-class people and I adore them. Always have, always will. I was born there and shall die there. Whenever I return from trips or holidays, Heywood gives me a cuddle. I can feel its arms going round me, enfolding me. I am just Julie to all the locals and the tradespeople, and I know they are quietly proud of me.

I was shopping in the Heywood Morrisons one day, as normal, when a local lady called Ethel shouted across the isle: 'Julie, they're at it again! They're calling you a bloody gay icon now! Will the bastards never leave you alone?' I replied, 'Don't worry, Ethel. I think it's a compliment.' She said, 'Well it doesn't bloody sound it to me. Keep your chin up, love, and don't worry.'

With all those tall mill chimneys, it really is like stepping into a Lowry painting – I love the architecture, think it's beautiful, because I've grown up with it. Probably because I was born on 29 March, I particularly love it when the daffodils start to come through and the first blossom springs to life on the trees. Spring is a very special time for me. It's like a rebirth every year and I've planted hundreds of daffodils and wild primroses at the farm where I now live.

The farm is just heavenly, especially because I missed so much natural beauty during all those years when I was working in studios. I feel so lucky when the swallows come back to nest in the eves and stables. The pleasure I now have seeing the seasons change is beyond description. A favourite saying, which hangs in my house, is, 'With all its sham, drudgery and broken dreams, it is still a beautiful world.' Also, I must add, if you are going to be miserable, it is so much easier being miserable in comfort rather than in poverty! I *can* say that because I have experienced both. Of course, money makes a difference. We must never, however, make it our God.

I can think of no better point than this to write a proper account of my very dear friend and guardian angel Edna, who came into my life just after I got the more permanent job in *Coronation Street*. From that time on, because I was working such long hours at the studios, I couldn't also cope with domestic things such as cleaning, which I must confess I never particularly enjoyed – and I certainly can't iron. In fact, when Bet was given an ironing scene in *Corrie*, my antics reduced everybody on the set to near-hysterics. I couldn't even set up the ironing board without it collapsing again; I was just as hopeless at that as I am with deckchairs. There is just something about such things, which means I can never make them stand up properly or do anything for me.

Originally the script cue read, 'Bet puts up the ironing board in the Rovers living room and the scene begins there.' Not a chance – sorry. In the end, after several complete cock-ups, the scene had to begin with the ironing board set up in advance. And I am ashamed to say that the floor manager also had to take the fuse out of the iron, so that I didn't keep burning holes in the clothes I was supposed to be ironing – and, for that matter, myself!

At one stage I remember the director saying in a very weary voice, 'Julie, think of the iron as a ship. The pointy end should face forward.' So, to add to my humiliation, I was even holding the bloody thing the wrong way round. Oh, how I needed an Edna in my life – and in she came. Originally from Wigan, she is my kind of person, and had had, I soon learned, a *very* tough childhood. Her father used to hit her around the head and ears and, one day while she was still little, he punched her so hard she became deaf. Life didn't get much better when she grew up because she found herself in an abusive marriage.

From day one Edna and I bonded, and she started cleaning and looking after me (and Alice, Bill and Gary) on a regular basis. This was at a time when we were all still living together in the house that Bill built, the one that had all the brand-new fitted carpets and everything. Sadly, though, it was becoming a bit of a tip, which I couldn't stand. I need order and cleanliness in my life. That is a must.

Edna calls what she does 'bottoming'. Looking round a room, she will say, 'That needs bottoming,' and, my goodness, can she bottom! She is just fantastic. She has now been with me thirty-three years, a lifetime. Faithful, loyal, endlessly reliable, she is everything you could ever wish for in a friend and guardian angel.

Sometimes Edna arrived to the sight of between thirty and forty hacks milling around the house; having put the lock on the door, I'd be cowering inside. I would hear the clip-clop of Edna's stilettos – which she still wears today, aged seventy and what's more can run in them – coming up the path and the reporters would be circling like vultures with a barrage of questions. All Edna would say was, 'Oh, piss off. I'm deaf, you silly buggers. Anyways she's done nowt wrong. Have you no bloody homes to go to?' Then she'd come in, calling out, 'Where are you, cocker? Take no notice of 'em. What you supposed to 'ave done this time? Come out from wherever you are. I'm gonna get this kettle on. Let's 'ave a brew.' And, as I listened to her voice, everything in my corner would come right again.

After Alice died, I gave Edna her mink coat, and that coat, I can tell you, has been out playing bingo on many an occasion since. Edna always called me 'cocker'. I filtered that endearment into Bet's dialogue. I was often misquoted by the press as saying 'chuck' (pronounced 'chook' of course), but that was Hilda Ogden's word. I always said 'cocker'.

During most of the years Edna came to the house, I rarely saw her because I was always out at work. But I remember one particular morning when the phone rang while I was still at home and, to my surprise, it was Edna on the line.

'Hi, Edna,' I said.

'I'm just phoning because I am going to be a bit late this morning, cocker. Jed's dead.' Jed was her husband. But, before I could say, 'Have the day off, for God's sake. Don't come in,' she'd gone. That's how amazing my friend Edna is.

When my mother died, Edna insisted, as a mark of respect, on walking behind the coffin on its way to the church. She was, you see, a friend of the whole family, including my son, and we all adore her. She's got quite a few kids, grandkids and great-grandkids of her own. She's a living guardian angel who cares for me and asks for nothing in return.

I remember when Bill passed away, Edna and I were down at the local chapel of rest together. She's not a demonstrative person, but, as we stood side by side looking at Bill in his coffin, I felt her arm go around my shoulders. Such a gesture was very unusual for Edna and, as I glanced at her, she said very quietly, 'Never mind, cocker, things can only get worse.'

'Oh, no,' I thought. But Edna was right, has always been right. There was just as bad to come then, and even worse to come later.

TEN

All the Way

Mam obviously thought I was asleep and couldn't hear what she was saying. She was in the next room on the telephone to her sister, my Auntie Florrie, and she was whispering because the news could not have been worse. You never actually said the word 'cancer' then, and you certainly didn't discuss *that* illness without lowering your voice.

'Is that you, Florrie?' the conversation began. 'I've got some awful news to tell you. It's about our Julie. She's got to go to hospital . . .' There was a pause, then she added, 'Yes, she's got, you know, the word that we don't say . . . Yes, yes, I'm afraid she has. She's got to have an ex-directory.'

That was so typical of my mam. She was always getting her words mixed up, and ex-directory and hysterectomy sounded very much alike to her. There were many moments in a similar vein. 'Just look at the condescension on these windows,' she'd say. And, 'I really like this seduced lighting, don't you?' Talking about a couple of pedigree Dobermanns: 'Those bloody Dormobiles have had me up all night.' She also once said excitedly, 'Oh, you've got to go and have a look at her bathroom, Julie. You'd love it; she's had a Suzuki fitted.' Now even I knew that a Suzuki was a motorbike, and what she actually meant was jacuzzi. If I ever tried to correct Alice, though, she'd brush me off by saying, 'You know perfectly well what I'm talking about. Stop trying to be clever. Don't get above yourself.'

The awful news she was sharing with my Auntie Florrie in 1979 was right, and, as I lay there I found myself thinking back to the moment when I'd joined the queue outside the mobile screening unit in the Granada Studios car park.

As I stood there during my lunch break, along with all the other actresses, typists, canteen ladies and cleaners waiting for their routine cervical smear tests, I was feeling relaxed and happy. This was the very last thing I had to do before going home and packing my cases for the holiday which No Name and I had been looking forward to for weeks.

After the nurse had taken the swab, I left the unit and didn't give the test another thought. Two weeks later, though, when I returned from a really good break in the Canary Islands feeling fit, tanned and healthy all that was about to change. Waiting for me in the pile of post was a letter that made my blood run cold. The smear test, it explained, had revealed abnormal cells clustered around my cervix and I was asked to contact my doctor. I was devastated. This could only mean one thing – the 'big C' – and in an instant I felt fear coursing through my body.

'Tests can be wrong,' I consoled myself. 'Mistakes can be made. The second test might place me in the clear. It could all come to nowt.' But somehow I knew this scare was for real.

On the day I went to Christie's Hospital, Manchester, for test number two, I was greeted by a grave-faced nurse who handed me a leaflet on breast cancer. 'Oh my God!' I muttered under my breath. 'Does that mean it's already spread from my cervix to Newton or Ridley? If so, Bet Lynch will be the first bionic barmaid in the country.' There are times, I find, when humour, even if it's black humour, is the only thing that does the trick and gets you through a situation.

On 11 January 1979, a day I will never forget, I received the second lot of test results. It was the news I'd been dreading. The test had confirmed the presence of cancerous cells and had revealed that the cancer had already spread from my cervix to my womb. I was only thirty-six years old and my life was on the line. 'Still,' I thought, finding refuge once again in black humour, 'if the cancer hadn't been detected, I wouldn't have known I had it and it wouldn't have been long before Annie Walker was looking for another barmaid.'

Apart from my immediate family, my partner No Name, my producer Bill Podmore (who I called Podders) and a handful of the *Coronation Street* cast, I didn't tell anybody about my troubles. And, within days, Bill had arranged for me to be written out of the script for nine weeks. During that time (February–April 1979) I was to be admitted to St Joseph's Hospital, Manchester, for the necessary – and hopefully life-saving – hysterectomy operation.

The good news – and, by God, I needed some – was that Sister Margaret, a Catholic nun who belonged to the order of St Joseph, would be there, helping to prepare me for the surgery the following day. I'd met this lovely person, a fully qualified nursing nun, on several occasions when she'd nursed my mam through various problems brought on by her eating disorders. We'd become dear friends, and I was very glad that it was her who was going to be looking after me.

During the preparations, a young student nurse came in to shave my pubic hair. 'Standard procedure,' I was told! She had obviously recognized me as Bet Lynch from *Coronation Street* and was a bit embarrassed. My heart went out to her. Being shaved is not very dignified, and not surprisingly the atmosphere was a little strained as she got on with the job. To lighten the situation, she asked, 'What's Annie Walker like in real life?'

'Why?' I asked. 'Have you found her down there?' That broke the ice and, having had a laugh together, we became pals.

Any woman who's been through the kind of experience I'm writing about here will understand that you soon learn to just sit there with your legs open! It really is a black-comedy situation in which you've got to learn to detach yourself from whatever's happening. It's a series of 'Carry on' moments. I had to sign a consent form, of course, giving Mr Jones, the surgeon, permission to do whatever was necessary, and to confirm that any bits and pieces that had to go, could go. I must have been very ill because I remember being told that the priest would be coming round for a visit. That did it! 'There's *no* way I'm having the last rites,' I whispered to my mam, who was visiting me, and, between us, we managed to get me to the loo. Once inside, we were like two giggly kids, determined not to come out until we knew he had gone.

Joking aside, this was of course a devastating time for Alice, Bill and Gary, and a very frightening time for me. To need so much looking after – physically, mentally and spiritually – was a terrible shock to my system; I was somebody who was more used to looking after others. Lying in hospital, then, on the eve of the operation, I could have been forgiven for thinking that things couldn't get worse. Well at least not until the operation was over.

Wrong! I hadn't reckoned on No Name freaking out. As I lay there in my hospital bed, with Sister Margaret sat alongside me, I was looking forward to No Name's early-evening visit.

'You'll like Mr Jones, the surgeon, Julie,' Sister Margaret was saying. 'He's shy, just like you.'

'What a strange job for a shy person,' I replied.

'Yes, 'tis so. But I know you will like him, and get on like a house on fire.' And we did. 'Cancer isn't something to be frightened of,' Sister Margaret added. 'It's simply something that needs to be faced up to and treated as quickly as possible. Catching it in the early stages makes all the difference.'

By then, I'd been given something to help me relax. I'd labelled my nightdresses Monday, Tuesday, Wednesday, Thursday, Friday, and hung them all up in the wardrobe. Everything I could think of had been organized. So, lying there, listening to Sister Margaret's gentle Irish lilt always so full of love and compassion, was very soothing. Having been told how important it was to go down for an operation in a good positive frame of mind, I was feeling, given the circumstances, reasonably relaxed. To say that Sister Margaret's presence had given me strength and confidence would be an all-time understatement. She was just wonderful.

Peter Adamson, who played Len Fairclough, one of my ex-*Street* lovers, came in to see me. 'We want you to know we're all with you, kid,' he whispered, as he sat there holding my hand.

So, all was as well as it could be under the circumstances, and that's how it stayed until the moment No Name entered the room, and stood hovering, ashen-faced, by the door. I was very glad to see her, but I could tell immediately that she was not herself and feeling very uncomfortable. If she had been her normal self, she would have come straight over to me, put her arms around my shoulders and given me a hug. But she just stood there inside the door, as if nailed to the spot.

'Ah!' I thought, trying to justify her strange behaviour. 'She's embarrassed because Sister Margaret's in the room. I can understand that. I must tell her that Sister Margaret knows all about us.' But when Sister Margaret smiled, said hello and got her a chair, No Name still stayed where she was – didn't thank her, didn't move, made no effort to sit down. That was very unlike her, and so was the fact that her eyes hadn't met mine at all. She just stood there, head lowered, biting her lip and looking down at the floor.

'Are you all right, luv?' I asked, bewildered.

Then, as if she'd been rehearsing what she was about to say for hours, the words gushed out, each following the other in quick succession, no pauses in between: 'I-know-you-will-understand-because-you-are-older-than-I-am,' she mumbled, 'and-a-lot-stronger-but-I-can't-cope-with-this. I'm-*terribly*-sorry-but-I'm-going-home-tonight-back-to-my-parents.' She skidded to a halt, but only for a second. 'I'm-sure-you'll-be-fine-and-I-know-you-will-be-well-looked-after. So-that's-it-really-good-luck.'

'What about the dog?' I gasped, stunned.

'I'm-sorry-I-have-to-go-now,' was her only reply.

'But . . .' My voice trailed off. I was too shocked to say anything.

'I think you *had* better go,' Sister Margaret interrupted. 'This isn't a place for you to be. Would you leave now, please.'

I looked at Sister Margaret, then at No Name, but no words would come. It was as if I was falling into a black hole and there were no words left to say. The next moment Sister Margaret crossed the room, opened the door and No Name left through it without a backward glance. I lay there, chilled to the marrow. The person I'd lived with for four years, and who I'd expected to spend the rest of my life with, had just walked out of the door; had abandoned me on the eve of major surgery. The next moment my thoughts returned to our red setter bitch, Sweep. Who would look after her tonight, tomorrow, forever, if need be? I *had* to make a phone call to ensure she'd be all right, and Sister Margaret arranged for me to do that.

I phoned Alice and Bill who were very surprised that No Name couldn't take care of Sweep but, when I made no further comment, they reassured me that Sweep would be fine – that of course they'd do whatever was necessary.

It was a long, long night, and that was when I nicknamed Sister Margaret Wonder Woman because her kindness was something I knew I would never forget – and I haven't. She knew, because I'd told her, that No Name and I were in a long-term same-sex relationship, but she wasn't at all judgemental, just incredibly sensitive. She really did help me get through that night, and when it became impossible for me to have any more pre-meds to help me stay calm, she stayed with me, just letting me unburden myself and talk. At other moments, when it all became too much, she held me in her arms, stroked my hair, sang to me, did whatever was needed to get me through the darkest hours before dawn. She knew how important it was for patients to go down to surgery with a positive attitude and she was only too aware that, after No Name's visit, I'd gone from being very positive to feeling totally negative.

Thanks to her support, though, I was able to smile again by the next morning, and was even able to resort once again to black humour. As they put me on the trolley to wheel me to the operating theatre, I placed a placard that I'd made across my tummy. Then, with Sister Margaret walking on one side and another nun on the other, we set off for the theatre, with the following words printed in capital letters: IN CASE OF RAPE, THIS SIDE UP.

When Mr Jones came to greet me, he looked down, read the placard, and his eyes filled with tears. 'Oh, God! I'm really buggered now,' I thought. 'How can he possibly do a good job if he can't fucking see?' I don't remember much after that. I was gone – put under – and in his hands. Or, as Alice was fond of saying, 'in the lap of the gods'.

The first thing I saw when I came round in the recovery room, still wearing the white regulation hospital gown, was the face of Jesus! For a moment I thought I was in heaven and someone heard me murmur, 'I'm very pleased to meet you, sir. I'll try not to be too much trouble.' In truth, though, the face of Jesus turned out to be his face on the crucifix hanging around Wonder Woman's neck.

During the agonizingly painful post-op period, I had another placard displayed on my door, which this time read: SILENCE. CUP FINAL IN PROGRESS! Eventually, I also got a little bar set up in the corner, which dispensed tots of brandy. I did this because my visitors kept passing out when they caught sight of my open wounds! I was the lucky one. I had a cage placed over me which meant I was the only person who couldn't see them. I knew they were there, though. They hurt like hell and I kept saying, 'Thank God for morphine.'

As soon as I came off that blessed stuff, I wanted a fag. I'd given them up as soon as I was told I needed surgery and had to clear out my lungs, but it had been very hard and I couldn't wait to start smoking again. When I asked Sister Margaret for a cigarette, she said, 'Oh no,' but she still gave me one.

As soon as I was sitting up in bed, Podders and others at Granada were on the phone wanting to know how long I would be in hospital, and when I would be back at work. As I didn't know the answer, I said I would ring them as soon as I saw the surgeon and found out. At this stage I hadn't even managed to get out of bed to use the little commode in the corner of the room, and I knew that was going to be the first major hurdle.

When I put Granada's question to Mr Jones, he was astonished. 'You've had a lot of surgery – *major* surgery,' he emphasized. 'And I really can't say, at this stage, how long you'll be with us. But it's very important for you to take things easy and be very careful. We'll just wait and see; take it one day at a time.' So, I couldn't give Granada the answer they needed, and this question-and-no-answer period continued for most of my nine weeks in hospital.

I totally respected Granada's need to know, though. They had storyline conferences to consider, and had to plan things well in advance. As a professional, I understood that there were constant deadlines to meet, and getting on with the job and putting everything else to one side had become second nature for me too.

When, at last, the day came for me to get out of bed, I was more than ready for the challenge; Wonder Woman, bless her, had decided that I could now make the journey to the commode. This was only a few steps away, but that's a very long trip when you've had five hundred or so stitches inserted in your body. Anyway, with a nun on each side of me, gripping an arm apiece, we were off, making very slow progress towards the corner.

Having made it – still with a nun on each side – I started to lower myself very gingerly onto the commode, where nature would, hopefully, oblige us and take its course. It had a wooden top with a sort of plastic pan inside it, and as I sat down, the legs collapsed and broke, and both nuns lost their grip on my arms. The next moment I hit the floor. I'd love to say that my language was terribly refined, as it should have been in front of two nuns, but no, the air was blue. 'What the fuck . . .' I kept repeating as I lay there, writhing in agony.

Emergency buzzers joined my expletives and, within seconds, I was being rushed back to the operating theatre. In addition to being a post-op cancer patient, I now had wooden splinters in my arse! Looking heavenward, I muttered, 'Now come on! This is not funny, no joke. Give me a break.'

Apparently, I'd torn myself falling to the floor. I was now haemorrhaging, and needed the internal dressings to be repacked. In telling my story, the last thing I want to do is alarm any other cancer patient who's in a similar situation. Every case is different, treatment varies from patient to patient – the chances of a commode collapsing under you must be one in several thousand. All I can say is that I was unlucky – accident-prone and very slow to heal – and the last time I needed to be repacked, I was asked if I'd like to spend the night in the shrine of St Emily, situated in the hospital. The question, I might add, didn't scare me. By that stage, I'd gone beyond fear.

'Yes, I would – please,' I replied, and my bed was wheeled into the shrine. It may have been the medication I was on – I'll never know for sure – but, later that night, as I looked at the statue of St Emily, which was lit by candlelight in the little chapel, I was suddenly aware that there were tears running down her cheeks.

'Oh God! That's it!' I thought, alarmed. 'My number's up. It must be. She's crying. It's obviously my time.'

It was another long night!

At daybreak, the nuns, who I knew had been checking up

on me throughout the hours of darkness, came back for me. 'I've got to tell you,' I exclaimed. 'A really strange thing happened during the night.'

'What was it, me darlin'?' Sister Margaret replied in her beautiful, gentle, Irish voice.

'You're gonna think I'm crazy,' I replied.

'Not at all. Tell us what happened.'

'The statue cried,' I blurted out.

'Now, isn't that *wonderful*?' she said. 'And you haven't realized what that means?'

It wasn't quite the response I'd expected. 'Well, to be honest with you, I thought it meant my number was up.'

'No, no, just the opposite.' She laughed. 'You're going to live.'

'I'm going to live?'

'You're going to live. Another miracle has been worked.'

Was it an hallucination? Was it the medication? Was it a miracle? You decide. Apparently, St Emily is the patron saint of incurables – and Emily is my granddaughter's name. And I'm still here.

I got visitors and phone calls all the time I was in hospital. Doris Speed brought me in a frothy pink bedjacket; Pat Phoenix sent a card saying, 'Keep fightin' it darlin''; Madge Hindle, who played Renee Roberts, brought me a white nightie; and Geoffrey Hughes, who played Eddie Yeats, turned up with armfuls of tinned baby food, which reduced me to giggles. The cast of *Corrie* had always been one big family, and once again, 'Kick one and we all limp' proved to be the case. Hundreds of cards also arrived from fans, some simply addressed, 'Bet Lynch, Heywood, Lancashire', and my room was like a florist's shop.

All this helped to keep my spirits up – as did my little bar. I was very glad to have a little drop of brandy nearby.

On one occasion Podders, a great pal who I adored and had been around the world with while promoting *Corrie*, phoned up and said, 'Now, come on, Julie, *bloody hell*! How long have you been off now? How long is it?' Podders had been with the series as a cameraman and director since 1961, but he'd replaced Susie Hush as producer in 1976. It was always good to hear from him and, in a strange way, his nagging kept me going, was just what I needed at the time. He had risen from the shop floor to get where he was, and by then had forgotten more than most people in the biz ever learn. He could take over any aspect of the work, if needed; just come down from his office and do whatever was necessary. He was 100 per cent talented and, because we were such good friends, could say anything to me. I might be in hospital, recovering from surgery, but the *Street* was his number-one priority.

'We've established that you're all right,' he kept saying. 'But we still don't know when you're bloody well coming back and how long we'll have you for. I bet you've not bloody asked that surgeon how long you've got to live?'

'Shit! No, I haven't,' I exclaimed.

'Aw, come on! That's not like you, Julie. Go on, have a word with him.'

'I will.'

'Then phone me and let me know. There's a bloody job to be done here.'

'I know! *I know!* You're right. I will.'

So the next time the surgeon came in to see me, I said, 'I'm *really* sorry to trouble you, Mr Jones, but could you possibly tell me how long I've got to live?'

211

'What?' he replied, startled.

'Have you any idea of how long I've got,' I repeated. 'You see, we have long-term story conferences.'

'I've never heard the likes of this,' he replied.

'I'm terribly sorry, but I have to ask. I promised I'd phone my producer back.'

'What sort of people are they?' he gasped.

'They're *wonderful* people,' I replied. 'You don't understand; I've gotta let 'em know. It's important. We've a lot of viewers, you see, and a lot of people depend on *Coronation Street*.'

'Really?' he grunted, looking rather wild-eyed. 'Well, I'll have to think about this . . . Normally patients receive counselling, are spoken to at some length, and there are all sorts of different—'

'I'm sure there are,' I interrupted, 'but we had that kind of conversation, if you remember, when you told me my womb needed to be removed. You said then I'd probably need counselling. D'you remember?'

'Yes, I remember.'

'Well, you'll remember me saying then, "I won't need any counselling because if there is a bonus to having cancer, it'll be losing my womb."'

'Yes, and I found that rather strange.'

'But I can only tell the truth,' I said. And it was the truth. Ever since Gary's birth I'd always had terrible trouble with my periods, so that was one aspect of my life I was more than glad to see the back of. Now all I wanted was for Mr Jones to tell me how long I'd got to live. That wasn't too much to ask, was it?

Having gone away and considered the matter very carefully, he came back and said very gently, 'In my opinion, and you can never really tell to the day, we all have a time to be born and a time to die, and we don't arrive or go a minute before we should. So, we all have our time. But, hopefully, you can expect a year.'

'Fantastic!' I said. 'Thank you!'

And with that, I grabbed the phone and rang Podders. 'Good news,' I said when I got through to him.

'Go on.'

'A year.'

'Terrific,' he replied. 'Thanks, kid.' And he put the phone down.

I didn't go away to convalesce when I left hospital; I was just glad to get home to Sweep. Every step I took was hard, and most of the time I was very frightened. The nurses weren't there at the end of the bed any more, and I had to go upstairs, one step at a time, on my bum. I was so weak I couldn't lift a kettle and, to begin with, I was frightened Sweep would jump up at me and burst my stitches. I needn't have worried. She greeted me by coming towards me on her belly and seemed to know exactly what she should and shouldn't do, which I found absolutely incredible. She never left my side. The runt of the litter, who was gonna be put to sleep (which was why No Name and I had chosen her), she was a wonderful companion and friend who really helped me to get well. As soon as I was up to it, we used go out together into the field at the back of the house. She lived to be sixteen, kept going until her back legs gave way. But, before she died, I reminded her she was the pride of the litter, not the runt.

When, at last, I returned to Granada in 1980 hordes of well-wishers were waiting both outside and inside to wish me luck;

thrilled to be back, I organized a champagne celebration to thank the cast for all their support.

Somehow, during those days, I always managed to blank out that I'd only been given a year to live. I just kept going, day by day, and decided that whatever time I had left, I would live to the full. After all, Bet hadn't got cancer. And this meant that every time I went to the make-up and costume departments, I could leave Julie behind and turn into her. That was marvellous – wonderful. Whatever problems Bet was dealing with, they were nowt compared with mine.

As for the aftercare, that could be dealt with in my lunch breaks. I'd go, come back, and pick up exactly where I'd left off. None of the treatment was short term. Like most cancer patients, I needed ongoing treatment and check-ups for five years after surgery, and my heart was often in my mouth during this time. I'd made friends with a group of women who I'd met when I was first diagnosed, and one by one they had died.

'They had their allotted time,' I kept reminding myself. 'Will it be my turn next?' I didn't know. But the year I'd been given came and went and I was still alive at the end of it. Once you've had cancer, though, the fear of it never quite goes away. But what can you do? You can either get on with your life, or curl up in a corner and surrender. Those are the only two choices.

As it happened the disease was to haunt my life for many years to come, hovering over our family like a huge black cloud. After my own cancer, my dad's cancer was diagnosed, and then my mam's. But I'll come to that later.

After that occasion the night before my operation, No Name never came to visit me again while I was in hospital. She got back in touch soon after I came out but, as far as I was

Me and my Dad leaving for the church for my second marriage, to Tony Rudman – minus bouquet.

Me with my bridesmaids – Jenny Moss and my cousin Irene.

With Tony Rudman, and a Saracen tank in the background.

Bet, where she belongs,
behind the bar.

Left. Showing Norma Major
how to pull a pint.

Below. Margaret Thatcher
visits the Rovers (when
I told her she had lippy
on her teeth).

Taking delivery of a brand new MGBGT, and so-called cross-dressing. Yeah, right!

Life begins at forty. Please, God – forever the optimist.

Above. On the Russell Harty
show with the fabulous
Barbara Windsor.

Left. Me with Shirley Bassey
and George Peppard,
when Granada hosted
the Bafta Awards.

Below. Me and my dear
friend Bill Podmore – the
headlines say it all.

After surgery for cancer, with Doris Speed, Lynne Perrie, Peter Dudley, Fred Feast and Pat Phoenix.

Receiving my MBE at the Palace in 1996 – a very proud day.

My wedding to Richard Skrob – third time unlucky!

Above. Me with some of the cast and crew celebrating my twenty-five years in *Corrie*.

Right. The Brighton spin-off. The look on my face says it all!

Left. My leaving party. No – it wasn't my ciggies but the fireworks in my cake that set all the fire alarms off!

Above. Nicky and me
in New Zealand.

Left. Janet and me on
holiday in Lanzarote.

Me with Vicki – Vicki's late mum, Mary, is on the left
and I'm holding Dizzy.

Left. With my
guardian angel, Edna,
acting daft in the snow.

Below. Me and
Wonder Woman,
Sister Margaret,
in the shrine
of St Emily.

Me and Scott in springtime.

concerned, the relationship was over – finished. She wanted a reconciliation, but that was impossible. The trust had gone. I must add, however, that cancer is a very tough thing for anyone to deal with, particularly for partners and family. Sometimes when somebody thinks they're going to lose you, they panic: harden their hearts against the pain of loss, and discover they can't cope with you or it. I understand that because as well as having cancer myself, I eventually had to cope with both Bill and Mam's.

I've come to believe that No Name behaved as she did because she was in a blind panic; couldn't cope with me being in a life–and–death situation and needing such invasive treatment. When you're that scared, it can become a fight or flight survival situation – and that, I believe, is what happened. It was tough on me, though, because her leaving me the night before major surgery came as a complete shock and I had no choice but to deal with being abandoned on top of what was about to happen to me. She did, though, see me through the early stages of being diagnosed, waiting for the second test results and then being told I needed to have my womb removed, and I know I was very demanding throughout all that because I was scared shitless. With hindsight, perhaps I should have realized just how bad things were for her, but I didn't. Up until that moment in the hospital she had been completely supportive, but I can see now that she must have been going through her own kind of hell that included every emotion in the book.

Right now, though, I'm remembering Frank Sinatra singing one of my favourite songs, 'All the Way', which goes, 'When somebody loves you, it's no good unless they love you all the way . . .' Well, that's how I thought things were between No Name and me. I thought we were an 'all the way' couple –

together for the duration – and I was wrong. But, hey ho! As I said, at least Bet hadn't got cancer. My dual life was my salvation, and I've always been the first to admit it.

So, having survived the year I'd been given to live and received the all-clear, I could, I hoped, get on with life and face a less troublesome future. I ought to have known better; I'm Julie Goodyear. Even as I tried to repay some of the blessings I'd received by doing some good for other cancer sufferers, the storm clouds were gathering in the form of a courtroom drama that would end up with me in the dock!

ELEVEN

I Made It Through the Rain

When I was thinking about the horrors I'd just lived through, I became obsessed with wanting to know what a smear test actually looked like. Where, for example, did the swabs go that day when they left the mobile unit in Granada's car park? Who looked down the microscope and saw that I had cancer? It seemed a very strange way for anyone to earn a living, but thank God somebody did it. Was it, I wondered, a man or a woman who had spotted those cancerous cells that had threatened my life? And would it be possible to meet and thank them in person?

These were questions, I decided, that needed answers, and, having set things in motion, I found myself en route to a smear testing centre situated just by the side of the Christie Hospital in Manchester. When I arrived, I could hardly believe my eyes. In fact, for a moment I thought I was in the wrong place. It wasn't at all what I'd expected. I couldn't have been more grateful to my surgeon Mr Jones, the doctors, Sister Margaret and the other nurses who had helped me through some of the darkest days of my life, but I was appalled by the conditions I found in the smear testing centre. Built in 1944, just two years after I was born, the Cytology Block, as it was called, was an eyesore and an embarrassment to the hospital, to the people who worked there and to the patients it cared for.

The lab, in fact, was no better than a Nissen hut. The roof leaked, the ceiling, which sagged, was on the verge of coming down, the walls were full of cracks and covered with peeling paint, and the ill-fitting windows, I was told, turned the building into a fridge in bad weather. The toilet facilities were not much better and the offices were unbelievably cramped. How on earth could anybody work in such conditions? How could they be efficient? There were slides all over the bloody place. I found myself shuddering and thinking, 'Surely, mistakes are made in these conditions, surely lives are put at risk.' I really was appalled because I, for one, knew what a mistake could mean to the patient concerned. I'd been lucky, and I wanted every woman to have the same chance I'd had.

At one point I became aware of a lab technician watching me from the far end of the room, and I noticed there were tears running down her cheeks. I walked down the room and put my arm around her shoulders. 'Was it you who dealt with my test?' I asked.

'Yes.'

'Thank you,' I said, giving her a big hug. 'Thank you so much for the work that you, and everybody else, is doing here.'

Before I left that day, I'd learned that the staff who worked in these primitive conditions were expected to deal with smear tests from women all over the north-west of England. I also learned that Christie's management team had estimated that it would cost £500,000 to build a new lab, but, once built, this would allow them to deal with even more cervical smear tests and reduce the current death toll from cancer of the cervix then running at about 2,500 women a year. So many women, and one of them could have been me. For a moment I was overcome, but I vowed there and then that somehow, even with the workload I'd got at Granada and my ongoing treatment, I would do summat to improve the terrible conditions for the people who worked there and for the patients whose lives depended on their tests.

So, that's how I became a registered charity and launched a £500,000 appeal to replace the test centre with a new, purpose-built unit. Called the Julie Goodyear Trust Fund, the charity was set up correctly, with all the usual legal safeguards in place, and from then on every minute I could spare I was out there flying the flag, drumming the drum, rattling the tins, raising the money.

Anybody reading this who has ever tried to do something serious for charity will be the first to understand that it's utterly impossible to do everything yourself and keep your eye on every single aspect and angle, and raffle ticket that's sold. Fund-raising is a tough job, it truly is, and you always need helpers. But if a charity has your name heading it and summat goes wrong, it's you who takes the rap, you who's held responsible. That was not something I knew when I set up the Julie Goodyear Trust Fund. I should have done, though, because in 1982 something went wrong and I found myself in trouble – serious trouble – with the law, trouble that threatened my freedom and meant that I could end up with a jail sentence.

The first whiff I had of this came just after my son's twenty-first birthday in 1981, when there was a knock on the door. There on my doorstep were two policemen. Minutes later, Janet Ross (my new PA at the time) and me were asked to accompany them to Rochdale police station, and before we knew what was happening, we were put into separate panda cars and driven there.

Jan was also my second same-sex relationship, and as this was still relatively new the court case put a massive strain on it. We were both in shock, but at least I wasn't on my own this time. I met Jan in a gay club I'd gone to with friends in late 1980. It was almost a repeat of the No Name situation. At the end of the evening she asked me for my phone number and, as she'd been such good fun, I gave it to her. Jan wasn't quiet, which made her an unusual choice of partner for me. She was an extrovert, but maybe at that stage in my life that was what I needed. She'd moved from Scotland, where she'd come from a large family, and when I met her, was working in a factory in Blackpool.

I found her accent quite difficult to follow at first, but we still managed to get on very well. We just teamed up, as it were, and became pals. With all the charity work, I desperately needed a PA at that time – as well as a bloody good friend – and Janet fitted the bill perfectly. She was boyish, bubbly, full of fun and an eternal optimist, the kind of person who never shuts up and can't sit still for a minute. So it's not surprising she used to drive me round the bend sometimes. Edna's nickname for her was 'Trouble in a Bubble' but she was also very fond of her.

Although Jan moved in with me in Heywood, the pull of the bright lights of Blackpool always remained very strong where she was concerned, and we were forever having spats about that. At one stage she had a parrot called Oscar, who must have been a very carsick bird, because every time we had words, he was put in the car and whisked up and down the M62. This happened so often, it was ridiculous. But one or other of us would phone and say, 'This is daft, you know,' and we'd get back together again – and everything would be fine until the next spat. That's how we were. I know I'm not the easiest person in the world to live with but, apart from the fact that she was always buggering off to Blackpool, we got on really well. We had some marvellous times, and went on some wonderful trips together. When we went to Israel, for example, we took a Bible with us as an *A–Z*.

'Well, we did Bethlehem yesterday,' I'd say. 'What shall we do today?'

'How about the Garden of Gethsemane?'

'Yeah, let's do that.'

Another bonus was that Mam and Jan got on really well. In fact, we all did. I met her mum, dad, brothers, sisters when they came down to Manchester, and we got on like a house on fire. Despite the spats, then, we had a very good friendship, and drifted in and out of each other's lives for twelve years. We're still the best of pals today. I never suffered from people's attitudes to gay issues. In the world I moved in, such relationships were common and just accepted. There were no snide remarks or pointing fingers. Alice and Bill were still alive then, and thought nothing of it.

During that time, however, I remember a huge fuss being made in the press when I turned up at a club dressed in a man's suit and tie. But that sort of thing was fashionable then. It caused so much unpleasant publicity, though, that I only wore the outfit once and threw it away. How could the hacks portray *me* as a cross-dressing butch? Look at me, for God's sake! Do I look butch? I just don't get it. Personally, I think the combination of masculine and feminine – particularly in a good photograph – is very attractive. All I was trying to do was take a lead from Liza Minnelli in *Cabaret*, but for some reason on the one occasion I did it I was portrayed as a freak!

But back to me and Jan in the police car. It was surreal. Ridiculous. I'd only been trying to help cancer patients and there I was in a police car being driven to a lock-up shop! 'They've made a mistake! They have to have done! It's a joke!' I kept telling myself. But once we got to the station, I could tell from the expressions on their faces that this was no joke. They were deadly serious. I kept trying to make jokes, but none of my black comedy was working and nobody was laughing. What the hell was going on?

Looking at the woman sergeant, I said, 'Aw, come on now, luv, this has got to be a gag. I'm Jack the Ripper, yes?'

'By the time we've finished with you, Ms Goodyear,' she replied without smiling, 'you'll wish you were.' That was the moment the enormity of what was happening began to sink in and I became *very* frightened. After that I gave up making wisecracks and just sat there in silence, staring out of the window.

Somebody must have made a phone call, because a short time later a solicitor who I'd never met but who is now a very dear friend entered the room, carrying an impressive-looking briefcase. 'My name is Roger Harper,' he said, introducing himself. 'I'm from George Davis and Company.'

Turning from the window, I glanced at him and said, 'No wonder Gracie Fields fucked off.'

'Quite!' he replied, clearing his throat. 'I'm very pleased to meet you, Ms Goodyear.'

Despite his presence, things then went from bad to worse, as they so often did – and do – in my life. All my good intentions had, it seemed, backfired. The present mess had come about because, to give the fund-raising a boost at a time when Manchester seemed to be suffering from charity fatigue, I'd agreed to a raffle being organized. I'd handed control of the raffle over to William Clarke, a thirty-three-year-old market trader, and his twenty-five-year-old business partner Rodger Forster. They'd offered to help the trust, along with lots of other people, and I had no reason to question their integrity.

The prize for the raffle was a Datsun car worth £2,650, but as this exceeded the maximum prize value of £2,000 allowed for raffles at the time, they had decided to turn it into a game of skill and charge 25p per ticket for people to guess the mileage the car could cover on one gallon of petrol. Having set this in motion, Clarke and Forster had then taken the car to various shopping precincts and public places to sell the tickets. And when a certain Vicky Montague was pronounced the winner at the draw, which took place at Rochdale Market in March 1981, she'd told the press that she was going to sell the car and give the proceeds back to the charity.

At the time I just thought that was a wonderful gesture and said so to the journalists. That, I thought, was that – a good piece of fund-raising. *Wrong.* The next thing I knew I was under arrest along with William Clarke, Rodger Forster, Vicky Montague and my PA Janet Ross, on a charge of 'conspiring to defraud the charity'. 'The competition,' it was alleged, 'had been fixed so that Vicky Montague could win, enabling her to sell the car and deposit the proceeds in the Fund.' Well, this was all news to me, but the nightmare had begun.

Having been taken to Rochdale, I was then transported by van to another police station to be formally charged and finger-printed. I suspect it was done this way because word had got around and it was thought that *Coronation Street* fans would start to congregate and make a fuss outside the police station. That's how protective the fans were – have always been – and for that they have my undying gratitude. When I was fingerprinted I looked down at my stained fingers and thought the ink looked just like blood. I really couldn't believe any of it was happening. (Later on, after the court case, I asked for my fingerprints back; I wanted to frame them. But the request was refused.) Anyway, I was charged – The Queen versus Julie Goodyear. I'd never actually met the Queen at the time, but that's what it said on the charge paper. Placed on bail for twelve months, I was then told I could carry on recording *Coronation Street*.

The press, of course, soon got hold of the story, jumped on the bandwagon and the circus hit town! The law of this country is that you are innocent until proved guilty. That might be the law, but I was found guilty every single day in the newspapers. Somehow, though, my fans, the viewers, knew this was a farce and I hadn't done owt wrong. I knew that from the volume of post that was coming in.

So-called friends, however, scattered like sewer rats – couldn't be seen for dust! My phone stopped ringing. To make it easier for me to accept why this was happening, I had the number changed. After all, if nobody knew the new number, nobody could ring. I know that sounds daft, but it helped me at the time. All the parties these 'friends' had come to at my house, all the fancy-dress dos, the cocktails, the beautiful buffets, the fab nights, were forgotten. They'd deserted me because of this court case hanging over me. How the hell did they think I felt? How could they even think I might be guilty? *How?* Because they didn't know me, that's how. But I hadn't realized that until then. The fact that they could even think such a thing, after I'd had surgery and my life had been spared, amazed me. Sister Margaret, my Wonder Woman, kept in touch, of course; and Lois Richardson, my make-up girl, stood strong and firm. But, dear God, I could count those who did on the fingers of one hand.

After what seemed an eternity, the day arrived when the five of us were due to appear in the dock at Manchester Crown Court, accused of 'conspiring together and with persons unknown to defraud people into buying tickets for a competition in aid of the Julie Goodyear Trust Fund, by falsely representing that the trust was conducting a genuine and honest competition. The charge alleges that a false winner had been pre-determined and that the car was destined for sale and the proceeds were to be contributed to the fund.'

To my astonishment, William and Rodger admitted the charge. Janet and me, as well as Vicky Montague, however, pleaded not guilty. 'I would never have allowed such a thing to happen if I'd known,' I kept saying to anybody who'd listen. And, although I was innocent, I felt dirty – tainted; and still, throughout it all, I was receiving aftercare treatment for cancer.

All five of us were given unconditional bail at the first hearing and my trial date was set for 1 March 1982. On 4 February 1982 William Clarke and Rodger Forster, who'd admitted the charge, were given six-month sentences, suspended for eighteen months, for their part in the fraud. I couldn't have been more distraught and worried. My trial was coming up the following month and if, against all odds, I was found guilty, my career would be destroyed. I certainly didn't think Granada would continue to employ an actress who was a convicted fraudster. And that thought was a killer, too terrible to contemplate.

'Come on, Julie, luv, stop all this nonsense,' I muttered to myself, as that lovely Barry Manilow song 'I Made It Through the Rain' started to run through my mind. 'You've made it through the rain before – and you will again.' Meanwhile, thank God for Bet. As always, she was the wind beneath my wings, and at least for the moment I could continue to turn into her at work. 'Thank you, Bet. Thank you,' I kept murmuring on a daily basis.

None of it, though, made any sense to me, and the strain it was putting Alice, Bill and Gary under was absolutely intolerable. 'Well, you've done it now,' Alice kept saying to me. 'After this, you just remember charity begins at home. After this, no more – that's *it*.' I totally understood how she felt.

During the trial, which began three months before my fortieth birthday, I was taken down to the cells, where I found out that the 'screws' – the warders – are changed every day so they don't get too fond of you. I also discovered that I had to pee down a hole in the floor, which I hated doing because, although my warders were female, I always felt like I was being watched. I knew Janet Ross was out of her mind with worry. Janet suffers from claustrophobia, so I realized that when she was taken down to the cells it would be even worse for her than it was for me.

Each time the jury was brought back into court, I tried to read their faces, and I often felt as though I was watching a scene from the *Crown Court* series being filmed at Granada Studios. The public gallery was crammed solid to watch Roger Harper, my solicitor, and Harold Singer, my barrister, standing absolutely firm. 'Maybe this time I'll make it through the rain,' I kept telling myself. But, if so, that would go against the usual grain of my life, and it was the hardest thing in the world to keep my spirits up.

On the fifth day of the hearing, the day when the verdict was due to be announced, someone pushed a tablet into my hand as I was brought back up the stairs into the dock. 'If they bring in a guilty verdict, take it,' they said. 'You'll never stand it in prison.' I've no idea what the tablet was, and as I dropped it when the verdict was announced I'll never know.

As I stood in the dock I kept scrutinizing everybody's faces, including the judge's. What were they thinking? What was running through their minds? I was facing a possible sentence of seven years in Holloway. *Seven years!* How could I survive that? My mam, dad and Gary hadn't missed a single day in court, but I'd sure miss them if this was not to be my day.

Suddenly, as I sat there thinking these thoughts, a shaft of light shone through the courtroom, and, as I glanced sideways, I saw Sister Margaret coming in. As she smiled and sat down a wonderful calm descended on me and I just knew it was going to be all right; that neither Janet nor I would be going to prison.

And I was right!

Judge Basil Gerrard suddenly stopped the trial, instructing the jury to 'return formal not guilty verdicts' on Janet, myself and Vicky Montague. He addressed the jury, saying 'there was no corroborative evidence' and that 'it would be wrong for persons such as these, of good character, who must be enduring quite a lot, to be made to go through any more when your decision would have been bound to be not guilty'. Oh my God, so many words to focus on and to take in at once. But all I knew was that we had been found *innocent* – I could have kissed him. For once in my life I *had* made it through the rain!

For a moment, as a cheer went round the courtroom, I thought my knees were going to give way, I really did. And, although I could hardly walk, all I wanted was to get out of that courtroom and back into the fresh air. I needed to breathe; couldn't wait to see daylight again.

When I did, I discovered that most of Fleet Street was there, shoving and pushing each other, with some actually falling over. When I instinctively bent down to help a photographer, I was shoved and nearly floored as well. It was just one massive sea of people, and there were banners being waved out of nearby office windows, reading, WE LOVE BET. I'd never seen anything like it. Crown Court Square was full to overflowing with cheering, happy people, reflecting exactly how I felt. It truly was incredible but I hadn't got the strength to join in.

As I was giving my mam, dad and Gary a hug, somebody shouted in my ear, 'Where do you want to go?'

'Back to work,' I replied.

I wanted to get back to the safe surroundings of Granada Television. That was my true home, where, let's face it, I'd spent more time than in my own home for many years. The court case had cost a fortune and I was cleaned out again, but all that mattered at the time was that I'd been found innocent, had my name cleared and was a free woman again.

As soon as the verdict was reported in the tabloids, I couldn't move for flowers. All the messages on the accompanying cards said that the senders knew I was innocent, but had thought I needed some space. Like twelve months' space! I love flowers, but I couldn't bear to have any of those in my home, so I took them to Heywood Cemetery and placed them on every grave that didn't have any. By the time I left, the cemetery was a riot of colour. And I've never had anything more to do with the people who didn't give me their support while I was waiting to go to court. As far as I'm concerned, a friend is there for you in bad as well as good times, and I've no time for fair-weather friends.

Talking of friends, I'd just like to add that Janet Ross, who stuck by me through that horrendous courtroom drama, remained an excellent PA on and off for eleven years after our relationship came to an end. She was very good at looking after me and Alice right up to my mother's death in 1987, and not surprisingly is now a carer and lives with another carer called Gwen. When she and Gwen went through their civil partnership ceremony in June 2006, they came on afterwards to my retreat in Spain and spent their honeymoon with me while I was working on this book.

My own relationship with Jan had ended on a very happy note. For us, it couldn't have finished any other way. Gwen knows how close we still are, and also knows how delighted I am that Jan has met somebody who is so right for her.

As soon as I got my breath back, and against Mam's wishes, I carried on raising money for the Julie Goodyear Trust Fund. Having started the job, I was determined to finish it, and eventually the Julie Goodyear Laboratory at the Christie Hospital was built. Podders came with me to its opening day in 1983. He made it very clear he was proud of me; and I was very proud to be there. It really was a marvellous feeling. But at what a price! But then I was getting used to those kinds of prices. Given my experience, would I ever become a registered charity again? Never. These days, I do what I can for charity very, very privately.

There is a PS and a PPS to the above tale of woe.

In 1996 the Julie Goodyear Rose, a beautiful, very fragrant yellow bloom, was bred in Yorkshire, on the estate of Lord and Lady St. Oswald. The honour of having a rose named after me was more than enough for this girl, so I said my share of any money from sales should be donated to my charity. Everybody was shocked. Apparently nobody else had ever done that when roses were named after them. But I was just thrilled to be able to do so.

Now for the PPS. About two years ago I went to the annual Tatton Park Flower Show. I love going there before it gets too busy, and I just wander through the gardens smelling all the different fragrances. While I was standing in the middle of one particularly beautiful plot, I suddenly realized it was the Christie Hospital Garden. 'Fancy that,' I thought, and I sat down.

A few minutes later, a couple of the people who had organized the stand recognized me. I didn't know them, but they came over to chat and asked me if I would do something for the hospital. 'I don't think so,' I replied politely. 'There's already a laboratory in my name at the hospital, and I got into a spot of bother about that at the time. I do, though, wish you every success with whatever the next project is.'

At first, they both looked as if they didn't know what I was talking about, but then one of them obviously twigged. 'Oh, *that* laboratory,' she said. 'It's now a block of offices.' I was stunned; couldn't believe my ears. The laboratory I'd nearly done time for was now a block of offices! 'But we do like to remember people who've done something for us,' she added. 'So, if you'd like to pop in to see us one day, we could name a ward after you.' I declined.

I've since found out that the Julie Goodyear Citology

Laboratory was relocated four years ago and amalgamated into a much larger screening centre as part of the Greater Manchester Health Authority services. The original building is now the finance department of Christie Hospital. I'm so grateful that my contribution has become part of bigger and better facilities, and means that even more women can be screened in the greater Manchester area.

As I mentioned earlier, my parents were in court throughout the trial, and I'm absolutely convinced that the shock of what was happening to their daughter on top of the fact that I was still receiving treatment for cancer couldn't possibly have done their health any good whatsoever. And, indeed, the result of that shock manifested itself very quickly.

I was on my own at home. It wasn't unusual for my dad to call round, not at all out of the ordinary. Always a smartly dressed man, I can see him now, clear as day, in his suit and trilby as he came through the kitchen door and I met him in the hall. The only thing different about him that day was the fact that he was carrying a very long stem of orchids.

'Are they for me?' I asked, surprised, because he'd never brought me flowers before, just wasn't that sort of man. He was very much a man's man and not very demonstrative. He didn't get married until he was forty, and if he hadn't met Alice, I'm convinced he'd have remained a bachelor all his life. But there he was that day, a working-class gentleman, carrying a stem of the most beautiful orchids.

'For me?' I said again, as he passed them to me. 'What's the occasion, Dad?' And I noticed that his lovely blue eyes were unusually watery.

'Let's sit down together,' he said gently, 'and have a chat.'

'A chat?' I repeated, suddenly anxious. 'Is me mother all right?'

'Yes, yes, she's fine, luv. I just wanted to talk to you on your own.'

An instant feeling of foreboding crept over me.

'You haven't got a drop of whisky, have you?' he asked as we went through to the lounge.

'A whisky, at this time of day?' I said, astonished.

'If you've got one, I'll have one.'

'Jesus!' I thought. 'This must be bloody serious.' Crossing to the bar, I poured him a tot before asking, 'What would you like with it, Dad?'

'Just as it is – that'll be fine.'

He took the trilby off his shiny bald head which over the years I'd grown to love so much, and I sat down, still holding the stem of orchids. 'Dad, what is it?' I asked. '*What's wrong?*'

He knocked his whisky back in one go and said, 'Now, look, what I'm going to tell you – you must give me your word that you'll never repeat it to your mother.'

'Me? Not tell me mother? You know what we're like, Dad.'

'No, give me your word.'

'If it's that important to you – and obviously it is – of course I'll give you my word.'

'Good – *good*. Because we don't want to go upsetting—'

'*Upsetting?* What in God's name has happened, Dad?'

'Well, it's not good news, Julie. I'm the one with cancer now.'

'What?'

'Aye. It's my turn now. Don't tell your mam.'

The world had stopped turning.

'Another whisky, Dad?' I whispered as soon as I could.

'Aye, please. That'll be nice.'

I got him his drink then sat there, looking down at the orchids, thinking, 'How the hell will I keep it from me mam?' I'd never kept a secret from her in my entire life. But I did keep my word because I knew Dad found it all much easier with her not knowing. When he went into hospital for what he told my mam was a 'routine man's problem', they did what they could. But the treatment had come too late. He was on a large, all-male ward, and when I went in to see him one day, he said, 'Can you get me home, luv? I'm ready to go home now.'

When I went to see the doctor, though, he said, 'There's no point taking him home – you know that.'

'He wants to go home,' I said.

'Well, you'll have to sign. We can't take responsibility.'

'I'll sign. If he wants to go home, he's goin' home.'

'You can't have an ambulance.'

'Can I not? Watch me.'

Just outside the hospital, I found a couple of ambulance drivers and asked if they would do the job for me privately.

'Course,' they said.

I went back into the hospital, got a wheelchair, and started to get Dad's stuff out of the locker for him. 'Hey, hang on a minute,' he said.

'Why?'

'You know them photos that you have for your work – those publicity shots – have you got any in t' car?'

'Yes?'

'Bring a few in for me.'

Now this was not my father; Alice, yes, my dad, no. But I went back to the car, got the photographs and brought them back in. Before he left the hospital, he explained, he wanted me to take him round every bed in that ward and introduce myself as his daughter. I was choked, couldn't speak, but I did as he asked, including signing a photograph for every man who wanted one. Which was all of them.

The two ambulance lads were fabulous. They got him back from the hospital to Heywood, took him upstairs on a stretcher, and then wouldn't take a penny for their kindnesses. When I next saw Dad, his pale blue eyes were shining brightly and his face was beaming. He was home, in the house he had built, and back where he wanted to be. Then there was my mam, of course. 'What are you two doin' back?' she asked when she got back from shopping.

'He got bored; didn't like it in there,' I replied.

'Oh, right.'

As there are certain things a daughter can't do for her dad – or at least I couldn't – like washing and shaving, I employed a male nurse. He was smashing, really fond of my dad, and they became great pals. So Dad was in his own bed, comfortable in his own room and that was what mattered.

My mam was completely oblivious to the fact he was dying. The very idea would have been impossible for her to accept. This was a man who had always been strong, who had virtually rendered her helpless, as so many husbands do. She didn't know how to write a cheque, pay a bill – do anything like that for herself. (I used to wonder what it would be like to be that kind of woman with that kind of husband. But that remained a luxury I couldn't afford.) Anyway, my mam didn't even guess and why should she? She'd been through enough with her daughter, and for lightning to strike twice in the same house was impossible,

234

wasn't it? Yes, summat was wrong with Bill, but he'd get better. Of course he would.

Gary was away on holiday with a couple of his mates at that time. 'Thank God for that,' I thought. He was very close to his nan and granddad, and although I knew I'd have to tell him as soon as he got back, at least it gave me a little breathing space. It was bad enough coping with my mam not knowing, without having to tell Gary straight away. The moment he came home, however, I told him, and understandably he freaked out.

'Your nan doesn't know,' I kept saying, 'and that's the worst part. But we've got to go along with it for Granddad's sake.' He just nodded; was marvellous. 'Go upstairs and see your grand-dad,' I added. 'He's been hanging on, waiting for you to come back.' It was true. Gary was the apple of Bill's eye; had always been more like his son than his grandson.

During those final days my dad couldn't come downstairs because he was too weak, and I never smoked in front of him. One day, though, when I was up in his bedroom and there was a lull in the conversation, I said, 'I won't be long, Dad.' We'd been chatting for about three quarters of an hour, and I was desperate for a ciggy. 'I'm just popping downstairs a mo.'

'Are you going downstairs for a fag?' he asked.

'Yes, I am,' I said.

'Will you do me a favour?'

'I'll do anything, you know that, Dad.'

'Then light one up in here.'

'You're joking, Dad.'

'Julie,' he said, 'what difference will it bloody make? Go on, have it with me.' It felt really strange smoking in front of me dad, but he wanted me to so I did it.

He was a good man, he truly was. He was the best husband my mam could ever have had. He worshipped her – *adored* her. And he taught me so many things: dignity, pride, self-respect, standards to live by, the value of money – pay your bills, don't short-change in your work. It must have been wonderful for Alice to be so loved by him. I'd witnessed it, but never had that kind of love in my relationships – not that I'd have minded a bit. If I'd married Geoff Cassidy, I'd have had it all right; but I didn't love him and couldn't short-change him. I know a lot of women would have compromised – I've often met them – but I couldn't. Surely there was a happy medium, though!

I've never forgotten wheeling Bill around that ward, with those publicity photographs he'd asked for. He'd never done anything like that before, but his pride just spilled over that day. A non-smoker all his life, he died of lung cancer on 4 September 1982. It was only six months after the court case, so he must have been ill all the time he was present in court. But, then, that kind of courage was so typical of him. I was *very* privileged to know Bill (William) Goodyear. He was a *really* good man, and I loved him.

TWELVE

That's My Life

One of the biggest shocks of my life happened two years before Bill died, on 8 October 1980 to be precise. It really was a shock, and came on the back of two others. Yeah, well I am Julie Goodyear! The first had kicked in earlier that year when I was on holiday in Tunisia with a girlfriend called Sam. While there, I met Andrew McAllister, a restaurant manager, taking a break from his job at the Langtry Manor Hotel, Bournemouth (once a love nest for Lillie Langtry and the Prince of Wales who became Edward VII). Andrew's entry into my life was very timely; he arrived just as I was trying to escape the unwanted attention of some Arab gentlemen. Impressed by his kindness, I accepted an invitation to go dancing with him later at the hotel disco. Then, having enjoyed each other's company during the holiday – and become absolutely inseparable – we kept in touch by phone on our return.

Three days after our homecoming, Andrew, who was thirty-two years old (six years younger than I was), admitted he was head over heels in love with me. He then added he'd packed his bags, was waving goodbye to the Langtry and was coming to be with me in Heywood. Not long afterwards on St Valentine's

Day he proposed marriage, I accepted and we got engaged. *I know!* History keeps repeating itself, but I still thought that this time I might be lucky.

The 8 October shock, which came just six months later, also began in a very pleasant way. I caught a train with Podders, the *Street*'s producer, for what I believed – and that would certainly have been enough excitement for one day – was a journey to London to discuss me making some personal appearances in Australia. But when we arrived at Euston Station and got off the train, the first thing I saw was a red carpet leading to a brass band that immediately broke into a welcoming fanfare. As Podders ushered me up the platform in the direction of a group of beaming faces, I kept looking over my shoulder, wondering who on earth this red-carpet treatment was for.

'What a lovely way to arrive,' I joked as we came to a halt. 'But you really shouldn't have! Who are you waitin' for?' Just as these words died on my lips, I saw him out of the corner of my eye, the famous red book clutched in his hands.

'*Julie Goodyear*,' he boomed in that all too familiar voice I'd heard so often on TV, '*this is your life!*'

I was absolutely gobsmacked. 'Eamonn,' I stuttered, when I got my voice back. 'Eamonn Andrews.' Then, still not quite believing what was happening, I added, 'Is it a series?' Given my life, it would need to be!

Before I could ask any more questions, though, I was abducted, bundled into the back seat of a waiting limo, covered with a rug, and whisked off to God knows where. It was surreal, and all the time I was wondering who on earth they would pull out of the hat, who was going to be there. So far, nobody had told me owt. All I found out was that I was on my way to

Thames Television in Teddington, Middlesex, where the show would be recorded.

Once we arrived at Thames, young researchers kept tripping past me, saying things like, 'I *loved* that chandelier in your dining room.' To me they were complete strangers who I'd never invited into my home, but they knew all about me because they'd been working in secret for about six months on my *This Is Your Life* file. At one point I remember saying to one of the researchers, 'How's me mam? Is she all right?'

'Oh, don't worry, love, everything's gonna be fine. Fantastic.' And it was.

A few hours later, dressed in a pale-blue, full-length chiffon evening gown, I came in through the audience and onto the stage set, taking my place alongside Andrew. When Eamonn asked Andrew about his relationship with me, Andrew's answer was: 'Julie told me she couldn't promise me very much, but life would *never* be dull.' Given what happened later that day, though, I think that was one occasion when the boot proved to be on the other foot! But back for now, as they say, to the studio.

Alice, Bill and Gary came in first and took their places next to Andrew, then the cast of *Coronation Street* (all well used by then to making appearances on *This Is Your Life*) made their entrance. When Chris Quentin came on, he lifted me up off the floor, swung me round and gave me such a big hug that he nearly burst all my stitches. When Doris Speed walked on, I very daintily lifted the skirt of my long dress and knelt in homage at her feet. She then paid me the following tribute: 'Television is a very nervy business,' she said, 'and we are grateful to anyone who relieves the tension. Now, Annie Walker may have her doubts about Bet Lynch, but Doris Speed has nothing but gratitude for Julie Goodyear because she has quite deliberately made me laugh and relax on so many occasions before we played a scene.'

My cousin Irene Hawksworth then told the viewers how we had shared and fought over the most comfortable bed when we were teenagers, and how I'd once knocked up the local greengrocer in the dead of night to get her a slice of melon when she was laid up with tonsillitis.

Peter Dudley, who played Bert Tisley in the *Street*, came on dressed in a Roman toga to remind me of the time we'd been in rep together, appearing in *A Funny Thing Happened on the Way to the Forum*. Having recalled me playing Vibrata, a sexy slave girl who he kept calling Vibrator, he then went on to say that, having blacked up my face for the part, I'd suffered an allergic reaction which left me looking like a piece of milk-chocolate peanut brittle. True!

The *Corrie* lot were then joined by my old teacher Tony Whitehead and school mates Anita Simpson, Sydney Yates and Peter Birchall, and also Sue Skelton, my best friend and jiving partner during my Carlton days.

The evening went marvellously well: the audience were so warm and loving, and it was surprise after surprise as people kept appearing. 'This is quite summat,' I remember thinking. 'I'll treasure the tape of it for ever.' And I have. Then Eamonn, who always liked to end the show with a big surprise for the guest, surpassed himself. Somehow he'd worked a small miracle by getting permission from Sister Margaret's order for her to leave the convent and attend my big night. I was totally overwhelmed. She'd only recently nursed me through cancer – saved my life – and I was absolutely overjoyed to see her again. Although I never cry, as that show came to an end it was, I can tell you, a tearful reunion with her. I felt I was dreaming. It was all wonderful.

After the show everyone was invited to a party in the Thames studios. The moment the credits stopped rolling I couldn't wait to get out of my long dress, slip into something more comfy, and have a relaxing drink and a proper natter without the cameras whirring. I also couldn't bear to let go of Sister Margaret's hand. 'Come on,' I said. 'Nip back to the dressing room with me while I get changed.'

Then, with her in tow, I headed for the dressing room for a quick change before the drive to Regent's Park. When I flung open the dressing-room door, however, I was in for the shock of my life. There, with a boy, was Andrew. We had caught them in an embarrassing clinch. As Sister Margaret's gasp joined mine, I pulled the door shut on all the sighs and heavy breathing we'd interrupted on the other side.

'That,' I said, shocked to the very core of my being and taking her by the hand and leading her away, 'is my life.'

As we drove over to Regent's Park, I couldn't help recalling the message Violet Carson had recorded for me from her Blackpool home: 'Hello, Julie. Sorry not to be with you, but I send my love and hope you will have a thoroughly enjoyable evening.'

Thoroughly enjoyable evening! Thank God Violet would never have to know what really happened, what Andrew had had in store for me. After our experience, Sister Margaret and I did a runner. Having hailed a black cab, we travelled through London together – a nun and a so-called star – both still deeply shocked.

Life, as they say, is full of surprises, but some really are more shocking than others. That man had the cheek of the devil and took some getting rid of, he truly did. He kept turning up at my home and it got so bad that I had to ask the police to help get rid of him. Thankfully they did, but I couldn't believe that yet again an engagement had gone so horribly wrong. I'll say it again: I've suffered so many times from being too trusting and believing what people, and men in particular, say to me. Nobody will be surprised to learn that my next relationship was with a woman!

Thanks to *Corrie* I've travelled the world and met some fantastic people over the years, and I'm forever grateful for that. Along with all the tragedies in my life, I've had some marvellous experiences and I've never become blasé. How could I? I still mop my own floors!

I first met the Queen and Prince Philip in May 1982, when they came to visit the set of *Coronation Street*. I was really excited. I'm an out-and-out monarchist, and so proud of our royal family. I think every country in the world is jealous of what we have, and rightly so. On this royal occasion I was standing next to Doris Speed, who was first in the line-up; the rest of the cast were standing outside their fictional homes. We'd all been told to address the Queen as ma'am (to rhyme with jam) and how to behave. But me, being me, should have known summat would go wrong.

As the Queen came towards us, Doris looked at her, then turned to me and said in a very loud voice, 'Oh, dear, isn't her make-up dreadful?' I know the Queen heard – could tell by the glassy look in her eyes – and I just wanted to die! There were times when I wondered whether my beloved Doris, who was no longer a spring chicken, just forgot herself, but maybe she just did such things on purpose. I will never know. What I do know is that Doris's remark had completely thrown me – scattered my composure to the four winds. Completely over-come, I found myself bowing first to Doris, and then curtseying to – and saluting – the Queen. By then, I didn't know what the hell I was doing.

I fared a bit better with Prince Philip. For the occasion I was wearing a pair of Diana and Charles earrings which I'd had made specially, and my hair, of course, was piled into a beehive. The Duke peered at my earrings and said, 'I think I recognize those two.' I didn't answer. By then, thanks to Doris, I'd lost the plot.

Afterwards, I asked Doris why she'd said what she had.

'Don't be silly, dear,' she replied. 'You must be hearing things!' But it wasn't just me; others, further down the line, had heard the remark. Once again, I was left thinking that Doris had very convenient lapses of memory, as well as a bloody good sense of humour!

While Margaret Thatcher was prime minister, she also came on a visit to *Coronation Street*. I'd never met her, but I'd always admired her strength of character. For me it was another of those special moments. As she came into the Rovers Return, accompanied by her aides, the first thing I noticed was that she'd got lipstick smeared all over her front teeth. 'Oh, my God,' I thought. 'If I can see it, surely her aides must be able to see it too. Why haven't they told her? If that were me, I'd much rather someone tell me than say nowt.'

Anyway, as I didn't want her to go on camera looking like that, I waited until she came alongside me and our eyes met, then I ran my little finger very deliberately over my teeth. She clocked what I was doing straight away and dealt with the problem in her usual decisive way. Then, having given me a very gracious smile, she walked on. I thought that was fabulous, and I'm convinced that was why I received an invitation, soon afterwards, to visit Number 10 Downing Street.

What should I wear? I had no need to worry. Dobbsy – Peter Dobbs – was there for me, and found me a fabulous, deep purple, beautifully tailored suit for the occasion. I was very grateful, and couldn't wait to go and see what Number 10 was like for myself. In the event, it turned out to be a truly marvellous occasion. I've never been very good at mingling – and I'm not good at networking either – but I love standing at the edges and taking everything in. At one moment I couldn't help noticing that Denis Thatcher, who was circulating and getting ever closer to me, had had one or two (or maybe even three) drinks more than he should have. And, as he kept eying me up, I began to feel a bit uncomfortable.

When he eventually landed at my side, obviously a little the worse for drink, he leaned in close to my Newton and Ridleys, then, as I stood there chatting politely to him, leaned in even closer and sort of patted Newton. Now, women from my background are quite used to dealing with fellas who become too familiar. We knee them in the bollocks, and, as Denis remained standing there, my right knee had instinctively gone into lift-off mode. Luckily for him, though – or perhaps luckily for me as his wife's guest – I was wearing a tightish skirt, which meant that, without hitching it up, it wasn't easy to see the action through. So I forced my right foot back down onto the floor, and the next time he made to move his hand, this time in the direction of Ridley, I smiled very politely but slapped his hand down at the same time.

It was quite a loud slap and I thought, 'Oh God. I'm going to finish up in the bloody Tower of London.' But no; the PM glanced across at me, took in the situation, winked, and carried on with her conversation. I went to the loo very quickly after that, and then kept out of Denis's way for the rest of the evening. If Denis was in a fit enough state to learn anything that night, I hope it was that we Northern women are renowned for our toughness. Centuries of bringing in the coal have seen to that.

All I can add, to sum up the Denis kind of experience, is that some men are predatory, and as you grow up you have to learn how to sidestep or handle such encounters. In my long experience, there are tit men, leg men and pinch 'em on the bum men, and as I've said, dealing with them by kneeing them in the balls is the done thing up North. Interestingly, it doesn't matter how big the fellas are; they'll still drop to the ground if you knee 'em in the right place. I must say, all those years I spent in the room overlooking the Gents' toilets at the Bay Horse Hotel held me in good stead for such moments. It was, I can confirm, a good education in the university that's called life. I might add, too, that although men are supposed to hate women who smoke and who dress too sexily, I remember reading that Bet has topped the chart for 'the woman most men fancy' in at least a hundred surveys over the years.

Writing about this has also reminded me of a time when I was working with a lovely actress called Jill Summers, who came into *Corrie* to play the part of Phyllis Pearce at the Capricorn nightclub. Jill was getting on a bit when she came into *Corrie*, and I absolutely adored her. As a child she'd been adopted and, later on, having worked in variety comedy and as a singer, she became a hit in musical revues. When she was working in Manchester, she used to have a suite in the Portland Hotel, and I often collected her on my way to work at Granada Studios. The story I'm about to tell sums this lady up.

We were in our car waiting at some traffic lights when a seedy-looking chap came round the corner and stopped level with us. Then he opened his mac and flashed at us. Winding down the window of the car, Jill smiled angelically at him and said, 'Oh, you are a sport.' You've never seen anything shrivel quite so fast. Jill had ruined the flasher's career. She was absolutely brilliant!

From Heywood market to Buck House, 10 Downing Street and then the Ritz Hotel, London, were huge steps for this piece of womankind called Julie Goodyear. On my first visit to the Ritz I was given a fabulous suite next door to Joan Rivers, and I was made to feel as at home there as I was in Heywood. To be able to walk past all the posh ladies having their afternoon tea and have the pianist look up, clock me, then tinkle out the theme of *Coronation Street* on the ivories was just fabulous – yet another high spot of my career.

I've been so privileged to meet the people I've met, and to visit the places I've visited. Thanks to my work, I've been lucky enough to travel the world and be wonderfully well looked after. Although sometimes this meant just seeing the inside of a luxurious hotel room, I also have many extraordinary moments to look back on. How many people, for instance, have been given a full Maori welcome as their plane touched down on the tarmac in New Zealand? I did! And, going into man-hungry Bet mode, I said jokingly to Podders, who was with me on that trip, 'I'll have the one on the left with the long tongue'!

It was just as well there were so many good moments, because, steel yourself, there were yet more bad ones en route. To be serious for a moment, though, *Coronation Street* gave me so much that whatever price I paid to be in it for twenty-five years I paid gladly. To this day I think of Bet with phenomenal affection, and it tugs at my heart strings every time a complete stranger comes up to me and says, 'You know, it's never been the same since you left.' And this still happens all the time, both in the UK and in Spain when I'm on holiday.

While I was in *Corrie*, I was very lucky with all my producers and I'd never hear a bad word said against any of 'em. Obviously, given the length of time I was there, producers came and went, as did directors and members of the cast, but I found something likeable in each and every one of them, and had fabulous working relationships. It's great to be able to say that.

Whenever I was summoned up to the office, though, I used to go into panic mode and think, 'Oh God! What now?' Once upstairs, we were always kept waiting in the secretary's area for a while, just to let the tension build a bit. Inside there was a desk with the boss behind it, and a chair placed in front that I nicknamed the naughty chair. I called it this because it was just a bit too low, which immediately made whoever sat in it feel very small. This was why, on many occasions, I used to ignore the chair and sit on the edge of the desk. But it took me a while to build up to that.

On one occasion during the 1990s when I was sitting in the naughty chair, it wasn't bad news. This time I was there because my producer Carolyn Reynolds wanted to tell me she was pregnant. Given the kind of publicity I'd been receiving in the newspapers I said with a mischievous glint in my eye, 'D'you think the press will claim I'm the father?' And we both fell about laughing.

THIRTEEN

Maybe This Time

Remember the saying 'Third time lucky'? Well that's what I hoped it would be when I agreed to let American businessman Richard Skrob become my third husband. But, no, it proved to be third time unlucky! It began well, though, which I'm sure by now you'll appreciate is not unusual in my life, and there were a number of times when I thought, 'Yep, maybe this time it'll all work out for the best.'

I first met Richard in June 1981 on my way to New Zealand with Podders to work for the charity Telethon and to promote our beloved *Coronation Street*. A marathon of a trip had been organized, and it was VIP treatment all the way. I'd never known the like of it – first-class lounges at airports, first-class compartments on the plane, gourmet food beautifully presented, exotic drinks – it was enough to turn a girl's head. Just great. I'd better make it clear here that there was never anything other than a working relationship and a good friendship between Podders and me; indeed, he was using the trip to reflect on his life and make the very tough choice between his wife and a friend of mine called Millie.

I'd first noticed Richard, who was travelling on his own, in the first-class lounge. Tall, skinny and wearing specs, there was nothing about his appearance that would stand out in a crowd, except he looked very lost and sad. When we got on the plane, I noticed he was seated on our left and that he was still looking lost and sad.

As soon as we were up up and away, Bill ordered some drinks and it turned into party time, and after a few glasses of champagne I found myself thinking, 'Why don't I invite that miserable bugger over there to come and join us and have some fun?' So, acting on impulse, I crossed the aisle and said, 'Hello. We're having a party – come and join us.' Richard nodded politely and I handed him a glass of champagne. By this stage of the flight I'd got nearly everybody in the first-class compartment joining in and having a good time.

When I sat down next to Richard, he told me that his wife had recently died.

'Oh my God,' I thought, mortified. 'I've been so insensitive.' It was obvious, though, that he needed a friend at that moment and my heart went out to him. I can't quite remember where the first stopover was for that leg of the journey, but I think it was Los Angeles, where we were due to change planes and Richard was destined to get off. By then, Podders, who'd had a lot to drink, was more than merry, and I had quite a struggle getting him off the plane and into the lounge to wait for our next connection. Mr Skrob, however, proved to be a total blessing and helped out. Having then thanked me for my kindness and understanding throughout the flight, he gave me a friendly farewell hug and went on his way.

That might have been that, but it wasn't. He came straight back. 'I'm worried about you,' he said. 'Your producer's in a bit of a state and I'm concerned that you won't be able to get him on the next plane on your own.' It was obvious he wanted to return my kindness and so he stayed and helped me with Podders – and then just stayed all the way round the world!

Wherever I went, there he was, clutching a huge bouquet of flowers, and whenever I booked into a new hotel, he was there waiting. It was all very flattering, head-turning stuff. This cultured American millionaire was pursuing me, and Podders, for one, was very impressed; thought it was fabulous.

Each time we met, our friendship grew and blossomed. We often talked about the death of his wife, which had obviously affected him very deeply. At other times, I talked to him about my work and home life – about my mam, Bill and Gary – and he told me about his children Ray and Cathy – and Steve, the son who'd been banished from the family because he was gay.

'But that's terrible,' I said, instantly upset for Steve.

'I think it is now,' Richard agreed, 'but at the time my wife was very distressed by his homosexuality, just couldn't come to terms with it.'

'But that's awful,' I kept saying. 'How must that boy have felt then? And how does he feel now?'

Not long after our first meeting, Richard invited me to visit him in the States. I agreed to come as long as I was allowed to pay my own expenses – both travel and accommodation. I've always been a very independent woman where financial matters are concerned. An airline executive, Richard was, by anybody's standards, a very wealthy man who had a truly beautiful home, and, although wealth and trappings never bother me, I really enjoyed that visit. Having met Ray and Cathy, I then insisted on meeting Steve, who proved to be adorable. The reunion between him and his father was very emotional, very special, and I was really proud to have been instrumental in bringing it about.

So, happy to have Richard in my life, I decided to invite him to Heywood to meet my family. The moment my mam heard he was coming, she decided she would detest him.

'But why?' I said. 'You haven't even met him yet.'

'I don't have to,' she replied. 'He's a Yank! A bloody Yank! And, although we've been through some pretty awful things together, Julie, this one takes the bloody biscuit. A bloody Yank!'

'Look, Mam,' I pleaded. 'Have a heart! His wife died recently, so a bit of compassion wouldn't go amiss. He's a kind man, honestly. A gentle soul, you'll see.'

'He's a bloody Yank.'

'Well, yes. But just give him a chance.'

'You don't give Yanks a bloody chance,' she retorted. '*You* don't know what they were like during the war, young lady. *I do.*'

And she would start all over again, bombarding me with tales of what had happened to friends of hers during the war. Yanks, as far as Alice was concerned, were definitely 'oversexed, overpaid and over here'. And because you couldn't get your hands on a pair of silk stockings or a bar of chocolate – blah blah – they took advantage, often made young girls pregnant, and then buggered off back to America.

'Mam,' I said, wearily, 'the war's been over for donkey's years – it's done and dusted.' But not as far as Alice was concerned.

Despite my mam's views, Richard's pursuit of me continued, and flowers carried on arriving at Granada Television. There were so many over-the-top bouquets I became embarrassed and had to ask him to send any further offerings to my home. It all smacked of showing off to me.

Life soon had another shock in store for me – this time another life-threatening one. On one of our dates, Richard told me that because he'd been feeling unusually exhausted and under the weather, he'd been to see his doctor and, after various tests, had been told he had leukaemia and hadn't that long to live. Before I'd had time to absorb this terrible news, he then added, almost in the same breath, 'So, will you marry me?' How could I refuse? I know this may sound daft to some and a ridiculous reason for accepting a proposal of marriage, but I knew how much he needed me at that moment and, despite my resolution never to risk a third-time-unlucky situation, I felt I had to say yes.

I only made two conditions: that he would respect my need to continue playing Bet in *Coronation Street*; and that, after we were married, he would come and live in England. Both were essential because there was no way I was going to give up Bet or, for that matter, leave my mam and Gary to go and live in the States. 'If you agree to those two conditions,' I said, 'I'll be a good and faithful wife, and always look after you.' He was thrilled and kept repeating I couldn't have made him happier. We then went on a lovely holiday to Mexico, where we spent a very gentle time during which we made our plans, even though we knew they weren't going to be long term. Our attitude was 'Let's be happy while we can!'

On New Year's Day 1985, the day we were due to get married in Barbados, the paparazzi, tipped off by some prick, had other plans. I ended up hiding in a sugar-cane field. We'd hoped to have a romantic beach wedding but, once the snappers descended, Richard quickly rearranged everything and we were actually married in a little church nearby. The paparazzi, serve 'em right, never got a single shot. In fact, the picture published in this book is the only picture that has ever been seen of my marriage to Richard Skrob.

Richard's daughter Cathy and his son Ray were our two witnesses at the wedding. My mam hadn't had a change of heart and remained absolutely disgusted with me. 'As usual, you're doing it for all the wrong reasons,' she grumbled, 'doing it because you're sorry for him. You've always been a soft touch. I reckon they see you comin'! I know you – know what you're like. It'll all end in tears. But, you'll suit yourself; you always do. You'll go through with it, but you'll see.'

One of Richard's favourite hobbies was sailing. He'd told me when we first met that the sea was – and always had been – his mistress. Even so, I thought it was very strange that he went out in his yacht on his own on our wedding night. But, as I sat there celebrating our marriage with his son and daughter, it was obvious they thought this was quite normal behaviour. Things got worse – it could only happen to me. We were supposed to be on honeymoon, but he didn't come back for three days. I had to remember, though, that this man had leukaemia and probably wasn't in a normal frame of mind. Anyway, in the event I made up my mind not to say anything negative or be angry with him. After all, it wasn't his fault that I didn't like sailing and was prone to seasickness.

After the wedding, I also couldn't help but notice that Ray's and Cathy's attitudes towards me had changed, and *not* for the better. I couldn't understand why at first, but I got the message by degrees. Over a period of time it was made very clear to me by both of them that their concerns were purely financial – they were very worried about their inheritance. I was shocked. On top of everything else that had been suggested about me in the past, I could now apparently add 'gold-digger' to the list. But I decided not to rock the boat and remained patient with them.

My concerns were very different from theirs. As I mentioned earlier, Richard had accepted before we got married that my work on *Coronation Street* would come first and that I would continue playing Bet, who was about to become the Rovers' first single landlady, with the sign '*Elizabeth Theresa Lynch licensed to sell intoxicating liquor to be consumed on or off the premises*' above the pub's front door, and I was really looking forward to him coming to live in England. I realized, of course, that we might not stay in my home, but just thought we'd get somewhere else to live.

So, when I returned home alone, I thought this was only a temporary situation and was happy for a while to speak on the phone and to meet up with him in Paris. It was all very exotic and, yes, I was chuffed. I'd never been to Paris before and we stayed at the very grand George V Hotel. It was fun – just great – and I made absolutely sure I paid my own share of the bill. I'd always done that and wasn't going to change now. I was no gold-digger.

As time went on and Richard still made no plans to move to England I kept making excuses for him. After all, although he seemed fine on the health front, he was having treatment in the States, and I could understand him feeling more secure in his own country.

★

A much happier moment occurred with my own son, who was now twenty-six, on 4 October 1986. Gary, now a car sales executive, married Suzanne Robinson, a secretary he'd met when he was on holiday in Spain and had been knocking around with for some years. I guess I was a typical mother-in-law-to-be. As far as I was concerned, the girl hadn't been born who was good enough to be Gary's wife, but Suzanne and I did get on really well.

For the big day, I chose a lovely lilac suit and matching hat, and Richard came over to accompany me to the bride's home in Sheffield. It should have been a very happy time for all of us. But it wasn't! Four days before the ceremony, the spoilers were out in force again – the hacks were busy once more dishing out the dirt about my personal life. A taxi driver who'd once been a friend of mine, had told the *Sun* and the *Daily Star* that I was a lesbian with an insatiable appetite for visiting seedy gay clubs – the seedier the better – pulling girls and so on and so forth.

With the papers full of this crap, the church in the village of Dore, where Gary's wedding was taking place, was besieged by reporters. Holding tightly on to Richard's hand for comfort, I paused on my way into the church and gave them a quote: 'I love my husband,' I said, 'and that's all I want to say on this happy day, except that I wish Gary and Suzanne a wonderful life together. I'm feeling very proud of myself. I have a wonderful son, a beautiful daughter-in-law and a fabulous husband. What more could a girl ask for!'

Gary was my only son and all I wanted was everything to be perfect for them, that they would live happily ever after. Sadly, though, their marriage hit the rocks nine years later. But at least by then they had had three lovely children – and I had three wonderful grandchildren to thank them for – Emily, Elliot and Jack.

I feel another PS coming on! This was a black-comedy moment during the period when I was being outed in the papers. Millions of viewers saw me rendered speechless for an instant when TV presenter Fern Britton made a deliberate *faux pas* while interviewing me. She was supposed to ask me when Bet would be getting a new boyfriend, but instead said, 'When is Bet Lynch going to get a new girlfriend?' Hastily correcting herself, she added, 'I mean boyfriend.' After a second's pause, I roared with laughter at her slip of the tongue and retorted, 'Shame on you, Fern, is that an offer?' And she blushed to the roots of her hair.

Richard and I couldn't, of course, continue our commuter-style marriage, living 7,000 miles apart in different countries. Long-distance marriages may work for a time, but there is usually a crunch point. This came for me the very last time I tried to speak to him, long distance, on the telephone. By then, after just over two years, things had become almost farcical and I knew he was never going to make the move from the US to England. In fact his children were making that very clear to me on a regular basis.

When I rang his home phone number – and here we go again with another black-comedy moment – his recorded voice on the answer machine, said, 'Hi there, Dick is unavailable.' Something clicked at that moment. Placing the phone down, I said quietly to myself, 'You're bloody right. Dick *is* unavailable.' So, much to my mam's delight, I told her it wasn't third time lucky; I was going to get a divorce. Overjoyed, she retorted,

'See, told you. What did I tell you? Those bloody Yanks are all the same. They've not changed, ne'er will!'

As always I understood. Throughout our marriage, he had been having treatment for leukaemia, which is hardly the time to change countries and start a new life. Of course I wanted things to turn out differently but there was nothing I could really do and I was just sad that he'd lost his life.

Another PS!

When the divorce came through in January 1987 Alice was terminally ill with cancer. When I went into her bedroom to tell her the news, not really knowing whether she was conscious or not, I said, 'I don't know if you can hear me, Mam, but my divorce papers from Richard have just come through, and you were right: I shouldn't have married him. I hope you can hear me, but if you can't, I understand. I just wanted to tell you anyway.'

As there wasn't even a flicker of an eyelid, I turned to walk out of the room. But then, from the bed, I heard the cry, '*Yippee!*' And, as I turned round to look at her, she said without even opening her eyes, 'Well, let's have a drink then, to celebrate.'

'I'll go and get 'em,' I said. 'I'll go and get 'em.'

FOURTEEN

On the Wings of Angels

Many years after my son Gary was born and at a time when abortion had become legal a very dear friend of mine who I'm not going to name for obvious reasons found herself pregnant and in a position where she felt there was only one path she could take. Having arranged to go into hospital for a termination, she asked me if I'd visit her there.

'Of course I will,' I said. I really was very fond of her.

When I arrived at the hospital, I discovered she was on a very large ward and I noticed at once that there was a horrible atmosphere. I've always been very sensitive to such things and I was immediately on my guard. Hospitals, of course, are not always like that. I've been on cancer wards, for example, and visited terminally ill people on many occasions when there's been laughter and a happy atmosphere. In fact, I've even joined in black-humour songs – the one I'm remembering right now goes, 'All my life I've been a'kissin' / Your left tit because your right one's a'missin' / Oh boy, when you're with me, oh boy . . .' Shared moments like that, when the morale is good, despite the circumstances, are pure magic. But there was none of that on the ward where my friend had landed, and I found myself wondering why. Then, suddenly, as I turned round, I saw the reason. There *she* was, the same ward sister who'd been at the horrible hospital when I was giving birth to Gary. It was obvious that she hadn't changed one iota. This time, though, it was my turn.

'Remember me?' I said, marching towards her, and it was obvious from her face that she did. 'You're the one who said to me, "We get your sort back in here every year," the one who refused me a whiff of gas and air when I needed it! And here you are still inflicting pain on those who can't help themselves.'

Like all bullies when they finally meet their match, she collapsed. She was cowering away from me as I moved ever closer. Then, fired up by the memory of what she'd done to me and was still doing to others, I gave her the hiding of her life. Literally. Before I knew it, I'd beaten her to the floor and, throughout it all, there was total silence from everybody else on the ward.

I realized later that any one of the young women lying there waiting for their terminations could have grassed on me. I could have been had up for assault and it could have cost me my job on *Coronation Street*. But not one of them did. And soon after, I heard – praise the Lord – that the sister had taken early retirement. Interestingly, it was only after I heard that that I stopped having the nightmares I'd always had about her.

If Alice hadn't been so close to me, she'd have given up on life the day after Bill died, but, as it was, she lasted another five years. During that time I tried everything in the book to keep her spirits up, keep her with me and keep her alive – holidays, day trips, weekends away – but I always knew we were running out of time. She was growing weaker before my eyes, and keeping her going was getting harder all the time. Even before she was diagnosed with cancer of the oesophagus, she'd had surgery to remove part of her intestine. I was very afraid that she'd need to have a colostomy, which I knew she'd hate. And because this was a possibility for a while, I took to wearing a colostomy bag about the house to reassure her and make her laugh. In the event, she survived that operation, thank God, and didn't need a bag.

Although mam had always adored my hands, especially my manicured nails, she'd always bitten her own nails, and had been unable to break the habit since she was a child. The plus side, though, was that when she needed to have her teeth removed, for the very first time she grew her nails and I could start treating her to manicures. That took her mind off losing her teeth!

Since developing anorexia after her mother's tragic death, she'd never been very strong and the damage to her body caused by lack of food over the years was pretty dreadful. Even when Alice was a child, her mam's nickname for her was the nine-penny rabbit because, even then, she didn't have much meat on her bones. It was a miracle really that she got to the age of sixty-four, and every time I went to see her after she became really ill, I lived in fear that it would be the last. The nursing staff adored her, were determined to keep her going, and I filled every room she was in from floor to ceiling with flowers.

Having overcome my own horrendous struggle with cervical cancer in 1979, to watch my mam losing her battle with cancer of the oesophagus in 1987 was almost unbearable. Having been told she needed surgery on her throat, I set about finding the best surgeon for the job, then booked her into a hospital in Manchester as a private patient. The first night she was in there, the surgeon asked to speak to me. 'I'm not at all sure,' he said, 'that your mother is strong enough to make it through the operation, and you must prepare yourself for the worst.' That was a *really* bad moment, very difficult to cope with, but I managed to keep myself together for her sake. My mam had been a smoker all her life and the surgeon said such operations were rather like emptying an ashtray, then seeing how far the cancer had spread.

She looked so tiny, so vulnerable, when they were wheeling her down to the operating theatre, and I so wished it could have been me; that I could have gone through the operation for her. I could only wait. As I sat there watching the hands of the clock, each minute felt like an hour. When they eventually brought her out, she was put into intensive care, and there were tubes – so many tubes – inserted into her. My heart was breaking.

The next thing I knew the surgeon wanted to see me again, and I could tell from the expression on his face that it was bad news. Having had cancer myself and dealt with my father's cancer, I could read all the signs by now, but I didn't want to hear what he had to say. However, I steeled myself for what I knew would be like a hard smack in the face.

'It's even worse than I'd anticipated,' he said. 'I'm so sorry.' They're always sorry, aren't they? But do they really mean it? Are they really affected? I'm never quite sure. 'You know,' he continued, 'it's very difficult with these old people to—'

'Stop right there!' I said. 'My mother *isn't* old.'

'I apologize,' he replied. 'I didn't mean—'

'Just try to remember that,' I said. 'She *isn't* old.'

I'd found his comment very offensive, but then we're hypersensitive at times like this. My mam wasn't old, but I have to say if she'd been 164, it would still have been too soon for me to hear those words. I did realize, though, that he was trying to prepare me for the end, and I knew I needed to get her home as soon as possible. As I couldn't do that until she came out of intensive care, I moved in with her, which they weren't best pleased about. I sat on the floor underneath the washbasin by her bed and, after a while, the staff just forgot I was there. I became part of the furniture and could wait and watch. During that time I became utterly convinced that if I took my eyes off my mam or the monitors, they'd stop and she'd die. I couldn't look away, couldn't move a muscle and just stayed there. The staff were fantastic, dashing in and out as they cared for Alice and all the other patients, but I still thought that if I stayed, at least I could make sure that if anything bleeped or stopped I could get hold of somebody quickly enough to save her life.

I had to get her home. She couldn't die in there. Just like Bill, I knew she'd want to be at home. The wait seemed to go on forever. Days became nights, nights became days, but eventually she was moved out of intensive care into her own little room. Everybody was amazed that, at only five stone (if that), she'd survived the operation and pulled through the recovery time in intensive care. And I could hardly believe it myself when I was told I could take her home.

By then, she'd left the house that my dad had built because there were too many painful memories there. Instead, she was living in a little flat, but there was no way she could look after herself and go back there. She was coming home with me. Of course she was. I got her room ready, decked it out with even more flowers, and organized lovely nurses to help out. Janet Ross was, thank God, still in and out of my life at that time, and we took it in turns to look after Alice. For most of that period we had a party, which was fabulous, and caring for my mam turned out to be one of the most rewarding things I'd ever done in my life. Lucky, Mam's little mongrel, was often in the room with her, and if I ever needed to go out for a breather or a fag, or to use the toilet, Janet took over. Alice adored Janet, so I always knew she was in safe hands.

This takes me to my favourite book, *Jonathan Livingston Seagull* by Richard Bach. When I first read this, it made perfect sense to me. It really is what it says on its back cover, 'a story for people who follow their dreams and make their own rules; a story that has inspired people for decades'. 'For most seagulls,' the cover says, 'life simply consists of eating and surviving. Flying is just a means of finding food. However, Jonathan Livingston Seagull is no ordinary bird. For him, flying is life itself . . . This is a fable about the importance of making the most of our lives, even if our goals run contrary to the norms of the flock, tribe or neighbourhood. Through the metaphor of flight, Jonathan's story shows us that, if we follow our dreams, we too can soar.'

Emotionally, I really identified with that, and especially with the part of the book that read, 'The bird sees farthest who flies highest.' I loved that book so much and I wanted my mam to read it during the last few months of her life.

'Why the bloody hell did you give me *that*?' she asked when she finished it.

'I thought you might like it, Mam,' I replied. 'It's one of my favourite books.'

'Oh, give over. It's about bloody seagulls! Have you lost the plot, or what?'

And we ended up rolling about laughing together.

I'd explained to my bosses at Granada that I'd be taking time off to nurse my mother. By then I'd built up my holiday entitlement to four weeks, but for storyline reasons I was never allowed to take all four weeks at once. I totally understood that, so I'd take two weeks at the beginning of the year and two weeks towards the end. I'd be written out during these periods, and one thing I could guarantee was that during those precious weeks I'd be poorly, go down with a cold or the flu. It was almost as if my brain was telling my body, 'You're in your own time now, so you can be ill if you like.' That's how it was.

Mam wasn't happy about me taking time off. 'I'll be all right,' she kept saying. 'I'm comfortable and, anyway, you've organized the nurses to come in.' Then she'd add, 'Look, Julie, I don't want you to lose your job.'

'There are lots of jobs,' I'd reply, 'but I've only got one mam.'

One day, as her eyes filled with tears when I said this, I looked at her and thought, 'When do children become their parents' parents?' I'd suddenly realized that, in a strange kind of way, I'd become her mam when my grandma died when I was just thirteen. That didn't matter, though. Like I said, 'You only ever have one mam,' and I'd have done anything for her.

Nevertheless, for the last three months of her life Alice couldn't stop worrying about me losing my job. I have to say I wouldn't have missed those last three months, not for the world. To be able to spend those weeks with her was just wonderful. Anything we hadn't said before – and God only knows we were always close – we were able to say then. And it didn't matter whether it was day or night, whatever she wanted, she got: a little bit of baby food, anything just to see her smile, just to make her comfortable.

Being off work, though, was very unusual for me, and it wasn't long before the hacks cottoned on. One night in 1987 when I knew they'd been outside the house for quite some time, Janet was downstairs and I was upstairs, sitting on the floor next to my mam's bed. That was the night when my relationship with the press reached an all-time low, hit rock bottom, which is saying summat. Unbelievably, one of the hacks outside began shouting through the letter box, 'C'mon Julie, we know you're in there. We know your mum's dying of cancer. Just let us take one picture and we can all bloody well go home.'

As I looked into my mam's eyes, I felt a mist of red anger rising from the soles of my feet and travelling all the way through my body. I knew my mam had heard what he'd said and at that moment I wanted to kill him. As Alice's eyes locked on to mine, though, she smiled the most beautiful of smiles and started to sing, 'A, you're adorable; B, you're so beautiful; C, you're a cutie full of charm; D, you're delightful; E, you're exciting; F, you're a feather in my arms.' As ill as she was, *she* was pulling *me* through; she'd stopped me from going out there and doing something I might regret. That, however, was the most despicable thing the hacks had ever done to me. Here was this tiny, shy woman who'd never had any desire whatsoever to be in the public eye, and they wanted a picture of her dying?

After she died, I even had to put bouncers on the door because, having failed to get photographs of her during the last days of her life, they wanted pictures of the body. Were there no depths those sewer rats would not go to? Apparently not. Each time after that first time, though, whenever a member of the press hollered through the letter box, my mam would lie there, singing, 'A, you're adorable; B, you're so beautiful; C, you're a cutie full of charm . . .'

I just loved her singing that; could have listened to it forever. Her all-time favourite song and singer, though, was David

Whitfield singing 'Cara Mia', and long before I joined *Coronation Street* I'd been lucky enough to get his autograph for her on one of his large glossy publicity photographs. She was so thrilled and always treasured that photograph. It was because of that experience that I never forgot how much a signed picture could mean to a fan. As a result, whenever I got fan letters, there was never one that remained unopened or unanswered. I'm not claiming I did all this myself. Because I got sackloads, I had to employ somebody to help out, but not one of my fans was ever ignored and their phone calls were always returned.

Just before my mam passed away, a change came over her, and for the first time in my life I became frightened of her. Both her face and her personality changed during this time – neither Janet nor I recognized her. She became bad-tempered, vicious even, and we didn't know what the hell was going on. Was it a reaction to the medication she was on? But how could it be? She was hardly on anything, except some pain relief. This was *not* Alice, and Janet and I were alarmed by the venom she spat out whenever we went into the room.

In desperation, I contacted Sister Margaret and described the situation to her. She seemed to understand totally, but then she always did. She organized things so that she could get time off from the convent and come to the house. It was such a relief knowing she was coming. Things were so bad by then that Janet and I were even frightened of Sister Margaret (who my mother was very fond of and knew very well) going into the room. Alice was behaving like a caged animal: her face was often contorted and, although she'd hardly ever sworn in the past, the stuff that was now coming out of her mouth was horrendous.

'Leave it to me,' Sister Margaret said calmly when she arrived and we voiced our fears. 'You two sit down and get yourself a nice cup of tea, and *don't*, however much noise there is, come upstairs.'

'Oh my God!' I thought, wild-eyed with fear. 'What on earth's going to happen? What's she going to do?'

Anyway, Sister Margaret went upstairs and Janet and I sat at the table, clasping hands, holding on to each other for dear life. It was a beautiful day, but all of a sudden lightning flashed across the sky, thunder roared, and we sat there astonished, paralysed by fear. It was as if what was going on inside Alice was also going on outside as well. Had the world gone completely mad? The storm seemed to go on for ages, before the thunder began to roll away and the lightning ceased, and everything went very quiet and calm in the house. By then Janet and I were shaking and, to this day, I can remember saying to her, 'She must be dead.' Janet replied, 'Yes, she must be. That couldn't go on any longer.' Trembling from head to foot, I said, 'I hope Sister Margaret's all right.'

And she was. There, suddenly, in the kitchen doorway, was Sister Margaret, looking very tired but smiling her beautiful smile. 'It's all right, darlin's,' she said. 'You can go up now. The devil's gone on his way.'

'But is she still alive?' I sobbed out.

'Of course. Go upstairs and see for yourself. This is the mother you know.'

As I climbed the stairs my knees were knocking. I'd become so afraid of the other person, the person that wasn't my mother, but when I walked into the bedroom, there was my mam sitting up in bed. And her face was beautiful again – *radiant*. The relief was indescribable. I don't know what Sister Margaret did that day; I've no idea as I wasn't in the room. I can only add, from conversations I've had with her since, that often on the point of death or just before, the devil can move in to claim a soul. It was something Sister Margaret had seen on many occasions and she was able to deal with it. I'm just so glad she was in our lives and able to help that day.

I should also add that the Macmillan nurses who looked after Alice were absolutely wonderful, before my mam reached the stage where she didn't want anybody else to wash, clean her or do any of those things that you are privileged to do for somebody you love. I remember writing on a piece of paper at that time, 'The hardest thing I've ever had to do in my life is to look death in the face and kiss it.'

Mam's doctor, who she thought the world of, used to call on a regular basis, just to check that she was comfortable. One night not long after Sister Margaret's visit Alice took a turn for the worse and was very uncomfortable. When, late that night, I called the doctor and he came, I remember my mam saying to him, 'Eh, what are you doin' here at this time of night?'

I didn't know then that those were the last words I'd ever hear her say.

A few minutes later, Janet came running downstairs and said, 'I think you'd better come up, Julie.'

'What is it?' I asked, trembling.

'The doctor's stuck a needle in the back of her hand.'

'He's done what? Why?'

'I think you'd better come up.'

'What is it?' I asked as I entered the room and stood looking first at the syringe and then the doctor.

'It's intravenous Valium,' he said. She was being sedated to make her comfortable.

'Is she going to be all right?' I asked, my heart beating so loud it seemed to fill the room.

'Try to keep calm,' he replied. 'She can still hear you.'

'But is she going to be all right?'

As he was speaking to me, I realized that there was another full syringe going in. Then he inserted a third loaded syringe into my mother's left hand. 'If she regains consciousness,' he said gently, 'one of you will need to press the plunger of that syringe in. But it probably won't be necessary.' And then he left. I have to say I could never have done that, and I don't think Janet could either. Thank God, we didn't have to.

Meanwhile, in case my mam could still hear me, I kept talking to her. I talked to her about all the good times we'd had, all the places we'd visited, and I told her it was all right for her to go. It was okay. I felt she needed to hear me say that. I told her I'd be fine. Her body was wasted – finished – but her heart, which was as strong as a lion's, didn't want to give up. 'I'll be fine,' I kept saying. 'You go, Mam.'

As she passed over, there was the most beautiful feeling in the room. It was just as if she was being lifted up and carried off on the wings of angels. Grief would come later, but the moment her spirit left was exquisite. It seemed to hover there above the now-empty shell that had been her body, and the room was filled with an incredible feeling of light and love. The next moment I saw her spirit rise, so gently, so slowly, and float towards the slightly open window. I smiled then because I knew she was free from pain and suffering, and I felt so privileged to be there with her as she started her journey to the other side.

During those last days my mam's little dog had hardly ever left her side in the room, but as Alice's spirit left her body Lucky moved closer and closer to my side, and then snuggled up against my leg. It was as if she was saying, 'It's time now for me to look after you. And here I am.'

Throughout those last three months there were regular phone calls from Granada. It is, after all, a business, and naturally they wanted some idea of when I'd be returning. I was constantly being asked how my mother was and, more pointedly, had I considered either putting her into a hospice or a nursing home? But I'd made my choice and I stood as firm as a rock.

One of the things Alice said to me just before she died was, 'You know, Julie, the thing most people find very hard to live with when somebody dies is the guilt. The guilt at what they might have done, perhaps should have done, the missed opportunities, the things that weren't said.' At the time, I wondered if she was talking from personal experience and thinking of her own mother. Then she looked at me, smiled and said, 'Julie, you'll *never* know what that guilt is. Take my word for it, you will never, ever, luv, need to feel that.'

After she died, I knew exactly what I wanted her to wear and how her hair should be done. Because I'm a local lass and they know me at the Chapel of Rest, I was able to go in and assist with all that. We placed her in a beautiful pure-white coffin, and she looked absolutely gorgeous. She had just the right amount of rouge on her cheeks and I made sure her nails were perfect, with just the right colour nail varnish. Then my mam's body was brought back to my home – as was still the custom at that time – and put in the dining room with a candle at each end of the open coffin. We then had a little service inside the house and Lucky came in for that and sat next to me.

When everybody had left that room I had my final moment

with Alice. I kissed her, held her hand and then fastened the lid of the coffin myself. As the coffin went down the path from my house, its lid brushed against the deep-purple lilac tree at the bottom of the garden. It was like a farewell caress. The weather was beautiful that day, 11 May 1987, but I have to tell you that as the coffin was lowered into the ground the heavens opened and the rain poured down my face. 'The angels are crying,' I thought.

As I glanced up, there was Podders, my producer, such a good mate, standing a little way off. Later on, I was touched to learn that one of the many books written about *Coronation Street* had a dedication inside it which read, 'In memory of Alice and William Goodyear'. It was as if they credited my mam with giving birth to me so that the creation of Bet Lynch could happen, and also acknowledged the part that Bill had played. How Alice and Bill would have loved that.

While I was away from the set, the writers had been having crisis meetings and doing their best to keep ahead of the Bet situation.

The storyline in 1987 was that, after the fire when the Rovers had burned down, Bet became aware of Alec Gilroy, who ran the Graffiti Club where the locals gathered while the Rovers was being renovated. A sly weasel of a man, Alec set about fleecing the regulars, and when Bet reopened the Rovers, he tried to sell her the idea of hiring his cabaret turns. Although Bet was warned not to have anything to do with him, she ignored the advice of her friends and linked up with Alec, borrowing money off him to buy the pub.

We'd just reached that point in the story when real life took over and I had to be written out of the show for three months while I looked after my mam. To explain my absence, the writers had Bet running off and leaving Alec very concerned about his investment. When it was time for me to return, however, it was decided that Bet Lynch should become Bet Gilroy and marry Alec. It was not a marriage welcomed by my fans. When I arrived at the church for the filming of the wedding, I was greeted by crowds chanting, 'Don't do it, Bet. *Don't do it!*' Startled though I was, the fact that they thought the marriage was for real, bless them, was a great compliment to me, the writers, producers and directors.

Alec Gilroy's proposal took place in Torremelinos and it was a very difficult, sensitive time for me so soon after Alice's death. However, Roy Barraclough, a veteran actor and naturally funny man, did manage to make me smile one evening. We were sitting in a restaurant after a day's filming when I saw something absolutely astonishing. 'Roy, look over there; look at that!' I exclaimed. A boat was coming out of the water, carried on the shoulders of fishermen, and on the top of the boat, lit up, was a statue of the Virgin Mary. As they came along the street towards us, I sighed and said, 'Oh Roy, that's absolutely beautiful! It's obviously a sign from me mam.'

'Don't be so fucking daft,' he replied, quick as a flash. 'They do that every Tuesday.' I found out later he was right. They did!

Even if I say so myself, there'll never be another soap quite like *Coronation Street*, or a character quite like Bet Lynch! I for one loved her for her strength, her sense of humour and, above all, the soft centre beneath that tough exterior. She'd had fifteen screen flings, starting with long-distance lorry driver Frank Bradley in 1971, before she got round to marrying Alec Gilroy in 1987. What a woman!

★

When I met the next person who was to share my life, I'd been living on my own for some time, but as my work was all-consuming that didn't bother me in the slightest. At that time, 1988, twenty-eight-year-old Nicky Higgins was working as a freelance production assistant on *Coronation Street*, and when we first got together I'd absolutely no idea that she was married. In fact, if anyone had told me she was, I'd have laughed like a drain and thought, 'No, absolutely impossible.' By then I'd had a certain amount of experience of gay women – certainly enough to recognize a really masculine butch woman when I met one – and in Nicky's case I was in no doubt about her sexual orientation. This was doubtless why the question of her being married didn't at first crop up. Nicky, who was tall, never ever wore any make-up and let her brown hair grow rather wild, always dressed in rather masculine-looking tweed sports jackets and sweatshirts.

Our first date was a trip to The Stables, the local Granada pub, and we just hit it off straight away – got on really well. Then, because her work with Granada was pretty irregular and because, since Janet had left, I needed a PA, she took the job on. A very gentle soul, she proved to be absolutely brilliant. Her adopted mother had been a librarian and my filing system became 150 per cent perfect!

After our friendship blossomed into a same-sex relationship, I was startled to find out that she was married. I think she'd just done what society and her adoptive parents expected of her and hadn't known her true self at the time. When I discovered this I thought it was a joke at first, but that soon stopped when a story appeared in the press. I was absolutely devastated to be in the scandal rags again but, from Nicky's point of view, I think it was good it happened. It freed her, put her on the path she should have always been on. For me, though, after all my previous trials and tribulations, it was a case of 'I *really* don't need this' and the relationship ground to a sudden halt. It all worked out well for Nicky in the end, though. Shortly after the fiasco in the press, she met a charming girl called Jackie, and they've been together ever since. That's marvellous, and I'm really happy for them both. Nicky's done really well and is now a producer. I always knew she was very talented and I'm very proud of her. We rarely meet these days, but we still exchange Christmas and birthday cards.

For me, there's a world of difference between loving someone very much and being in love. Emotional and spiritual commitment are much more important to me than any physical aspect. While my same-sex relationships lasted, they were very special and important. I've always been the sort of person, though, who'd rather avoid great passionate bust-ups whenever I possibly can.

I've never liked the word 'lesbian' and I find 'dyke' offensive. I don't mind 'gay', though, which someone told me recently stands for G-A-Y: 'good as you'. The truth, however, is I don't like labels; I think they're unnecessary as well as misleading. I don't look at somebody and think, 'You're a woman' or 'You're a man' or 'You're this or that.' I see people as people. For the same reason, I've never thought of myself as bisexual. 'Bi', as far as I'm concerned, means two, and when I'm with somebody, I'm with that person, one person not two! And I expect the same in return from whoever I'm with at the time.

As it happened, the next person who came to live with me after Nicky and I agreed to part was another woman. This friendship blossomed into my fourth and last same-sex relationship. The fact that it was the last, however, is no reflection on

Vicki Claffey, who to this day remains my PA and still lives close by in Heywood. This relationship came about after I'd paid yet another visit to Hoar Cross Hall in Staffordshire, my all-time favourite health farm which has become my second home and somewhere I go a couple of times a year. I first went there to interview a gentleman called Steve Joynes, who owns it, an interview that was never shown. He'd started with a mobile fish-and-chip van, but by then was a multimillionaire. He, his wife and son are now three of my dearest friends. While there, I mix with mums, daughters and other women who arrive with their friends for the weekend, and, between having facials, manicures, pedicures and reflexology, I enjoy chatting to every-body. I also use the gym and have become very good at archery, which I enjoy very much; I'm proud to say I've won quite a few prizes.

It was during one of my regular visits there that I first met Vicki, who I realized straight away was gay. At that time she was working for a woman who made a point of complaining about everything under the sun. After our paths had crossed a number of times, I avoided her like the plague. Let's just say she wasn't my cup of tea. I did, though, feel very sorry for the staff of the health farm and particularly for Vicki, who used to bring her there, depart and then come back to collect her later. On one occasion when Vicki was waiting for her, we got chatting. In the right circumstances I'm actually quite a sociable person, who enjoys putting everybody I meet at their ease. Anyway, on this occasion poor Vicki was looking particularly down-trodden and, having sought her out to try and cheer her up, our friendship began.

After that day we kept in touch by telephone and the more I got to know her – and her mother Mary – the more I liked her and couldn't believe how badly she was being treated. I was particularly concerned that her National Insurance stamps were not being paid, which meant of course that she wouldn't be entitled to a pension when she retired. So – and, yes, here we go again – as I was without a PA and she needed a good job, I asked her if she'd like to come and work for me. Our friendship just developed from there.

She has now been my PA for sixteen years and, although our same-sex relationship finished many moons ago (and we have occasional spats and I sack her on a regular basis), we remain great friends. Her loyalty to me is phenomenal, and I would trust her with my life, I truly would. Friendship, as I have said before, is even more important to me than relationships. Vicki does a damn good job, always holds the fort when I'm away, and I always make a point of speaking to her at least once a day. And the first thing I did when she came to work for me was to pay up her National Insurance stamps, so at least she has a pension now.

When you're an actress – a known face if you like – and a good listener, attracting people (including the wrong kind of person) is an occupational hazard. Alongside the right decisions, I've made many mistakes in my life, but I've never hardened my heart and closed down. I've always been aware that if I did that, I'd never meet anybody and I'd be a bored-witless recluse. What a horrible fate. I'd rather go on taking risks and making mistakes. When things do work out – as they have, for example, with two of my PAs, Janet and Vicki – I've proved over and over again that I can be a very good friend, and I'm very protective of the people I care about. When I really care for somebody, I'm always there to catch them when they fall. Nevertheless, I discovered many years ago that you can't protect other people from everything or live their lives for them, and that applies even if you've given birth to them.

I can't say I was sorry when the 1980s came to an end. One way and another, they hadn't been the best ten years of my life. New decades are like new beginnings, times when we feel we can turn over a new leaf, put behind us the bits we don't particularly want to remember, store the bits we enjoyed and, above all, look forward to what's still to come. I must have been born optimistic. As the nineties came in, despite everything that had happened to me, I thought, 'Bring it to me, baby. I'm ready!'

FIFTEEN

Life is What Happens

Between 1990 and 1994, I found myself dreaming about another kind of life. By then I'd done twenty-two years in *Coronation Street* and, although I was as fond of playing Bet as I'd always been, I kept remembering the resolution I'd made to quit at the right time. This, then, is how 21 September 1995 became another very big day in my life. That was the day I walked on to the set of *Coronation Street* to be filmed for what I'd decided would be the very last time. By then, twenty-five years had passed since I first joined the cast of the *Street*, and I'd decided that the time had come to hang up my leopard-skin and leave. I'd actually been ready to go three years before that, but Carolyn Reynolds (my producer then) persuaded me to stay and make it a twenty-five-year silver anniversary. That aside, there was always a standing joke between us that I'd need to work out three years' notice before I left. And, as it happened, although I don't think she really thought I would leave, I did.

Walking away from my beloved *Corrie* was one of the hardest things I've ever done, harder even than I'd anticipated. But I was determined not to wait, as Doris Speed had done, until it was time to go straight into a nursing home or residential care.

Until I actually left the *Street*, my work had been the one constant in my life, and I wasn't at all sure how I'd feel during the inevitable adjustment period. At least, though, I had plans – plans which included lots of different kinds of work to keep me occupied. And at the time these plans seemed to be very promising and exciting. The fact that most of them never came to fruition – would never see the light of day – wasn't even a blot on the horizon then. And, although I've never regretted my decision to leave, I've always been the first to admit that my career since has been much more low key. The reason for that, however, will become clear.

I was absolutely heartbroken, for example, when my ambition to host my own daytime chat show on Granada, called *The Julie Goodyear Talk Show*, were dashed, and it took me ages to find out why. I couldn't understand what had happened – was completely bewildered. I'd worked really hard on the three-hour pilot, had some fabulous guests and studio audiences, and I knew it was quality. I'd done my homework, prowled around the set until I knew every square inch of it, and when the cameras started to roll, I was more than ready. At the end, although I was exhausted, I was pleased because I knew it was good.

Carolyn Reynolds had been observing and the first thing she said to me as I came out of the studio, looking totally knackered, was 'Now, will you come back into *Coronation Street*?'

'No,' I replied. 'That was good.'

For whatever reason it never got off the ground. Granada just kept saying its fate was in the hands of the ITV Network, which was responsible for giving regional programmes the national go-ahead. The next thing I heard was that Network Centre had viewed it, but ITV couldn't find a spot for it in their schedules. I begged, I pleaded, but Granada wouldn't budge. The director (Jane McNaught, who was later made producer of *Coronation Street*) knew it was a great show, but she also knew which side her bread was buttered and when to keep her mouth shut. Eventually the show was given an early daytime slot 'just to test the water'. The press followed their usual practice and came down on me like a ton of bricks, saying the show wasn't good enough – was so bad, in fact, it shouldn't be shown at all. I'd *never* done a shit job in my life, and that hurt me very deeply.

The truth is, when you've made the kind of cock-up I'd made of my personal life, your working life has to be perfect, otherwise everything's seen as a failure; and I actually said that to David Liddiment, a controller at Granada. He didn't reply. Eventually Andrea Wonfor, who knew I was distraught, called me in and told me what was going on. Her exact words to me were 'It is not in Granada's interests to allow you to be seen being successful doing anything else.'

At last I understood! My work was being canned – or at least put on the back-burner – because it wasn't in Granada's interests for me to be successful in anything other than *Coronation Street*. Now I could at least walk away from that mega-disappointment knowing there was nothing wrong with my work, never had been, never would be. It was still, though, a very bitter pill to swallow.

The words 'not in Granada's interests' kept running through my head for days. *Coronation Street* was Granada's flagship; it could never be harmed by any one member of the cast, past or present, letting the side down by being unprofessional. But I would never have let it down, would never have been disloyal or done anything to damage it. It was difficult to understand the reasoning behind the decision that had wrecked all my plans; I thought it was very short-sighted business-wise. On the other hand, I could see that if they let one cast member rise to prominence in summat else, others who'd found success in *Corrie* might also want to break free and do it. Internal politics were clearly at work and I had no option but to accept the decision made about my recorded chat shows. So d'you know what I did? I did a live programme – the *National Lottery Live*, to be exact.

'If it's going out live,' I thought, 'they can't interfere, can't stop it being transmitted.' Oh, how I enjoyed that. 'Live' had never frightened me; I absolutely loved it and never corpsed. It was, in the scheme of things, a small victory, but one that I treasured and one that was very important for me at the time.

However, another setback came my way in 1996, when I was informed I'd lost a dream TV role. I was meant to star in the gritty drama *Girls' Night Out* – a £2 million film penned by *Band of Gold* creator Kay Mellor. Granada TV apparently had second thoughts about me, and the part was given to Julie Walters.

A really big day – a day I could hardly believe was happening – was 21 February 1996, when, aged fifty-four, I went to receive the MBE I had been awarded for services to television and drama from the Queen at Buckingham Palace.

When I first heard I'd been awarded this, I was so over-come I burst into tears. I was a *really* happy Goodyear, and so proud! On the day, needless to say, I left Bet's leopard-skin and jangly earrings behind me and opted instead for a classy pale-blue suit and a white hat. My son Gary and his wife Suzanne, accompanied me, and as the hired Rolls-Royce broke down just outside London, we eventually arrived in style in the back of a twenty-seven-foot-long chauffeur-driven Cadillac Fleetwood.

It was a very special day. I was wide-eyed when we were met at the entrance by beefeaters and ushered into the grand ballroom – a gigantic luxurious room hung with huge chandeliers and priceless paintings. Given what I'd done for a living all those years, houses and locations always seem like studio or film sets to me – I thought Buckingham Palace was the most fantastic place I'd ever seen in my entire life. What a spectacle it was: the huge rooms, the cavalry, the colours. Everything about it was just mind-blowing. I was very nervous but then, thank goodness, I found someone even more nervous than me – a lollipop lady who'd also been honoured in the New Year's list.

When the Queen came into the room, I was instantly struck by her amazing blue eyes and very impressed by the different languages she spoke to the various recipients. As my big moment arrived, Her Majesty, who was known to be quite a fan of *Coronation Street*, took my MBE from a velvet cushion, pinned it on to my jacket, and then stood chatting to me for a couple of minutes. She was so natural, so good at putting me at ease. She spoke about the *Street*, told me how much she enjoyed watching the series, and then added how sorry she was that I had decided to leave. 'I very much look forward to what you are going to do next,' she said.

'So do I, ma'am. So do I.'

Throughout my time at Buckingham Palace, I kept glancing at Gary and thinking, 'Who could have predicted this? What a long way we've come together.'

After losing all those post-*Corrie* career opportunities through no fault of my own, I hosted a chat show for a satellite channel, Granada Breeze, which at least proved that I could do it, and do it well. I also did panto and some commercials as well as being given the honour of the post of cultural ambassador for Liverpool in 1998. Other good news was that I'd bought a run-down six-bedroomed farm, with eighteen stables attached, as a big renovation project for me and a team of builders. I wanted a spa bath put in and a balcony to overlook the spectacular views across my twenty-seven-acre plot. Completing the purchase in 1996, I used my new-found freedom from the *Street* to create my dream home on the farm in Heywood. I love the Lancashire way of life, feel secure there. I love the people and how they treat me. I'm nowt a pound in Heywood, and that's the way I like it.

I'd no idea when I started the farmhouse project that it would bring into my life Scott Brand, the man who was destined to be my next partner and to this day, ten years on – yes, a record for me! – is still in my life. But people always say, don't they, that life is what happens when you're making other plans!

The papers, needless to say, were determined to have a field day when this piece of news got out. Soon after I met Scott, I woke up one morning to the kind of charmless gutter-press headlines I was by now used to attracting. This time the story broke in the *Sun* – the front-page headline read 'BET'S GOTTA NEW TOYBOY! *Scott, 27, is half her age*'. The drivel beneath went on to say,

> Coronation Street legend Julie Goodyear has fallen in love with a van driver who is just half her age. Bisexual Julie, 54, took a fancy to six-footer Scott Brand as he delivered building supplies to her new £500,000 home. One minute he was dropping off supplies – the next he was being invited out for a drink by one of the most famous women in Britain. He didn't need to be asked twice and they've been dating

ever since. Dark-haired Scott lives with his shopkeeper dad Dave and mum Pat in Radcliffe, near Manchester. Her new romance is the latest chapter in an amazing love life which has seen her linked with a string of men and women . . .

Now for my version. Having gone from terraced, through bungalow and semi–detached, the farm was gonna be the big one – detached. Where I'd come from, a detached home with land attached was real wow factor, and I was really loving making my dream come true. And, although I had the builders running all over the property, there were also lots of laughs along the way. Then something quite extraordinary happened. While I was at the house one day, checking up on some orders and paperwork, there was a knock on the door. Nothing unusual in that, the builders were always in and out asking questions about this and that. But this proved to be a very different kettle of fish.

'Come in,' I called, and when the door opened, there in front of me was a six-foot-four-inch lanky bloke, with shoulder-length hair and piercing blue eyes, dressed in jeans and T-shirt. That was striking enough, but standing next to him was a little old lady from the spirit world. She was so tiny, at first I thought she was a dwarf or maybe a child. This sort of visitation doesn't happen very often, but when it does I know it can't be ignored. Having said that, instead of commenting on the spirit's presence, which I never do when I don't know somebody, I just said, 'Yes?'

Obviously shocked at being confronted by me, he replied, not altogether sure he could believe his eyes, 'Bet?'

That day I was wearing a chain around my neck with my name engraved on it, so I pointed to the chain and said, '*Julie*. Can I help you?'

'Eh?'

'Oh, c'mon,' I added, laughing. 'Put me clothes back on, luv. It's nippy in here.'

And that was how I met Scott Brand, who'd come to deliver a load of cement and needed his delivery note signed.

This was on the Monday; he returned, with deliveries, every day after that. Often they were things that weren't needed or had been brought to the wrong address, and once I realized he was just using the deliveries as an excuse to come and visit me, I thought, 'Oh, piss off.' But I was nevertheless intrigued because the tiny spirit woman came with him every time. 'Eventually,' I thought, 'if he keeps on coming, I'm gonna have to say summat to him.' That, though, is not an easy thing to do. There's always the risk, if you tell someone you don't know that there's someone from the spirit world alongside them, they'll freak out. And I didn't want to spook him. But, when he – and she – continued to come the following week, I thought, 'Right. Bloody hell. If this will get shot of him, I'll tell him.'

His visits were now becoming embarrassing and the other builders were cracking jokes. I was forever having to tell them to stop being cheeky buggers, get back to work and behave themselves. Anyway, on this occasion I took my by now troublesome delivery bloke round to the back of the farmhouse and sat down with him on a couple of railway sleepers.

'My name's Scott,' he told me.

'Yeah, and try to remember mine's Julie not Bet.' Then, plunging in, I added, 'Look, Scott, I have to tell you summat. Every time you come here, there's somebody from the spirit world with you.'

As the colour drained from his face, I paused, then added quickly, 'Are you all right with that piece of information? If not, it's not a problem, I won't carry on.' As I said this, though, the little old lady next to him was spurring me on, nodding her head vigorously. 'But,' I continued, 'I know she wants me to tell you – she's made that clear every time you've come here.'

'Can you describe her?' he asked nervously.

'Of course I can.'

'Then can you tell me is she all right?'

'She's laughing,' I said, 'so she must be all right.'

'Okay,' he said, making it clear he would like me to continue. So I described for him exactly what the little old lady was wearing, right down to her shoes and the style of her hair, the expression on her face and everything else about her. At this point he said, 'You've not got a whisky, have you?'

As he looked rather poorly, I went and got him a tot. 'Are you okay?' I asked after he'd knocked it back.

'It's my grandmother,' he explained, his eyes welling up. 'She died just before I came here to make the first delivery. We buried her last week.'

'I'm *very* sorry to hear that,' I said, 'but she's fine now and is obviously still looking after you.'

'She always said she'd do that.'

What she'd actually done, though, was bring Scott to me to look after! And that, I've always said since, was summat I could have well done without. Scott and I were both born under the star sign of Aries, which means we're not compatible. Nevertheless, at the time of writing this book, we've been living together for ten years. During that time I've been able to pass on to Scott some of the lovely things Geoff Cassidy passed on to me – how to put your knife and fork together and feel comfortable in really nice places, and suchlike. We've had some really good times together as well as some really bad patches but it's still the longest relationship I've ever had. I'm acutely aware, though, that if I'd still been in *Coronation Street* it wouldn't have worked, simply because my job always came first and I couldn't have given our relationship the time it needs. As things are, though, I've really been able to work at this one.

Even though I know Scott is going to read this book, I have to be honest and say our relationship is not *Love Story*. But I've had a great deal of fun being with him. Right at the start, the first time we ever went out for a drink, I said, 'Our relationship will have to be platonic, you know.' But his answer to that was to lean over and give me a French kiss! Talk about 'where angels fear to tread'!

The truth is ever since I was diagnosed with cancer, my attitude has been one day at a time. That's enough for me now. When you've been given a year to live and survived you don't get too greedy about how much longer you might have. And any woman reading this will understand. To quote many of 'em: 'I'd rather have a nice cuppa tea these days. So put the kettle on, luv. Right now, I'm just bloody grateful to still be here.'

I take great pleasure in the fact that Scott's much more confident now than when we met. At first he wasn't ready, in any sense of the word, for the kind of world I lived in. I wasn't surprised. My life can be very daunting for friends or partners who are not used to being in the public eye, and it's proved too much for some people over the years. I just have to hope that the person I'm having fun with – and leaning on – doesn't turn out to be cotton wool, or disappear and not be there for me.

Gary once said that Scott and I can be a bit like Howard and Hilda and I thought, 'Yeah, that's about right. That sums us up.' But having said that, we always pull together if some- body or something threatens us from outside. And Scott is very protective where I'm concerned. Although he's asked me to marry him every single day since we met, I keep saying, 'Nope! I'll never remarry now.' But I always feel dreadful because he's never been married, so who knows?

He might be twenty-five years younger than me, but he often seems to be the mature half of our relationship. I'm the one who still manages to get into scrapes of one kind or another, and his most constant cry, echoing my beloved mam, is 'What have you done *now*?' Age, to me, has always been irrelevant. As far as I'm concerned I'm about ten years old, the age of my youngest grandchild, Jack, and I will never lose the child in me. Like me when I was a girl, Jack spends an awful lot of time on his own. I see many similarities between him and me, so many it's quite uncanny at times. My other two grandchildren try to get him to join in, but he's so happy in his own company. He spends a lot of time in his bedroom pottering around, and when he catches me looking at him, he winks. It's unspoken, but I think he knows we're about the same age!

SIXTEEN

As If We Never Said Goodbye

In 1999, four years after I left *Coronation Street* and stopped being Bet, Granada issued a publicity statement that I was about to make a comeback, and that 'Bet would be even bolder and brasher than ever.' It was true! I'd taken some persuading, but I'd agreed to return for what was described as a 'spin-off' or a 'soap bubble'.

Sadly for some of Bet's fans, her shiny stilettos wouldn't actually touch the cobbles of the *Street* this time. The location, instead, was Brighton, where her step-granddaughter Vicki was running a bar and about to get married. The fun I had filming this with Ken Morley was terrific. The pair of us could hardly look at each other without cracking up, and to this day I've remained friends with Ken, his wife Sue and his son Roger. We often all go out for a meal together, and still crack up.

I had one particularly fraught day while filming the *Street* spin-off. Having dashed into the studio's en suite bathroom during a quick change, I got locked in. Becoming more and more panicky about getting out, I begged for someone to break down the door. A workman was summoned, put his shoulder to the door, heaved and fell into the bathroom, where I was cowering in the corner dressed only in my bra and pants. He was a gentleman. He grabbed a towel and threw it over *his* head to spare *my* blushes.

By the time I got home that day, I was really stressed out. So I got a drink and, barefoot, went out onto the balcony of my bedroom. Gazing out over the garden, I felt peace and calm returning. But when I tried to move again, I couldn't. My legs felt most peculiar – very heavy – and were rooted to the spot. Fearing some kind of paralysis I screamed for Scott, who came racing up the stairs two at a time. Having taken one good look, he then pointed out that the decking of the balcony had been freshly sealed with yacht varnish, and I was now stuck to it! He eventually prised me off with the only tool that seemed suitable for the job, a cake slice. Then, throwing me over his shoulder, he carried me into the bedroom and dumped me unceremoniously on the bed. Was I grateful for being rescued? No! I was yelling at him not to get varnish on the bedspread!

Whilst filming the spin-off I kept telling reporters, 'No, I've no plans to return to *Corrie* full time. There's one helluva difference between signing a six-week contract for filming a spin-off and signing a year's contract for weekly appearances. With the greatest will in the world I couldn't go back full time. I loved my twenty-five-year stint in *Corrie*, but I'm enjoying my freedom now and doing things this way leaves me time to be myself.'

I then admitted to feeling terrified when my return was first suggested. That was why I felt the need to do yet more research on my character's character. One night when I was in Spain I saw two women who were both definitely Bets. One was wearing scarlet lace and lots of pearls, with a scarlet silk flower behind each ear. The other was dressed in leopard skin with lots of gold jewellery. I simply had to get closer to see their make-up, the colour of their nail varnish and exactly how many rings they were wearing. When I did, it turned out they were Czech and ran a bar. Their heroine, they told me, was Ivana Trump.

'Don't be surprised,' I warned people at Granada on my return, 'if Bet now has a touch of Ivana about her and a flower behind her ear – two, if it's evening.' I also said the new Bet would be 'more canny'. 'She hasn't got that many tomorrows or much more earning potential left, so she's got to be more clever,' I added. 'But she'll still make the same mistakes in her personal life; still be as daft as ever.'

My so-called twelve-month return to *Corrie* should have been a happy experience, but it wasn't. It was a nightmare! The team spirit and camaraderie that we'd all taken for granted when I was last there had gone. The sets were still the same, but everything else – the entire way of working – had completely changed. The make-up and costume departments were, compared to what they used to be, virtually non-existent. As far as I was concerned, nobody could function efficiently in that situation. Everybody was expected to come through the door from outside in character and be ready to start the moment they arrived. It was mind-blowing, just like a conveyor belt. There was no laughter, no conversation, *nothing*. It just felt soulless and certainly wasn't the place for me, and I knew it. And you've got to remember that *Corrie* was now five episodes a week as opposed to the three when I was a regular.

The parts of the spin-off that had been shot on location in Brighton had given me a false sense of security, but had only been good because they weren't done in the studio. I didn't know that, though, when I went in through the studio door.

Once there, I discovered the scripts were changing by the minute, which meant that what you'd learned the night before was useless because you were no longer doing the scene anyway. Worse, sometimes you might find yourself expected to do a scene you hadn't learned, hadn't even got with you, because you thought you were doing something else.

'What d'you mean, you've not got it?' the director would bark.

'I've not got it because that's episode five and I'm supposed to be doing episode one!'

'Now, come on. Surely you know where we're up to? After all, you've done all this before.'

Then I discovered there was an early-morning scene about to be shot out of sequence and for that I shouldn't be wearing make-up. 'Oh, that doesn't matter,' was the response. 'We don't work like that now. It doesn't make any difference, and if you're going to take it off, you'll keep the entire studio waiting. So keep it on.'

But it did matter to me, and I'd been used to getting things right. Many years before I'd seen Diana Dors in the film *Yield to the Night*. I followed her example and never wore make-up if the scene didn't require it. Before Diana took all the 'slap' off to do the prison scenes, people just thought of her as a bubbly blonde sex bomb who couldn't act. But when they saw her in that film, they said, 'My God! She really can act.' Very few people in our business, though, are prepared to leave the slap off. And that's sad. Forget the vanity; get it off is what I say. Our first duty is to make the character and action believable. Nobody's going to believe you're anguished or in pain with full make-up and false eyelashes on. Give over. These are lessons everybody in the industry needs to learn, and thanks to Diana

Dors I'd learned them at an early age. The make-up department were constantly surprised when I'd say, 'No no, it's an early morning scene. Let's get this one done without the slap.' I don't think you should be in our profession if you can't be bothered to get things right.

Anyway, there were too many moments like this that went against everything I held dear. Learning a script the night before had become a waste of time, and respect for the actors and their characters was non-existent. Other members of the cast were by now used to this approach, but I wasn't. I hadn't been there when the changes took place, and I didn't like them. Most of the others had come in during the transition period, and some of the older members weren't doing that much and therefore weren't hit as hard. Maybe if they'd brought me back gently – eased me in – it would have worked, but they hadn't. I was in virtually every bloody scene and there was no support. In the end, I didn't know what day it was, what page I was supposed to be on or what scene it was. I didn't know what clothes I was supposed to be wearing, and there was nobody there to help me. With the best will in the world, I found it impossible to work like that.

I put up with the new way of working for about another fortnight, then decided enough was enough. There was no one to reason things out with; the directors didn't have time to talk to the cast, and were running around like headless chickens, churning episodes out. The shock to my system was phenomenal. I felt ill all the time and couldn't sleep. With nobody to ask what was happening next, I was going absolutely demented. To this day, I vividly remember Carolyn Reynolds, the producer, phoning me up at home when I was upset and saying, 'Now come on, Julie, think Beckham.'

'What? Who?' I spluttered.

'David Beckham? Think Beckham.'

'Why?' It took me a while to see what she was getting at, then I realized he'd been in the news for having a terrible time about being sent off – or something like that – and she was trying to get me to identify with somebody else in the public eye who was having a rough time.

'Okay!' I said, by now absolutely beside myself. 'I'm thinking Beckham, and shall I tell you what it feels like? I feel like I've got no fucking football boots, I'm in the wrong fucking position and I'm trying to stitch number seven on my own fucking back while the rest of the team, who are supposed to be on my side, are kicking the fucking ball at me.'

'Well!' she retorted crossly. 'If you're going to be like that, I'm going to put the phone down.' And that was the end of that conversation.

At least I'd got a bit of fight back, and that was very important to me. I'm nobody's doormat! It was, like, 'Hang on, Carolyn Reynolds, you're the woman who met me for lunch and asked me to come back as a favour. I didn't need to do it, for God's sake.' What's more I'd always got on very well with her and liked her as a person, and this was the main reason I'd agreed to go back in the first place.

Later, when I told her I was going, she said, 'But you've done the hardest bit, Julie.'

'Oh? What was that?' I asked.

'Walking in.'

True enough; that had been tough. I wasn't made to feel very welcome, but that's okay; I could have dealt with that. I only wanted to be a member of the team after all. Everyone else knew what they were doing, though, were used to the new way of working. It had obviously never occurred to anybody that I might need a little support while I was easing my way back in.

'Think Beckham.' Not bloody likely. I've never been into football and I can't think of anything more boring. Sorry, Becks. Nothing personal.

I should have known it would all end in tears. It had started badly and was now ending badly. When I went back for that ill-fated return to the set, the sound guys played 'God Save the Queen'. I know they meant well – doubtless did it out of love – but I felt absolutely choked and found it very hard to concentrate on my first scene after that. The pressure I felt was absolutely awful. Then I discovered the laughter had gone and the cast was no longer a family. When I'd first joined it was team work but, like in so many areas of life, that had gone. It was now, out of sheer necessity, quantity over quality and machines had replaced people. As Edna is fond of saying to me, 'It's not a world any more; it's a system.' We used to have such fun in the studio, but there was no time for any of that now: no time even to rehearse a scene, no time to get things right, let alone perfect. And, as I'm a perfectionist who can't compromise with my work, I found that way of doing things sheer hell.

When my doctor came to see me, she said, 'No, Julie. If you continue like this, you'll have another nervous breakdown. The alarm bells are already ringing.'

I'd done the special in Brighton, but now that I was too ill to complete the twelve-month contract, the press had a field day. Day after day they hammered away at me, but by then I'd passed through the pain barrier. At long last I couldn't care less; didn't give a shit. I only wished I'd gone through that pain barrier and come out the other side many years before. I told Carolyn Reynolds this, and she agreed with me.

Despite all this my love for *Coronation Street* never faltered, so when I was asked in 2002 to do another spin-off, in Blackpool, I only agreed after I'd made damn sure I knew what was happening in advance and checked and rechecked that everything was in place: make-up, costume, scripts and the rest. For me, that kind of order is essential and the only way I can enjoy my work and give my best. I worked with George Baker, a marvellous actor, and it proved a wonderful experience, which is how it should be. There was Cecil Newton, the brewery manager, just about to go into church to marry Bet when he had a heart attack and died. It could only happen to Bet! After that scene was screened, my postbag was filled with 'Congratulations on your wedding day' and 'Sincere condolences' cards all mixed up together. Rather like my life really!

There was other acting to be done beyond the *Corrie* spin-offs. I starred in two pantomimes – as Widow Twanky in *Aladdin* at the Royal Court in Liverpool in 1998, and as the Wicked Queen in *Snow White* at the Opera House in Manchester in 2001. As Widow Twanky I was making history because apparently the role had never been played by a woman before.

When I first saw the Royal Court it was obvious it hadn't been used as a theatre for many years. It was a ruin. There were no seats – nothing – just a big open space which I think had been used for raves. So that was another challenge. Then I met Jane and Barry Joseph, the panto's producers, and the actor, Danny McCall, who was to play my son Aladdin. Danny, who used to be in *Brookside*, became a great pal of mine. Having adopted me in real life as his second mum, he became my adopted son who I love very much.

Having accepted the role of Widow Twanky, I soon found

out why a woman had never played the part. The weight of the wigs bearing down on my head and neck was unbelievable, and the number of costume changes involved was phenomenal. Had I taken on too much? As it turned out, the answer was no. I'm from the North so I understood the Liverpool audiences, knew they'd take their time to make their minds up if they liked me, but that if they did they'd take me to their hearts. Big time!

Although we'd rehearsed and were more than ready for the opening night, I was still very apprehensive. The Royal Court's a big theatre, a 2,000-seater, and I could smell the audience even before they entered; I'm sure they could smell the fear on me. I knew they were sussing me out to begin with and I was as hesitant about them as they were about me. This continued until Danny and I got to the rubbing of the magic lamp scene, a scene where only he and I were on stage, appealing to the kids and saying, 'Whatever shall we do, children? Whatever shall we do?'

The idea, of course, was to encourage the kids to answer, 'Rub the lamp, rub the lamp,' so that the genie would appear. Well, whether we'd carried on too long with 'Whatever shall we do, children?' I don't know, but a little boy in the front row aged about four was obviously getting fed up. The next time I said, 'What shall I do, children?' he shouted out at the top of his voice, 'Just rub the fucking lamp.' What can I say? That heartfelt cry broke the ice and the wonderful Scouse audience burst into laughter – with Danny and I joining in. I've no idea who the little boy was, but I blessed him. He dispelled all my nerves, and from that moment on I fell in love with our Liverpool audiences and we played to packed houses.

At one stage during the panto I kept thinking there was a train rumbling past underneath us, which was rather disconcerting. Then I realized everybody was stamping their feet, which was just another way of applauding. I've always thought there's something very energizing about Liverpool and its people, I think they come out of the womb singing. Scousers also have a fabulous sense of humour and the women are renowned for nearly always having a little bottle of gin in their handbags so they can have a tipple or two during the shows. They also get their fags out. They're my kind of people, which was why I was so thrilled when I was made cultural ambassador to the city in 1998. I've still got the framed certificate in my home at Heywood.

While I was in the panto, Danny often handed me little bits of paper with names written on them of the children with birthdays in the audience, so that we could make their day by wishing them a happy birthday. On one particular evening when it was birthday time for the kids, Danny, knowing I wouldn't stand a chance with my Lancashire accent when I was reading this one out, passed me a piece of paper with the name Michael Hunt written on it.

'Right,' I said in all innocence, standing by the footlights, 'it's birthday time, kids. And it's Mike Hunt's birthday today. Where are you, Mike Hunt?'

It was only when the rest of the cast and all the grown-ups in the audience started to snigger, giggle and then laugh aloud every time I shouted out 'Mike Hunt' that I realized something was up. Everybody on the stage was now doubled up with laughter and the audience were in hysterics, as only a Liverpool audience could be. I didn't know what the hell was going on until Jane Joseph came on stage and whispered, 'Every time you say "Mike Hunt" it sounds as if you're saying "my cunt".' I was absolutely mortified and threatened to beat Danny within an inch of his life. We still dine out on that one, though, and I'm more careful with my pronunciation these days.

All this talk of pantomimes has jogged another very special memory. When my grandchildren came to see me playing the Wicked Queen in *Snow White*, I asked each of them in turn if they'd enjoyed it. The older ones said yes, it was marvellous, but when I came to the youngest, Jack, he said, 'Nah.'

'Why d'you say that, darlin'?' I asked.

'I don't like it when they boo you, Nana.'

'Oh,' I said. 'I know what you mean.'

'Couldn't you play Snow White next time?' he asked. I was so touched. There I was in my sixties and he thought I was young enough to play Snow White.

It was at that panto in Manchester when the three of them, much to Gary's delight, came up on the stage and stood with me for the finale. Gary's always been very quiet, probably because I've always been in the public eye and he doubtless took a lot of stick at school. So to see his children, with no inhibitions whatsoever and not needing to be asked twice, standing there with Nana, singing the finale in front of 2,000 people, was a moment he said he'd never forget. It was wonderful, after all we'd been through, him and me, to have a moment like that.

In 2002 I starred as Jacqueline in *La Cage aux Folles* in a three-month run touring the country. To put it mildly, the production was both well received and well supported by the pink pound. My song as Jacqueline, of course, was 'The Best of Times is Now', so as you can imagine my heart and soul went into that number.

Part of the tour took us to the New Theatre in Cardiff and one of my most memorable nights there was when there was a signer on stage to interpret the words for hundreds and hundreds of, would you believe, deaf leather queens! They'd turned out in full force and were truly fantastic, but how the hell I kept my face straight as the signer interpreted 'cock feathers' I'll never know. What a night, and we received a standing ovation.

Going back from the stage to TV, in 2003 I did a comedy sketch programme for BBC Scotland called *Revolver*. I had a wonderful producer called Gary Chippington and worked very closely with Melvyn Hayes who's a fantastic comedy actor. It was filmed on location in Glasgow and I played eighteen different characters, which for an actress is like giving a kid a bag of toffees.

When you've played one character for as long as I did, to be given that kind of opportunity was heaven. And all eighteen were a long way from Bet – like a meths-drinking old tramp on the docks; an agoraphobic; a pathologist; Hettie at the National Trust; and Joyce who ran a brothel with a stair-lift! I thought *Revolver* was a quality show and really hoped that it would be recommissioned. But sadly that wasn't to be, as so often happens.

I've dipped my toes into reality TV a couple of times, firstly in 2005 in *Celebrity Fit Club* which was hosted by the lovely Dale Winton. It was whilst taking part that I first met Tina Baker. Tina's mother had recently died and, much to my delight, she adopted me as her new mum and we've kept in touch ever since. The show itself involved three months of filming which I found gruelling but very rewarding.

As a result I was offered *Celebrity Age Swap*, with me shedding over twenty years to become Linda Hart, an American gothic TV producer. I absolutely loved doing it, especially as one of the challenges was to interview Tina Baker in character for a job in American TV. Tina totally believed that I was Linda Hart, bless her. And the Linda Hart character didn't end there –

I went on to judge a Bet Lynch lookalike competition in a gay club in Manchester. I never got sussed that night either, but you can imagine the gay lads' reaction when I finally did the reveal. The place went wild and it was drinks all round.

Having renovated the farm on the edge of Heywood, I enjoyed kitting it out with chandeliers and stained glass in a style that some have said is 'more reminiscent of Hollywood than Heywood'. But, eh, why not! I love it.

Throughout the renovation, which lasted into the new millennium, I kept the picture of how I wanted it to be in my mind's eye. I knew I'd bought an ugly duckling, but I also knew, thanks to Bill, my dad, the master builder, that it had potential; could be converted into a swan. I never doubted it was going to be hard work and that I would need to be very hands-on, but I didn't mind that either. It's just as well, though, that I didn't anticipate the troubles I'd have to go through to achieve my dream. But thank goodness I didn't, or I might never have taken it on, and I'm so glad I did now.

I love cooking good solid British fare, like roasts or liver and onions, and make a point of buying fresh produce from the Bury, Rochdale and Heywood markets. I also enjoy picking up local bargains. I've always been very careful with money and I'm proud of having no mortgage on my home. I love beautiful clothes, but I'm just as happy wearing a bargain picked up on a market stall as I am in an Armani. And, to this day, my beauty routine consists of washing every morning in cold water, a habit that dates back to the time when we were poor and there was no alternative.

These days, when I'm not otherwise busy, I love walking the boundaries of the farm's twenty-seven acres. I've created a lovely garden in part of it and I never tire of wandering around out there. Those acres of green mean so much to me, and the stable yard, which is currently home to fifteen rescue horses and an assortment of stray cats, is just lovely. The farm is a very peaceful place and the traumatized and injured recover very quickly there. One of the horses had been badly beaten about her head with a baseball bat before she came to me, and it took me at least six months to win her trust. When I first got her, she was wild-eyed and always reared back when approached. She was so frightened it was heartbreaking.

One day when I was on the verge of giving up trying to make friends with her, I leaned over her stable door and said, 'Well, I've done everything I can think of to win your trust. I've stayed in the stable with you all night, sat in the hay with you – and it's not working. I just don't know how to make you happy.' As I was carrying on like this, a tear began to roll down my cheek – and then it happened! The next moment I felt her tongue lick the tear away. So gently. I held my breath, didn't dare move a muscle, and from that moment on she stopped looking wild-eyed and we are now the best of friends.

I must add: please, having read this, don't send me any more injured horses or stray cats. You should see my vet's bills!

As I said, the farm is a very peaceful healing place, and my home there is full of treasured mementos of all the years I played Bet in *Coronation Street*. Needless to say, as a mark of my love and respect for her, there are some leopard-skin rugs and throws, plus other accessories scattered about here and there.

As I sit back in my chair, reflecting on that last sentence, almost the final full stop in this book, it's midnight and there's not a sound coming from outside. Yet, somewhere in the distance, I fancy I can hear music. Straining my ears, I realize that the sound is coming from *very* far away. It's faint, almost in-audible, ghostly even, but I can just catch the words: 'A, you're adorable; B, you're so beautiful; C, you're a . . .' It's Alice! But that song can't be true of me, can it, of someone so many have claimed to love but then left? For a moment, I feel tearful. Then, clear as a bell, my grandma's voice sounds in my ear as well: 'But remember your epitaph: "At least she tried."' And suddenly I feel calmer, more at peace with myself. I have always done my best and, if I failed, that's because at the end of the day I am only human – just Julie.

As I remain sitting here, with the moon shining through the darkness, I fancy one of its silvery beams is lighting up their faces, and each line of their sweet smiles is, once again, etched on my memory.

I stand up from the table.

'You're still here,' I say, greeting them softly. Then, crossing to the open window, I throw back my head and cry out into the night, 'Grandma, I always *hear* you. Mam, I always *feel* you. It really is as if we've never said goodbye.'

A chuckle seems to fill my small universe. I laugh back then I cry real tears, knowing why they've come to me tonight. They're giving this book, my life story, their endorsement, their seal of approval. I couldn't have asked for more. Raising my eyes to the heavens, I'm suddenly a little child once more, my face uptilted, my eyes shining as bright as the stars. 'Watch me run, Mam,' I cry out. 'Watch me, Grandma. Watch me, both of you . . . *watch me fly*.'

Awards

1987 – Woman's Own Women of Achievement Award
1990 – TV Times Top Ten Awards, Editor's Special Award
1993 – TV Times Silver Jubilee Hall of Fame Best Soap Actress
1996 – MBE
1998 – Radio Times 75th Anniversary Hall of Fame

Index

Index

Index

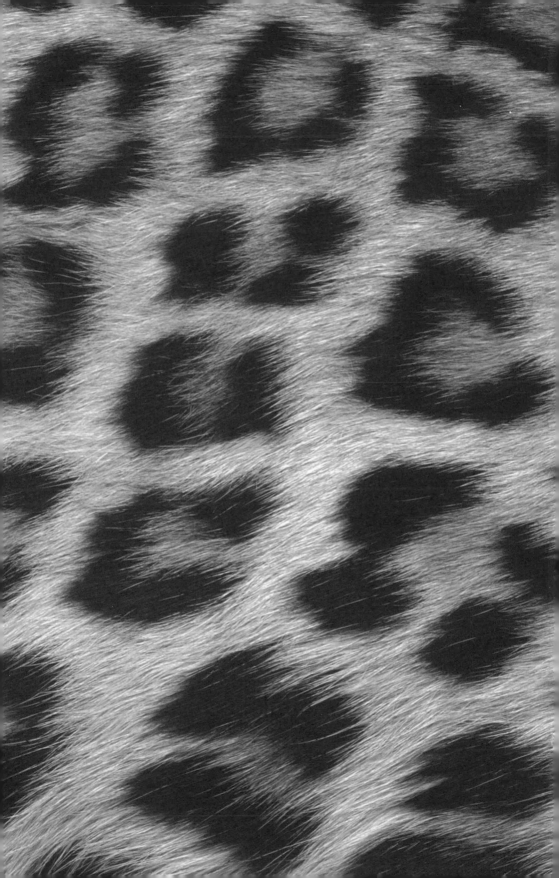